EGYPTIAN BOOK OF THE HIEROGLYPH TRANSLATIONS USING THE TRILINEAR METHOD

Understanding the Mystic Path to Enlightenment Through Direct Readings of the Sacred Signs and Symbols of Ancient Egyptian Language With Trilinear Deciphering translation Method

Vol. 1
by
Dr. Muata Ashby
©2016 Sema Institute

A Collection of Hieroglyphic Texts Translated by Dr. Muata Ashby from the Ancient Egyptian Books of The Dead

Cruzian Mystic Books
Sema Yoga
P.O.Box 570459
Miami, Florida, 33257
(305) 378-6253 Fax: (305) 378-6253

First U.S. edition 2016

The author is available for group lectures and individual counseling. For further information contact the publisher.

Ashby, Muata
EGYPTIAN BOOK OF THE DEAD HIEROGLYPH TRANSLATIONS USING THE TRILINEAR
METHOD: Understanding the Mystic Path to Enlightenment Through Direct Readings of the Sacred Signs and
Symbols of Ancient Egyptian Language With Trilinear Deciphering Method
Vol. 1.
ISBN: 1-884564-91-7

Library of Congress Cataloging in Publication Data

1 Egyptian Book of the Dead, 2 Egyptian Philosophy 3 Hieroglyphs 4 Meditation, 5 Self Help.

www,Egyptianyoga.com
www.Kemetuniversity.come

Table of Contents

Table of Figures

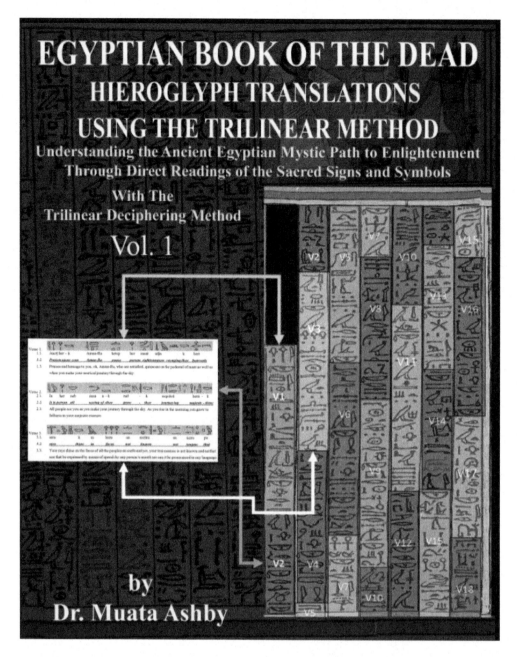

This new volume contains original translations of Chapters of the Ancient Egyptian Book of the Dead (Book of Coming Forth By Day) displaying the Ancient Egyptian Hieroglyphs with word for word translations plus the innovative "Trilinear System", a technique developed by Dr. Muata Ashby to bring out the depths of the Kemetic/Neterian *Sebait* or Ancient Egyptian Mysteries philosophy. This is an ideal study guide for approaching the Ancient Egyptian Hieroglyphic writing in a step by step manner through three layers of descriptive translation. This volume includes translations presented at the annual Neterian Conferences over the last fifteen years and also includes new texts never before published. This book provides new and deeper and direct insights into the Egyptian Mysteries for beginning, advancing and advanced aspirants alike as it may be used as a philosophy study reference, a textbook, or as a reader for daily spiritual study or ritual worship.

The True Name of The "Book of The Dead"

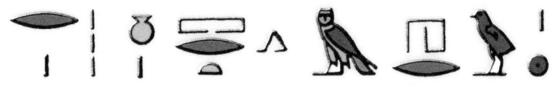

Rau nu pert m heru

=

The

"Chapters of going as light"

Or

The

"Book of Becoming Light"

Or

The

"Book of Enlightenment"

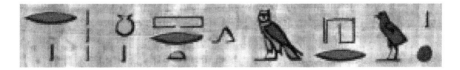

PART 1: INTRODUCTION TO THE PERT-M-HERU

Figure 1: A Papyrus Scroll of the Pert-m-Heru

Preface[1]

"The Egyptians neither entrusted their mysteries to everyone, nor degraded the secrets of divine matters by disclosing them to the profane, reserving them for the heir apparent of the throne, and for such of priests as excelled in virtue and wisdom."

—Clement of Alexandria (150?- 220?)

The Three Levels of Religion and the Mysteries

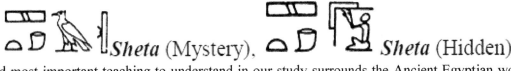

Sheta (Mystery). *Sheta* (Hidden)

The first and most important teaching to understand in our study surrounds the Ancient Egyptian word "Sheti." Sheti comes from the root *Sheta*. The Ancient Egyptian word *Sheta* means something which is *hidden, secret, unknown,* or *cannot be seen or understood, a secret, a mystery.* What is considered to be inert matter also possesses "hidden" properties or *Shetau Akhet.* Rituals, Words of Power (Khu-Hekau, Mantras), religious texts and pictures are S*hetaut Neter* or *Divine Mysteries. Shetat* or *Seshetat* are the secret rituals in the cults of the Egyptian Gods. *Shetai* is the *Hidden God, Incomprehensible God, Mysterious One,* and *Secret One.* One name of the soul of the Ancient Egyptian god Amun is *Shet-ba* (The One whose soul is hidden). The name Amun itself signifies "The Hidden One," "*Shetai.*" Sheti (spiritual discipline) is to go deeply into the mysteries, to study the mystery teachings and literature profoundly, to penetrate the mysteries. *Nehas-t* signifies: "resurrection" or "spiritual awakening." The body or *Shet-t* (mummy) is where a human being focuses attention to practice spiritual disciplines. When spiritual discipline is perfected, the true Self or *Shti* (he who is hidden in the coffin) is revealed.

Shetaut Neter
(Secrets about the Divine Self)

The *Book of Coming Forth By Day* represents the second level of Shetaut Neter. Shetaut Neter means "the way or wisdom of the hidden Divinity which is behind all Creation." Religion has three levels of practice. The first is the myth, which includes the traditions, stories and everything related to it. The next stage is the ritualization of the myth. The final stage is the metaphysical philosophy behind the teachings given in the myth. The book *The Ausarian Resurrection,* presented the complete myth of Asar (Ausar or Osiris), Aset (Isis) and Heru (Horus). The *Book of Coming Forth By Day* represents stage two, the ritualization of the myth of Asar, and through the practice of the rituals contained in the book it is possible to feel, think, act and ultimately experience the same fate of Asar, spiritual enlightenment. Thus, a spiritual aspirant is to understand that {he/she} has incarnated on earth and has been dismembered by egoistic thoughts and actions. However, by gaining an understanding of the hidden mysteries, it is possible to reach a state of beatitude and resurrection, just as Asar.[2]

Therefore, a serious spiritual aspirant should see every aspect of {his/her} life as a ritual in which the soul within them (Asar) is struggling to be reborn again. This spiritual rebirth is accomplished by the practices of listening to the teachings, practicing them and meditating upon them. With the understanding of the hidden knowledge, you can see that all of nature around you is Divine. This includes plants, animals, planets and stars, food, other people, etc. So, through your understanding of the myth and how it relates to your life, and by living your life according to this understanding (ritual), you can lead yourself to discover and realize (mystical experience) the deeper truth behind your own being. This is the true practice of religion. If you understand the superficial teachings of a religious myth, and you practice its rituals blindly

---

[1] Taken from the book Egyptian Book of the Dead by Muata Ashby ©2000
[2] See the book *The Mystical teachings of the Ausarian Resurrection: Initiation Into the Third Level of Shetaut Asar* by Muata Ashby

without understanding the deeper implications, you will not obtain the higher realization. Your practice will be at the level of dogma. This is why there is so much religious conflict in the world today. At the level of dogma, each religion has different myths and rituals and therefore, little if any, common ground upon which to come together. The results of this misunderstanding and ignorance have been personal disillusionment and wars. Yet, at the mystical or metaphysical level, all religions are actually pointing towards the same goal, that of spiritual realization.

A New Translation of the Prt M Hru

Why do we need a new translation of the *Ancient Egyptian Book of the Dead*?[3] If you have picked up a Christian Bible lately, you will notice that you do not have the original text. In fact, the present versions are centuries removed from the original scriptures which comprised the original texts. The Bible is one of the primary sources containing information regarding the beliefs of the Christian faith. It is a compilation of selected portions of writings[4] by different authors, written over a period of 1,000-2,000 years (1,500 B.C.E.- 200 A.C.E.). It is composed of two main sections, the Old Testament and the New Testament, which are made up of smaller books. The original form of the Old Testament is in the ancient Hebrew language. Later, about 250 B.C.E., the Old Testament was translated into Greek. The original form of the New Testament is in the ancient Aramaic, Greek and Hebrew. These forms serve as the primary "original" texts of the Bible. However, since most of the people of the world do not understand ancient Aramaic, Hebrew or Greek, it became necessary to make translations of the Bible into forms that people of modern times could understand. Translations of the Bible pose important problems because the church and religious scholars admittedly[5] do not understand the meanings of some of the ancient Hebrew words in part or at all. Present day English speaking people would not even be able to understand the original King James Version of the Bible which was written only 387 years ago, much less scriptures that were written over 1,700 years ago. However, the essence of a teaching can be discerned and brought forth by those who are initiated into the correct understanding and practice of religious philosophy in its three steps[6]. This is why updates to the translations are necessary.

However, at the same time, the necessity for translations opens the door to corruption and misunderstanding, as some translators may want to present a certain view of the scriptures to prove their own points or to mislead others, or they simply may not produce a correct translation because they do not understand the philosophy which the original Sages were trying to impart. Many people do not see the spiritual scriptures as books of spiritual principles being imparted through metaphors. Rather, they insist that they are to be believed word for word or not at all. If this is the case, and if certain words, customs or ideas cannot be understood by theologians and scholars, as they have already admitted, there is bound to be some misunderstanding. For example, people in modern industrialized countries live with modern plumbing and aqueducts. Their concerns are different than people thousands of years ago worrying about the annual Nile flood or rains for watering their crops. Since ancient spiritual scriptures are most often enveloped in mythology which has been blended with historic events and personalities, these will inevitably contain some information related by expressions that only people living in those times would understand. If the scriptures are interpreted strictly in historical or literal terms, they will become the object of many different interpretations and consequently, arguments and misinterpretation as well. For this reason, the religious beliefs of the translator of the particular text in question may or may not be in agreement with the original scriptural meaning, and may consequently influence the translation. Therefore, the reader should exercise caution when choosing a translation to use for study. Another important consideration is that the translator should be a practitioner of the philosophy as well, that is, one who is involved with the culture of the text. In this way, by living the teachings, they can draw from the feel of the teaching and thereby bring to bear the inner insight which comes from the Divine source.

Since languages and culture change over time, it becomes necessary to update translations on a regular basis. Another important factor is that there are new discoveries that arise from time to time which alter the understanding of the use of some terms or elucidate a new meaning of the old text, which in turn affects the understanding of the meaning of the teachings. Although revision work has been incorporated into this volume, its most important contribution relates to the interpretation of the scriptures from the point of view of a living mystical tradition.

---

[3] Pert m Hru-Book of Coming Forth By Day

[4] The Bible does not include the entire group of scriptures that were written in biblical times. See the book *Christian Yoga* by Muata Ashby

[5] By general admission; confessedly.

[6] Myth, Ritual and Metaphysical (Mysticism).

Unlike the Bible whose original texts were translated into many languages, the *Ru Pert Em Heru (Prt m Hru)* has not suffered removal from its original form, but from convention to suit modern culture. What I mean is that the pervasiveness of the Bible and its various versions has caused a situation in which many people, including scholars, have come to believe the Bible as being historically accurate, and the final authority on spiritual teachings. They also view the modern versions as being true to the original versions. While the study of the *Prt m Hru* has been mostly confined to scholars and a limited number of interested people, it has suffered from being interpreted by scientists instead of religious scholars and practitioners of the philosophy. Thus, the translations, while being accurate in many respects, have lost the deeper meaning which was originally intended. Yet, this meaning is as real today as it was seven thousand years ago when the *Pyramid Texts* were carved in stone, but it can only be discovered if the translation and interpretation has a spiritual basis.

Figure 2: An Ancient Egyptian tomb entrance at Sakhara (the land of Seker-Asar).

Author's Foreword

Who Were the Ancient Egyptians and What is Yoga Philosophy?

The Ancient Egyptian religion (*Shetaut Neter*), language and symbols provide the first "historical" record of Yoga Philosophy and Religious literature. Egyptian Yoga is what has been commonly referred to by Egyptologists as Egyptian "Religion" or "Mythology," but to think of it as just another set of stories or allegories about a long lost civilization is to completely miss the greatest secret of human existence. Yoga, in all of its forms and disciplines of spiritual development, was practiced in Egypt earlier than anywhere else in history. This unique perspective from the highest philosophical system which developed in Africa over seven thousand years ago provides a new way to look at life, religion, the discipline of psychology and the way to spiritual development leading to spiritual Enlightenment. Egyptian mythology, when understood as a system of Yoga (union of the individual soul with the Universal Soul or Supreme Consciousness), gives every individual insight into their own divine nature and also a deeper insight into all religions and Yoga systems.

Diodorus Siculus (Greek Historian) writes in the time of Augustus (first century B.C.):

"Now the Ethiopians, as historians relate, were the first of all men and the proofs of this statement, they say, are manifest. For that they did not come into their land as immigrants from abroad, but were the natives of it and so justly bear the name of autochthones (sprung from the soil itself), is, they maintain, conceded by practically all men..."

"They also say that the Egyptians are colonists sent out by the Ethiopians, Asar having been the leader of the colony. For, speaking generally, what is now Egypt, they maintain, was not land, but sea, when in the beginning the universe was being formed; afterwards, however, as the Nile during the times of its inundation carried down the mud from Ethiopia, land was gradually built up from the deposit...And the larger parts of the customs of the Egyptians are, they hold, Ethiopian, the colonists still preserving their ancient manners. For instance, the belief that their kings are Gods, the very special attention which they pay to their burials, and many other matters of a similar nature, are Ethiopian practices, while the shapes of their statues and the forms of their letters are Ethiopian; for of the two kinds of writing which the Egyptians have, that which is known as popular (demotic) is learned by everyone, while that which is called sacred (hieratic), is understood only by the priests of the Egyptians, who learnt it from their Fathers as one of the things which are not divulged, but among the Ethiopians, everyone uses these forms of letters. Furthermore, the orders of the priests, they maintain, have much the same position among both peoples; for all are clean who are engaged in the service of the gods, keeping themselves shaven, like the Ethiopian priests, and having the same dress and form of staff, which is shaped like a plough and is carried by their kings who wear high felt hats which end in a knob in the top and are circled by the serpents which they call asps; and this symbol appears to carry the thought that it will be the lot who shall dare to attack the king to encounter death-carrying stings. Many other things are told by them concerning their own antiquity and the colony which they sent out that became the Egyptians, but about this there is no special need of our writing anything."

The Ancient Egyptian texts state:

"Our people originated at the base of the mountain of the Moon, at the origin of the Nile river."

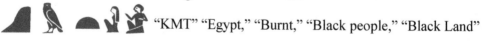 "KMT" "Egypt," "Burnt," "Black people," "Black Land"

In describing the Ancient Egyptians of his time, Herodotus (Greek historian c. 484-425 BC) said: *"The Egyptians and Nubians have thick lips, broad noses, wooly hair and burnt skin... ...And the Indian tribes I have mentioned, their skins are all of the same color, much like the Ethiopians... their country is a long way from Persia towards the south..."*

Diodorus, the Greek historian (c. 100 B.C.) said the following, *"And upon his return to Greece, they gathered around and asked, "tell us about this great land of the Blacks called Ethiopia." And Herodotus said, "There are two great Ethiopian nations, one in Sind (India) and the other in Egypt."* Thus, from these accounts we gather that the Ancient Egyptian peoples were of dark complexion, i.e. of African origin and they had close ties in ancient times with the peoples of India.

Where is the land of Egypt?

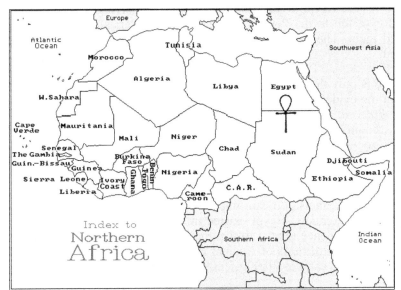

Figure 3: A map of North East Africa showing the location of the land of *Ta-Meri* or *Kamut,* also known as Ancient Egypt.

The Ancient Egyptians lived for thousands of years in the northeastern corner of the African continent in the area known as the Nile Valley. The Nile river was a source of dependable enrichment for the land and allowed them to prosper for a very long time. Their prosperity was so great that they created art, culture, religion, philosophy and a civilization which has not been duplicated since. The Ancient Kamitans (Egyptians) based their government and business concerns on spiritual values and therefore, enjoyed an orderly society which included equality between the sexes, and a legal system based on universal spiritual laws. The *Prt m Hru* is a tribute to their history, culture and legacy. As historical insights unfold, it becomes clearer that modern culture has derived its basis from Ancient Egypt, though the credit is not often given, nor the integrity of the practices maintained. This is another important reason to study Ancient Egyptian Philosophy, to discover the principles which allowed their civilization to prosper over a period of thousands of years in order to bring our systems of government, religion and social structures to a harmony with ourselves, humanity and with nature.

Christianity was partly an outgrowth of Judaism, which was itself an outgrowth of Ancient Egyptian culture and religion. So who were the Ancient Egyptians? From the time that the early Greek philosophers set foot on African soil to study the teachings of mystical spirituality in Egypt (900-300 B.C.E.), Western society and culture was forever changed. Ancient Egypt had such a profound effect on Western civilization as well as on the native population of Ancient India (Dravidians) that it is important to understand the history and culture of Ancient Egypt, and the nature of its spiritual tradition in more detail.

The history of Egypt begins in the far reaches of history. It includes The Dynastic Period, The Hellenistic Period, Roman and Byzantine Rule (30 B.C.E.-638 A.C.E.), the Caliphate and the Mamalukes (642-1517 A.C.E.), Ottoman Domination (1082-1882 A.C.E.), British colonialism (1882-1952 A.C.E.), as well as modern, Arab-Islamic Egypt (1952-present).

Ancient Egypt or Kamit, was a civilization that flourished in Northeast Africa along the Nile River from before 5,500 B.C.E. until 30 B.C.E. In 30 B.C.E., Octavian, who was later known as the Roman Emperor, Augustus, put the last Egyptian King, Ptolemy XIV, a Greek ruler, to death. After this Egypt was formally annexed to Rome. Egyptologists normally divide Ancient Egyptian history into the following approximate periods: The Early Dynastic Period (3,200-2,575 B.C.E.); The Old Kingdom or Old Empire (2,575-2,134 B.C.E.); The First Intermediate Period (2,134-2,040 B.C.E.); The Middle Kingdom or Middle Empire (2,040-1,640 B.C.E.); The Second Intermediate Period (1,640-1,532 B.C.E.); The New Kingdom or New Empire (1,532-1,070 B.C.E.); The third Intermediate Period (1,070-712 B.C.E.); The Late Period (712-332 B.C.E.).

13

In the Late Period the following groups controlled Egypt. The Nubian Dynasty (712-657 B.C.E.); The Persian Dynasty (525-404 B.C.E.); The Native Revolt and re-establishment of Egyptian rule by Egyptians (404-343 B.C.E.); The Second Persian Period (343-332 B.C.E.); The Ptolemaic or Greek Period (332 B.C.E.- c. 30 B.C.E.); Roman Period (c.30 B.C.E.-395 A.C.E.); The Byzantine Period (395-640 A.C.E) and The Arab Conquest Period (640 A.C.E.-present). The individual dynasties are numbered, generally in Roman numerals, from I through XXX.

The period after the New Kingdom saw greatness in culture and architecture under the rulership of Ramses II. However, after his rule, Egypt saw a decline from which it would never recover. This is the period of the downfall of Ancient Egyptian culture in which the Libyans ruled after The Tanite (XXI) Dynasty. This was followed by the Nubian conquerors who founded the XXII dynasty and tried to restore Egypt to her past glory. However, having been weakened by the social and political turmoil of wars, Ancient Egypt fell to the Persians once more. The Persians conquered the country until the Greeks, under Alexander, conquered them. The Romans followed the Greeks, and finally the Arabs conquered the land of Egypt in 640 A.C.E to the present.

However, the history which has been classified above is only the history of the "Dynastic Period." It reflects the view of traditional Egyptologists who have refused to accept the evidence of a Predynastic period in Ancient Egyptian history contained in Ancient Egyptian documents such as the *Palermo Stone, Royal Tablets at Abydos, Royal Papyrus of Turin,* the *Dynastic List* of *Manetho,* and the eye-witness accounts of Greek historians Herodotus (c. 484-425 B.C.E.) and Diodorus. These sources speak clearly of a Pre-dynastic society which stretches far into antiquity. The Dynastic Period is what most people think of whenever Ancient Egypt is mentioned. This period is when the pharaohs (kings) ruled. The latter part of the Dynastic Period is when the Biblical story of Moses, Joseph, Abraham, etc., occurs (c. 2100? -1,000? B.C.E). Therefore, those with a Christian background generally only have an idea about Ancient Egypt as it is related in the Bible. Although this biblical notion is very limited in scope, the significant impact of Ancient Egypt on Hebrew and Christian culture is evident even from the biblical scriptures. Actually, Egypt existed much earlier than most traditional Egyptologists are prepared to admit. The new archeological evidence related to the great Sphinx monument on the Giza Plateau and the ancient writings by Manetho, one of the last High Priests of Ancient Egypt, show that Ancient Egyptian history begins earlier than 10,000 B.C.E. and may date back to as early as 30,000-50,000 B.C.E.

It is known that the Pharaonic (royal) calendar based on the Sothic system (star Sirius) was in use by 4,240 B.C.E. This certainly required extensive astronomical skills and time for observation. Therefore, the history of Kamit (Egypt) must be reckoned to be extremely ancient. Thus, in order to grasp the antiquity of Ancient Egyptian culture, religion and philosophy, we will briefly review the history presented by the Ancient Egyptian Priest Manetho and some Greek Historians.

The calendar based on the Great Year was also used by the Ancient Egyptians. The Great Year is based on the movement of the earth through the constellations known as the precession of the Equinoxes and confirmed by the History given by the Ancient Egyptian Priest Manetho in the year 241 B.C.E. Each Great Year has 25,860 to 25,920 years and 12 arcs or constellations, and each passage through a constellation takes 2,155 – 2,160 years. These are the "Great Months." The current cycle or year began around the year 10,858 B.C.E. At around the year 36,766 B.C.E., according to Manetho, the Creator, Ra, ruled the earth in person from his throne in the Ancient Egyptian city of Anu. By this reckoning our current year (2,000 A.C.E.) is actually the year 38,766 based on the Great Year System of Ancient Egyptian history.

Egypt is located in the north-eastern corner of the African Continent. The cities wherein the theology of the Trinity of Amun-Ra-Ptah was developed were: A- Anu (Heliopolis), B-Hetkaptah (Memphis), and C-Waset (Thebes). The cities wherein the theology of the Trinity of Asar-Aset-Heru was developed were A- Anu, D-Abydos, E- Philae, F- Edfu, G-Denderah, and H- Ombos.

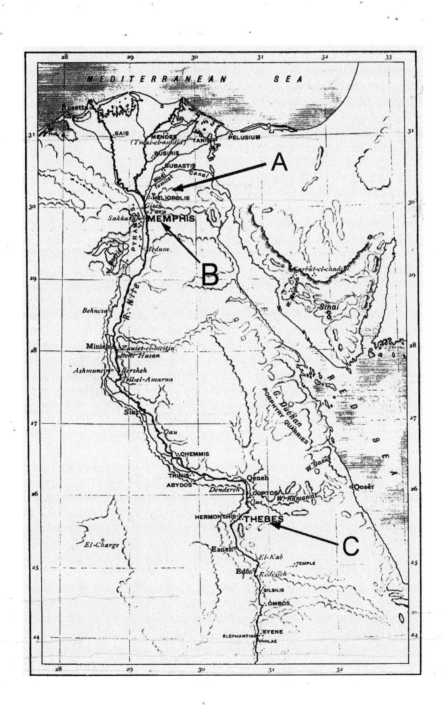

Who Am I?

Who am I? What is this mind which perceives? What is this universe made of? Is there a God?

Throughout history, these and many other questions have followed humanity from generation to generation. The need of human nature to experience, to evolve and understand has led to the invention of philosophies which assist the human mind in grasping the realities it seems to perceive in the world as well as those which it seems to perceive with the heart, but which remain intellectually unknowable. In ancient times these philosophies developed as myths, religions, yoga systems and in modern times they have taken the form of sciences called psychology, physics and non-religious philosophies such as Marxism and existentialism. Yet with all the developments of the past, humanity as a whole remains in search of the answers to happiness, health and peace. Has religion and science failed? Most importantly, throughout all the teachings embodied in religions and the discoveries of modern science, has humanity missed out on the benefits of religion and science? Is there anything useful in these endeavors for humankind? A deeper study into the history, meaning and practice of ancient teachings reveals a remarkable concordance with modern scientific discoveries. In essence, modern sciences such as Quantum Physics are leading scientists to contemplate life and our understanding of reality in terms which ancient philosophers and Sages espoused thousands of years ago. Science is a discipline which professes to shun non-rational thoughts, a common feature to both mythology and religion. So how is it possible that it would lead to the same conclusions about existence as mystical religions and Yoga philosophy?

Two of the most important areas we will look into are psychology and mythology. We will look at these from a yogic or mystical-symbolic point of view rather than a rational, literal or logical way. The reasons for doing this will become clear as we progress through the study. Mythology and spiritual symbolism were never intended to be understood as factual events which occurred in a particular place in time exclusively. Rather, they are to be understood as ever recurring principles of human life which need to be understood in their deepest sense in order for them to provide humanity with the benefit of their wisdom.

Psychology has been defined as the study of the thought processes characteristic of an individual or group (mind, psyche, ethos, mentality). In this work we will focus on religious mythology as a psychological discipline for understanding the human mind, its development and transformation. Mythology can be understood as a language, however, it is a unique kind of language. Certain languages are similar because they are part of a family of languages. For example: Italian and Spanish. This similarity makes it possible for a person whose native language is Spanish to understand the meanings of some Italian words so as to somewhat be able to follow along a conversation in Italian. Mythology is much more intelligible than an ordinary human language. Mythology is more akin to music in its universality. If the key elements of this language are well understood, it is possible to understand and relate any mythological system to another and thereby gain the understanding of the message being imparted. Setting up your own personal spiritual program will require that you develop a profound understanding of the psychological principles upon which ancient mythology is based in order to discover your special path on the spiritual journey.

In order to gain insight into the *"Psycho-Mythology"* or psychological implications of religious and spiritual mythology which promote the psycho-spiritual transformation of the individual leading to the attainment of Enlightenment, we must first define what is meant by the terms psycho and mythology. Here, the term *psycho* must be understood as far more than simply that which refers to the mind and its thoughts. We will be using *psycho* to mean everything that constitutes human consciousness in all of its stages and states. *Mythology* here refers to the codes, messages, ideas, directives and beliefs which affect the psyche through the conscious and unconscious mind of an individual, specifically those effects which result in transpersonal or transcendental changes in the personality as well as those which constitute anti-yogic, anti-transcendental movements.

While our study begins with Egyptian Mythology, Religion and Yoga Philosophy, it also necessarily relates to all mythologies, religions and philosophies around the world. Briefly, Egyptian religion is the oldest recorded religion in this historical era and in our book, *Egyptian Yoga*, we compiled the correlations between the religion which developed in Egypt and those which developed later around other parts of Africa as well as in Asia.[7] It becomes evident that what has been called Egyptian Mythology is in reality a highly sophisticated and advanced system of Yoga Philosophy. Yoga is a system of personal transformation by which we are able to discover our true Self wherein lies the answers to all of our questions about the purpose of our existence, who we are, how to overcome adversity and promote prosperity, and why we are in the situations of life in which we find ourselves. Most importantly, the idea is not to amass mountainous amounts of wisdom teachings but to discover their meanings and how to apply them in ordinary life to rise above it, as a lotus rises above the muddy waters without retaining a

---

[7] The term Asia includes Europe.

single drop of the dirty water on its petals. If this does not occur, then one is not practicing philosophy, religion or yoga, but something else. Initiation is therefore the process of coming into a philosophy and way of life which allows you to become free of any restrictions or impediments to your happiness. It is also a process of discovering how to end pain and suffering in life. Thus, it is a process of becoming established in your own inner support and inner peace without depending on the world.

What is Human Existence and What is its Purpose?

Human life is a process in which a human being experiences various situations, ranging from pain and suffering to happiness and pleasure, between the time span of birth and death. From a yogic point of view, all human situations are painful because they are distractions from the true source of bliss and abiding happiness within the heart. Attachment to objects and relationships outside of oneself seems like the normal course of human life, but the masses of people adopt this mode of existence out of ignorance. Ignorance of what? Ignorance of their deeper Self. If they had knowledge of the deeper Self within, there would be no need to seek personal fulfillment through worldly achievements, worldly possessions or worldly relationships. This endless search leads every ignorant human being to engage in various situations and entanglements, which in the beginning seem to hold the possibility of bringing about a happy circumstance, but which invariably leads to pain, suffering and frustration. A mature human being discovers that ordinary human life cannot satisfy the inner need of the soul because it is unpredictable and transient. So what should one live for? Did not the Ancient Egyptians build wondrous monuments and innovations in science, medicine, government, social order, etc.? They did not withdraw from the world, but they did not seek spiritual fulfillment through the world either. This is the first key to understanding Ancient Egyptian culture and spiritual philosophy.

You do not have to turn on the television or read a newspaper to see the miserable condition of most people. Think about your own life. Has there been any situation where happiness was abiding? Have you experienced any relationship with someone who never disappointed you or caused you pain? Has there been any possession you acquired which did not lose its power to bring you happiness or that you did not become bored with, even though it made you happy to possess it in the beginning? Even those people who say they are happy with life as it is are deluding themselves into believing that the happy moments balance the painful ones. This is not true because even the happy moments are setting you up for some painful disappointment in the future, because all worldly situations and relationships come to an end. Thus, by living in accordance with the ignorant philosophy of life, your happy moments cause longing for more happy moments, and when these are not possible, there is disappointment and frustration. The longing and frustration does not end at the time of death. When the body dies, the mind continues to hold the deep rooted desires for worldly fulfillment and this causes the soul to be impelled toward countless new lifetimes of karmic entanglements in search of worldly fulfillment. All of this occurs out of ignorance of one's true Self.

"The visible world is ephemeral, the spirit world is forever; gain strength from this since nothing physical can destroy you."

"Labor not after riches first, and think thou afterwards wilt enjoy them. He who neglects the present moment, throws away all that he hath. As the arrow passes through the heart, while the warrior knew not that it was coming; so shall his life be taken away before he knoweth that he hath it."

"There is no happiness for the soul in the external worlds since these are perishable, true happiness lies in that which is eternal, within us."

FROM: THE STEALE OF ABU: "Be chief of the mysteries at festivals, know your mouth, come in Hetep (peace), enjoy life on earth but do not become attached to it; it is transitory."
—Ancient Egyptian Proverbs

Becoming free from the clutches of ignorance is not as simple as learning about its cause. Even if you are honest and truly believe in the philosophy of yoga and mystical spirituality, all of your mental efforts to negate the ignorance will fail in the beginning. This is because your mind has spent many hours over a period of days, months, years, lifetimes and eons, believing in the illusion of human life. Even if you were to understand that it is your worldly attachments which are causing you mental agitation and suffering, the process of attaining Enlightenment is not as simple as saying, "O.K. since my possessions are distracting me and causing me agitation and worry, I will give them up and have peace." Even if you were to find yourself without possessions, your mind would be grieving over their loss, or preoccupied with how to regain them or how to survive without them.

Even if you give everything up and go to a distant cave away from civilization, you cannot escape from the world. There will still be ants and mosquitoes to bite you, cold weather, rain, wild animals, and the restless wandering of your mind thinking of the life you left! Initiation into spiritual life is the process of learning an art of living which leads to freedom even while involved in the world. Your goal is to become as the lotus which rises up from the muddy waters, able to exist in the world without being soiled by it, and having discovered the bliss of inner spiritual discovery, always abiding in that wondrous glory in any situation which life presents to you. Once the teachings of spirituality are understood and you have a firm conviction as to their reality, then you can begin the process of making them your reality. Spiritual realization requires sustained effort over a period of time wherein spiritual disciplines are directed towards overturning the mountainous creations, which the mind has produced in the past due to ignorance. The mind is like a river. Ignorant ideas are like logs, rocks, branches and dams in the river which block, divert or distort the flow of water. With the correct equipment (correct understanding and practice of the spiritual disciplines) and through sustained effort, the obstacles to spiritual realization can be removed allowing the river of the mind to flow freely toward the ocean of self-discovery. As the second stage in the practice of religion (ritualism), the *Prt m Hru* also encompasses the disciplines of spiritual practice which are in modern times recognized by the name "Yoga," especially the Yoga of Righteous action. These will be discussed in detail later.

If you have developed enough spiritual sensitivity to understand that there is no abiding peace or happiness to be found in ordinary human existence, you are qualified to study the deeper mysteries of spiritual life. This is the process of Initiation, which leads from ignorance to Enlightenment and self-discovery. It is the process by which a human being living an ordinary life is taught how to lead an extraordinary life and to attain superhuman expanded (enlightened) consciousness. Where is there an inexhaustible source of bliss and happiness, which does not depend on external factors? Where is it possible to find unending peace and tranquility and a joy which is not subject to external conditions of either prosperity or adversity? The initiatic process shows the way.

In order for the teachings of mystical spirituality to come true in your life, you must make them the central force in your life. You must center your life around them and infuse them into every aspect of your life. In this way you will become transformed into the ideal of what the teachings describe: an Enlightened human being. It is not possible to gain higher spiritual understanding of the practices in any other way except to live them. Thus initiation is a way of life and not a single event. It is a continuous process which leads to greater and greater awareness and expansion, culminating in the highest levels of Self-Knowledge, Stage Three of Religion.

Before proceeding with the main body of this work, it would be helpful to establish some working definitions for the disciplines which will be discussed in order to provide a common basis for understanding the journey we will undertake. These terms will be further defined and explored throughout the course of this work.

Philosophy

Philosophy has been defined as the speculative inquiry concerning the source and nature of human knowledge and a system of ideas based on such thinking. In this work, the idea of philosophy will be confined to the modes of thinking employed for the purpose of transforming the human mind, leading it to achieve transpersonal states of consciousness. In its original sense, philosophy is a mental discipline for leading a person to enlightenment. In modern times this lofty notion of philosophy has come to be regarded as unscientific speculation or even as an opinion or belief of one person or group versus another. Specifically, we will look at Kemeticism[8] as a philosophy of psychological transformation.

> "Never forget, the words are not the reality, only reality is reality; picture symbols are the idea, words are confusion."[9]

---

[8] Term coined by the author to signify Kemetic, based on the ancient words Kemet or Kamit, used in Ancient Egypt to describe the land and inhabitants of North-East Africa, meaning Ancient Egyptian- related to Ancient Egyptian culture, religion and mysticism. *"KMT" "Egypt", "Burnt", "Land of Blackness", "Land of the Burnt People."* This term is most appropriately used to refer to the religion of Ancient Egypt in order to relate it to the culture of ancient times. Another term, "Egyptian Yoga" meaning Smai Tawi, has bee introduced previously. Howevber, the proper name of Ancient Egyptian Religion is "Shetaut Neter," meaning "the hidden way of the Divine Self" (i.e. God).

[9] Hermetic proverb. Hermeticism is the later development of Kemetic Philosophy.

"The Self {ultimate reality} is not known through study of scriptures, nor through subtlety of the intellect, nor through much learning; but by him who longs for it is it known."[10]

One caveat which any true philosophy must follow is the understanding that words in themselves cannot capture the ultimate essence of reality. Words can be a trap to the highly developed intellect. Therefore, we must always keep in mind that words and philosophical discourse can only point the way to the truth. In order to discover the truth, we must go beyond all words, all thoughts, and all of our mental concepts and philosophies, because the truth, as *Hermetic* and *Vedanta* philosophy would say, can only be experienced; it cannot be encapsulated in any way, shape or form.

The study of philosophy in its highest form is to assist the student in understanding {his/her} own mind in order to be able to transcend it, and thus, experience the "transcendental" reality which lies beyond words, thoughts, concepts and mental notions. Mental conceptions are based on our own worldly experiences. They help us to understand the world as the senses perceive it. However, clinging to these experiences as the only reality precludes our discovery of other forms of reality or existence which lies beyond the capacity of the senses. A dog's olfactory sense and the vision of a hawk are much superior to that of the human being.

However, the human has one advantage which is superior to all senses and scientific instruments, the intuitional mind when it is purified by the practice of Yoga philosophy and disciplines. Ancient mystical philosophical systems have as their main goal the destruction of the limited concepts and illusions of the mind. In essence, the philosophies related to understanding nature and a human being's place in it were the first disciplines which practiced what would today be called Transpersonal Psychology, that is, a system of psychology which assists us in going beyond the personal or ego-based aspects of the psyche in order to discover what lies beyond (trans) the personal (relating to the personality).

Metaphysics

Metaphysics is the branch of philosophy that systematically investigates first causes of nature, the universe and ultimate reality. The term comes from the Greek "*meta physika*," meaning "after the things of nature." In Aristotle's works, he envisioned that the first philosophy came after the physics. Metaphysics has been divided into *ontology*, or the study of the essence of being or that which is or exists, and *cosmology*, the study of the structure and laws of the universe and the manner of its creation. From time immemorial, philosophers, such as those who wrote the Ancient Egyptian Creation myths, to Greek philosophers such as Plato and Aristotle, to more modern philosophers such as Whitehead and Kant, have written on metaphysics. Skeptics, however, have charged that speculation which cannot be verified by objective evidence is useless. However, these skeptics do not realize that what they consider as "objective reality" is not objective at all, since objectivity is based on the perceptions of the senses, and as just discussed, modern science itself has proven that the human senses cannot perceive the phenomenal universe as it really is. Further, the objective information that can be gathered by scientific instruments is only valid under certain conditions. This makes it relative and not absolute information. Thus, what people ordinarily consider to be real and abiding is not. Einstein's proof of relativity confirms this. There must be something real beyond the phenomenal world which sustains it. The search for that higher essence is the purpose of philosophy and metaphysics. Therefore, the value of metaphysical and mystical philosophy studies is evident.

Psychology

Psychology, as used by ordinary practitioners of society, has been defined as the study of the thought processes characteristic of an individual or group (mind, psyche, ethos, mentality). In this work we will focus on Kemeticism as a psychological discipline for understanding the human mind, its source, higher development and transformation. However, Mystical Psychology in reality does not relate only to the mind since a human being is composed of several complex aspects. The term personality, as it is used in Yoga, implies mind, body and spirit, as well as the conscious, subconscious and unconscious aspects of the mind. Therefore, the discipline of psychology must be expanded to include physical as well as spiritual dimensions. Once again, modern medical science has, within the last twenty years, acknowledged the understanding that health cannot be treated as a physical problem only, but as one which involves the mind, body and spirit. Likewise, spiritual teaching must be related as a discipline which involves not only the soul of an individual, but the mind and body as well – in other words, the entire human being.

---

[10] Indian Vedantic proverb.

Yoga

The literal meaning of the word Yoga is to *"yoke"* or to *"link"* back. The implication is to link back individual consciousness (human personality) to its original source, the original essence: Universal Consciousness. In a broad sense Yoga is any process which helps one to achieve liberation or freedom from bondage to the pain and spiritual ignorance of ordinary human existence. So whenever you engage in any activity with the goal of promoting the discovery of your true Self, be it studying the spiritual wisdom teachings, exercising, fasting, meditation, breath control, rituals, chanting, prayer, etc., you are practicing yoga. If the goal is to help you to discover your essential nature as one with God or the Supreme Being, Consciousness, then it is Yoga.

Yoga (Sanskrit for "union") is a term used for a number of disciplines, the goal of each being to lead the practitioner to attain union with Universal Consciousness. Present day Indian Yoga philosophy is based on several Indian texts such as the *Upanishads, Bhagavad Gita* and the *Yoga-sutras* of Patañjali, and several other Yoga treatises developed in India. The practice of Yoga generally involves meditation, moral restraints, and the awakening of energy centers (in the body) through specific postures (asanas) or physical exercises, and breathing exercises. All Yoga disciplines are devoted to freeing the soul or individual self from worldly (mental) restraints. They have become popular in the West as a means of self-control and relaxation.

The specific form of *"yoking"* or to *"linking"* back that was practiced in Ancient Egypt was called "Smai Tawi" or union of the two lands, i.e. the opposites, the Higher and lower aspects of self or soul and Spirit.

Religion

All religions tend to be deistic at the elementary levels. Most often it manifests as an outgrowth of the cultural concepts of a people as they try to express the deeper feeling which they perceive, though not in its entirety. Thus, deism is based on limited spiritual knowledge. Deism, as a religious belief or form of theism, holds that God's action was restricted to an initial act of creation, after which he retired (separated) to contemplate the majesty of his work. Deists hold that the natural creation is regulated by laws put in place by God at the time of creation and inscribed with perfect moral principles. A deeper study of religion will reveal that in its original understanding, it seeks to reveal the deeper essential nature of creation, the human heart and their relation to God, which transcends the deistic model or doctrine. The term religion comes from the Latin *"Relegare"* which uses the word roots *"Re"* which means *"Back"* and *"Ligon"* which means *"to hold, to link, to bind."* Therefore, the essence of true religion is the same as yoga, that is, of linking back, specifically, linking the soul of its follower back to its original source: God. So, although religion in its purest form is a Yoga system, incorporating the yoga disciplines within its teachings, the original intent and meaning of the religious scriptures are often misunderstood, if not distorted. This occurs because religions have developed in different geographic areas. As a result, the lower levels of religion which are mixed with culture (historical accounts, stories and traditions) have developed independently, and thereby appear to be different from each other on the surface. This leads to confusion and animosity among people who are ignorant of the true process of religious movement. Religion consists of three levels: *myth, ritual and mystical experience.* If the first two levels are misunderstood or accepted literally, the spiritual movement will fail to proceed to the next higher level. In order for a religious experience to lead one to have a mystical experience, all three levels of religion must be completed. This process will be fully explained throughout the text of this volume.

Mysticism

Mysticism is a spiritual discipline for attaining union with the Divine through the practice of deep meditation or contemplation, and other spiritual disciplines such as austerity, detachment, renunciation, etc. In this aspect, Mysticism and Yoga are synonymous.

Dualism

Similar to Deism, Dualism is the belief that all things in nature are separate and real, and that they exist independently from any underlying essence or support. It is the belief in the pairs of opposites wherein everything has a polar counterpart. For example: male - female, here - there, hot - cold, etc. While these elements seem real and abiding to the human mind, mystical philosophers throughout history have been claiming that this is only an outer expression of the underlying essence from which they originate. In reality, the underlying essence of all things is non-dual and all-encompassing. It is the substratum of all that exists. Modern science has been confirming this view of matter. The latest experiments in quantum physics show that all matter is composed of energy. Most importantly for this study, dualism is a state of mind that occurs at an immature level of mental understanding of reality. It is akin to egoism and egoistic tendencies which tend to make a person see {himself/herself} as separate and distinct from the world and from other living beings. Through the study and practice of mystical spiritual teachings, dualism is replaced with non-dualism and salvation, spiritual enlightenment, then occurs. Therefore, salvation or resurrection is related to a non-dualistic view of existence and bondage and death are related to dualism and egoism.

A dualistic view of life can lead to agitation, suffering and even catastrophic events in human experience because the mind is trained to see either good or evil, acceptable or unacceptable, you or me, etc., and not the whole of creation composed of many parts. In the dualistic state of mind, the attitudes of separation and exclusivism are exaggerated. These render the mind agitated. Mental agitation prevents the mind from achieving greater insights into the depths of spiritual teachings. Thus, agitated people are usually frustrated and unable to discover inner peace and spiritual fulfillment.

When societal institutions such as the church rationalize and even sanction dualism, then egoistic sentiments hold sway over the heart of human beings. In this sense, dualism and egoism go hand in hand. When universal love and humility are replaced by egoism and arrogance, then it becomes possible to hurt others and to hurt nature. When we forget our common origin and destiny, we easily fall into the vast pit of egoism. We see ourselves as an individual in a world of individuals, fighting a battle of survival for wealth in order to gain pleasures of the senses, rather than seeing ourselves as divine beings who are made in the same image, with the same frailties and potential. This degraded condition opens the doors to the deep-rooted fears and sense of inadequacy which translate into anger, resentment, hatred, greed and all negative tendencies in the human personality. The concept of dualism is the basis of the atrocities and injustices that have been committed in the history of the world. Under its control, human beings seek to control others and nature, and to satisfy their inner urges through violence because they cannot control themselves and express their deeper needs in constructive ways. In the Indian Vedantic tradition, duality or *dvaita* is seen as the greatest error of the human mind. For this reason all of the disciplines of Vedanta, Shetaut Neter, Yoga, Buddhism, Taoism and other forms of creation-centered spirituality are directed toward developing a correct understanding of human existence. When the underlying unity behind the duality is discovered, there can be no violence or ill will against others. This is the basis of non-violence. Harmony and spiritual enlightenment then arise spontaneously. Egoism now gives way to universal love and peace.

Spiritual Transformation

Transformation here is to be understood as not merely a change in specific behavior patterns or a change in feeling based on temporary circumstances, but as a complete re-orientation of the psychology of the individual. This re-orientation will lead to a permanent improvement in behavior and genuine metamorphosis of the innermost levels of the mind. Specifically, we will focus on Kemeticism as a system for psychological transformation wherein the individual ceases to be a limited individual, subject to the foibles and follies of human nature, and attains the state of transcendence of these failings.

Mythology

Most people hold the opinion that mythology is a lie, an illusion, fiction or fantasy. Mythology can be best understood as a language. However, it is a unique kind of language. An ordinary language is sometimes similar to another because it is a part of a family of languages. For example, Italian and Spanish words are similar. This similarity makes it possible for a person whose native language is Spanish to understand the meanings of some Italian words and somewhat follow along a conversation in Italian. Even so, mythology is much more intelligible than this. Mythology is more akin to music in its universality. If the key elements of this language of mythology are well understood, then it is possible to understand and relate any mythological system to another and thereby gain the understanding of the message being imparted.

Enlightenment

Enlightenment is the central topic of our study and the coveted goal of all practitioners of Yoga and Religion. Enlightenment is the term used to describe the highest level of spiritual awakening. It means attaining such a level of spiritual awareness that one discovers the underlying unity of the entire universe as well as the fact that the source of all creation is the same source from which the innermost Self within every human heart arises.

All forms of spiritual practice are directed toward the goal of assisting every individual to discover the true essence of the universe both externally, in physical creation, and internally, within the human heart, as the very root of human consciousness. Thus, many terms are used to describe the attainment of the goal of spiritual knowledge and the eradication of spiritual ignorance. Some of these terms are: *Enlightenment, Resurrection, Salvation, The Kingdom of Heaven, Christ Consciousness, Cosmic Consciousness, Moksha or Liberation, Buddha Consciousness, One With The Tao, Self-realization, Know Thyself, Heruhood, Nirvana, Sema, Yoga,* etc.

Yoga Philosophy and the World Religious Philosophies Defined

Yoga philosophy and disciplines have developed independently as well as in conjunction with religious philosophies. It may be accurate to say that Yoga is a science unto itself which religions have used and incorporated into their religious philosophies and practices by relating the yogic principles to symbols such as deities, gods, goddesses, angels, saints, etc. The following is a brief description of yoga philosophy in comparison to the philosophies which developed along side it.

Yoga Philosophy

Human consciousness and universal consciousness are in reality one and the same. The appearance of separation is a mental illusion. Yoga is the mystical and mindful (thoughtful, aware, observant) union of individual and universal consciousness by integrating the aspects of individual personality, thereby allowing the personality to be purified so that it may behold its true essence.

Vedanta Philosophy

Spiritual Philosophy of Mystical Psychology of Ancient India.

1- Absolute Monism: Only God is reality. All else is imagination.
2- Modified Monism: God is to nature as soul is to body.

Monotheism

Monotheism means the belief in the existence of a single God in the universe. Christianity, Judaism, and Islam are the major monotheistic religions. It must be noted here that the form of monotheism espoused by the major Western religions is that of an exclusive, personified deity who exists in fact and is separate from creation. In contrast, the monotheism of Ancient Egyptian, Hindu and Gnostic Christian traditions envisions a single Supreme Deity that is expressed as the Supreme Deity of all other traditions, as well as the phenomenal world. It is not exclusive, but universal.

Polytheism

Polytheism means the belief in or worship of many gods. Such gods usually have specific attributes or functions.

Totemism

Totemism is the belief in the idea that there is a relationship between kinship groups and specific animals and plants. Many scholars believe that religions which use these symbols are primitive because they are seen as worshipping those animals themselves. However, when the mythology behind the beliefs is examined more closely, the totems are understood as symbols of specific tutelary deities which relate the individuals to a group, and also to the greater workings of nature, and ultimately, to God.

Pantheism

1- Absolute Pantheism: Everything there is, is God. God and Creation are one.
2- Modified Pantheism: God is the reality or principle behind nature.

Panentheism

Term coined by KC F. Krause (1781-1832) to describe the doctrine that God is immanent in all things but also transcendent, so that every part of the universe has its existence in God, but He is more than the sum total of the parts.

Kemeticism: Shetaut Neter: Ancient Egyptian Philosophy - Egyptian Yoga

1-Monotheistic Polytheism - Ancient Egyptian religion encompasses a single and absolute Supreme Deity that expresses as the cosmic forces (gods and goddesses), human beings and nature.

Hinduism and Mahayana Buddhism
1-Monotheistic Polytheism.

The Tree Stages of Religion

While on the surface it seems that there are many differences between the philosophies, upon closer reflection there is only one major division, that of belief or non-belief. Among the believers there are differences of opinion as to how to believe. This is the source of all the trouble between religions. This is because ordinary religion is deistic, based on traditions and customs which are themselves based on culture. Since culture varies from place to place and from one time in history to another, there will always be some variation in spiritual traditions. These differences will occur not only between cultures, but even within the same culture. An example of this is Christianity with its myriad of denominations.

Therefore, those who cling to the idea that religion has to be related to a particular culture and its specific practices or rituals will always have some difference with someone else's conception. In the three stages of religion, Myth, Ritual and Mysticism, culture belongs to the myth stage of religious practice, the most elementary level.

Myth ⇀ Ritual ⇀ Mysticism

An important theme, which will be developed throughout this volume, is the complete practice of religion, that is, in its three aspects, *mythology, ritual* and *metaphysical* or the *mystical experience* (mysticism - mystical philosophy). At the first level a human being learns the stories and traditions of the religion. At the second level rituals are learned and practiced. At the third level a spiritual aspirant is led to actually go beyond myths and rituals and to attain the ultimate goal of religion. This is an important principle, because many religions present different aspects of philosophy at different levels, and an uninformed onlooker may label it as primitive or idolatrous, etc., without understanding what is going on. For example, Hinduism and Ancient Egyptian Religion present polytheism and duality at the first two levels of religious practice. However, at the third level, mysticism, the practitioner is made to understand that all of the gods and goddesses being worshipped do not exist in fact, but are in reality aspects of the single, transcendental Supreme Self. This is evident in the Prt M Hru.

In the area of Yoga Philosophy and the category of Monism, there are little, if any, differences. This is because these disciplines belong to the third level of religion wherein mysticism reaches its height. The goal of all mysticism is to transcend the phenomenal world and all mental concepts. Ordinary religion is a part of the world and the mental concepts of people, and must too be ultimately transcended.

Selected Spiritual Philosophies Compared

The Sages of ancient times created philosophies through which it might be possible to explain the origins of creation, as we saw above. Then they set out to create disciplines which could lead a person to discover for themselves the spiritual truths of life and thereby realize the higher reality which lies beyond the phenomenal world. These disciplines are referred to as religions and spiritual philosophies (mysticism-yoga). Below is a basic listing of world religious and spiritual philosophies.

Table 1: Religious Philosophies

RELIGIOUS PHILOSOPHIES				
Shetaut Neter	**Vedanta**	**Samkhya**	**Buddhism**	**Yoga**
Non-dualist metaphysics. God manifests as nature and cosmic forces (neteru). Union with the Divine through wisdom, devotion and identification with the Divine.	Non-dualist metaphysics. God alone exists. Union with the Divine through wisdom, devotion and identification with the Divine.	Dualist Philosophy. Discipline of understanding what is real (God) from what is unreal (transient world of time and space).	Union with the Absolute through extinction of desire.	Mystical tradition: union of individual consciousness with the Absolute Consciousness (God) through cessation of mental activity by wisdom, devotion and identification with the Divine. Example ↓ Egyptian Yoga Indian Yoga Christian Yoga Buddhist Yoga Chinese (Taoist) Yoga

Table 2: Religious Categories

RELIGIOUS CATEGORIES				
Theism	Atheism	Ethicism	Ritualism	Monism
Belief in a God which will save you.	Salvation by doing what makes you happy. There is no God, only existence, which just happened on its own without any help.	Salvation by performing the right actions.	Salvation by performing the correct rituals.	Salvation by understanding that all is the Self (God).
↓ Example Orthodox Christian Orthodox Islam Orthodox Judaism	↓ Example Epicureans Charvacas Atheists Existentialists Stoics Humanists	↓ Example Zoroastrianism Jainism Confucianism Aristotelianism	↓ Example Brahmanism Priestcraft	↓ Example Taoism Spinoza Cabalism Sufism Idealism Christian Science Gnosticism Gnostic Christianity Vedanta Shetaut Neter Buddhism

Origins and Basis of Mysticism in the Rau nu Pert em Hru

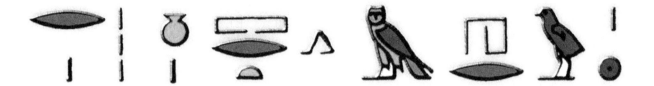

Figure 5: Scene from the *Prt m Hru* of Lady Taameniu

INTRODUCTION TO THE PHILOSOPHY OF The *PERT EM HERU*

What is The Rau nu Pert em Hru?

The scriptures presented in this volume come from the extensive body of texts known as the *Egyptian Book of the Dead*. These texts span the entire history of Ancient Egypt, beginning with the *Pyramid Texts* in the early Dynastic period. These were followed by the *Coffin Texts*, which were followed by the late dynastic texts which were recorded on a variety of different media, of which the most popularly known is papyrus.

The teachings of mystical spirituality are contained in the most ancient writings of Egypt, even those preceding the Dynastic or Pharaonic period (4,500 B.C.E.-600 A.C.E). The most extensive expositions of the philosophy may be found in the writings, which have in modern times been referred to as "The Egyptian Book of the Dead."

It was originally known as "Rau nu Prt M Hru" or "Rau nu *Pert Em Heru*" or "Reu nu *Pert Em Heru*."

> *Rau*= words, teachings, liturgy, *nu* = of, *Prt* or *Pert* = going out, *em* or *m* = as or through, *Hru* or *Heru* = Spiritual Light or Enlightened Being (the God Heru). This may therefore be translated as: ***"The Word Utterances for Coming into the Spiritual Light (Enlightenment) or Becoming one with Heru."***

Thus, the *Rau nu Pert Em Heru* is a collection of words used to affirm spiritual wisdom and to direct a human being towards a positive spiritual movement. Each *Rau* or *Ru* contains affirmations of mystical wisdom that enables a human being to understand and experience that particular aspect of Divinity. The collection of these verses has been referred to as "Chapters," "Utterances" or "Spells" by Egyptologists. While the teachings presented in the *Rau nu Pert Em Heru* may be thought of as being presented in Chapters and referred to as such, they must also be thought of as special words which, when understood, internalized and lived, will lead a person to spiritual freedom. In this volume we will refer to the groupings of subjects as "Chapters" which may be better defined for our usage here as: a collection of Hekau -words of power- which impart a spiritual teaching and affirm that teaching, and by their repeated utterance make it a reality. The term "Ru" may be used as a shortened version of "Rau." It was not until after 1,500 B.C.E. that the collections of Ru were compiled in the form of papyrus scrolls and standardized to some degree. However, this process of standardization was not as rigid as the canonization of the books of the Bible, which had been separate scriptures relating to Christianity and Judaism prior to around the year 350 A.C.E.

In Egyptian mythology, Hru is not only a reference to the god who is the son of Aset and Asar (Isis and Osiris), but Hru also means "Day" and "Light." In fact, Day and Light are two of the most important attributes of the god Heru who is understood as the highest potential of every human being. Therefore, the title may also read as **"The Book of Coming Forth by (into) the Day," "The Guide for Becoming Heru," "The Chapters for Coming into the Light,"** or **"The Book of Enlightenment."** The writings were named "The Egyptian Book of the Dead" by modern Egyptologists who obtained them from the modern day dwellers of the area (northeast African Arabs) who said they were found buried with the Ancient Egyptian dead. In the interest of simplicity and consistency, the name *"Pert Em Heru"* will be used throughout this text.

The *Pyramid Texts* and the *Book of Coming Forth By Day* are similar in scripture and purpose. It is correct to understand that the texts referred to as the *Book of Coming Forth By Day* evolved out of the *Pyramid Text* writings. This is because the *Pyramid Texts* are the early form of the well-known texts, which have been called the *Book of Coming Forth By Day*. The *Pyramid Texts* are hieroglyphic writings contained in the pyramid tombs[11] of the kings of the early Dynastic period. Both are collections of

---

[11] Not to be confused with the Pyramids in Giza.

utterances, originally recorded in hieroglyphic, which lead the initiate to transform {his/her} consciousness from human to divine, by purifying the mind with wisdom about the neteru (gods and goddesses, divine forces in the universe), and through the practice of rituals which promote personality integration and thus, spiritual transformation. Each of these constitute major treatises of Ancient Egyptian philosophy and together constitute an advanced, holistic system of spiritual development. All of these have as the main purpose to effect the union of the individual human being with the Transcendental Self. This philosophy of spiritual transcendence and enlightenment did not begin with the dawn of the Dynastic period in Ancient Egypt. The evidence from ancient texts and the history of Manetho show that the Ancient Egyptian history, which is known about, is only the descendent of a much more ancient era of Egyptian civilization.[12]

Ancient Egyptian Religion as Yoga

The Ancient Egyptians Practiced Yoga

> **yo·ga** (yō′gə) *n.* **1.** Also **Yoga**. A Hindu discipline aimed at training the consciousness for a state of perfect spiritual insight and tranquillity. **2.** A system of exercises practiced as part of this discipline to promote control of the body and mind. **--yo′gic** (-gĭk) *adj.*
>
> —American Heritage Dictionary

Most people have heard of Yoga as an exercise, however, Yoga is a vast science of human psychology and spiritual transformation which includes physical and mental health as the prerequisite for further progress. Yoga, in all of its disciplines, was practiced in Ancient Egypt (Kemet, Kamut, Kamit or Ta-Meri) and is the subject of the Ancient Egyptian Mysteries. Yoga, as it was practiced in Ancient Egypt, included the disciplines of virtuous living, dietary purification, study of the wisdom teachings and their practice in daily life, psychophysical and psycho-spiritual exercises and meditation. Practitioners of Indian Yoga, Buddhist Yoga and Chinese Yoga (Taoism) today refer to all of these disciplines as Yogic disciplines. Therefore, the Ancient Egyptians were the first practitioners of Yoga Philosophy in our history. Through a process of gradually blending these in the course of ordinary life, an individual can effect miraculous changes in {her/his} life and thereby achieve the supreme goal of all existence, the goal of Yoga: Union with the Higher Self.

The Term "Egyptian Yoga" and The Philosophy Behind It

Egyptian Yoga is what has been commonly referred to by Egyptologists as Egyptian "Religion" or "Mythology," but to think of it as just set of stories or allegories about a long lost civilization is to completely miss the greatest secrets of human existence. As previously discussed, Yoga in all of its forms was practiced in Egypt earlier than anywhere else in our history. This unique perspective from Africa provides a new way to look at life, religion and the discipline of psychology. Perhaps most importantly though, Egyptian mythology, when understood as a system of Yoga, gives every individual insight into their own divine nature. This is its true worth.

The teachings of Yoga are at the heart of *Prt m Hru*. As explained, the word "Yoga" is a Sanskrit term meaning to unite the individual with the Cosmic. The term has been used in certain parts of this book for ease of communication since the word "Yoga" has received wide popularity especially in western countries in recent years. The Ancient Egyptian equivalent of yoga is: *"Smai." Smai* (Sma, Sema, Sama) means union, and the following determinative terms give it a spiritual significance, at once equating it with the term "Yoga" as it is used in India. When used in conjunction with the Ancient Egyptian symbol which means land, *"Ta,"* the term "union of the two lands" arises.

---

[12] See the book *Cycles of Time* by Muata Ashby

Smai Tawi
(From Chapter 4 of the *Prt m Hru*)

In Chapter 4[13] and Chapter 17[14] of the *Prt m Hru*, a term "Smai Tawi" is used. It means "Union of the two lands of Egypt," ergo "Egyptian Yoga." The two lands refer to the two main districts of the country (North and South) In ancient times Egypt was divided into two sections or land areas. These were known as Lower and Upper Egypt. In Ancient Egyptian mystical philosophy, the land of Upper Egypt relates to the divinity Heru (Horus), who represents the Higher Self, and the land of Lower Egypt relates to Set, the divinity of the lower self. So **Smai Taui** means "the union of the two lands" or the "Union of the lower self with the Higher Self. The lower self relates to that which is negative and uncontrolled in the human mind, while the Higher Self relates to that which is above temptations and is good in the human heart. Thus, we also have the Ancient Egyptian term **Smai Heru-Set,** or the union of Heru and Set. So Smai Taui or Smai Heru-Set are the Ancient Egyptian words which can be translated as "**Egyptian Yoga.**"

Above from left to right are the symbols of Egyptian Yoga: *Sma, nfr, nkh, and htp.* The Ancient Egyptian language and symbols provide the first "historical" record of Yoga Philosophy and Religious literature. The Indian culture of the Indus Valley Dravidians and Harappans appear to have carried it on and expanded much of the intellectual expositions in the form of the Vedas, Upanishads, Puranas and Tantras, the ancient spiritual texts of India.

The hieroglyph Sma, "Sema," represented by the union of two lungs and the trachea, symbolizes that the union of the Higher Self and lower self leads to the One.

The hieroglyph, nfr, "Nefer," close in pronunciation to "Neter" (God), expressed by the union of the heart and the trachea symbolizes: That which is the most beautiful thing, the highest good, and the greatest achievement.

The hieroglyph, nkh, "Ankh," symbolizes the union of the male (cross-temporal) and the female (circle-eternal) aspects of oneself, leading to the transformation into an androgynous being. Thus, the two become One. The Ankh was also later used in Christianity and Hinduism as a symbol of divinity. Therefore, the Ankh is the unifying symbol, which links Egypt, India and Christendom.

The hieroglyph htp, "Hetep," symbolizes supreme peace, the final abode of all who satisfy the desire of their soul, union with its Higher Self: YOGA. Egyptian Yoga encompasses many myths and philosophies, which lead to the reunion of the soul with its Higher Self. Ancient Egyptian religion involves three major theological branches based on the Trinity (Amun-Ra-Ptah) which emanates out of the Hidden and nameless Transcendental Divinity. This Divinity is variously known under the following names: Nameless One, Nebertcher or Neberdjer, Tem, Neter Neteru, Amun, Asar, Ra, Kheper, and Aset. These names are to be understood as being synonymous. They refer to the same idea of an Absolute Supreme Being or transcendental reality from which the phenomenal world arises, as land rises out of an ocean.

The central and most popular character within Ancient Egyptian Religion of Asar is Heru, who is an incarnation of his father, Asar. Asar is killed by his brother Set who, out of greed and demoniac (Setian)

---

[13] Commonly referred to as Chapter 17
[14] Commonly referred to as Chapter 176

tendency, craved to be the ruler of Egypt. With the help of Djehuty (Djehuty), the God of wisdom, Aset, the great mother and Hetheru, his consort, Heru prevailed in the battle against Set for the rulership of Kemet (Egypt). Heru's struggle symbolizes the struggle of every human being to regain rulership of the Higher Self and to subdue the lower self. With this understanding, the land of Egypt is equivalent to the {Kingdom/Queendom} concept of Christianity.

The most ancient writings in our historical period are from the Ancient Egyptians. These writings are referred to as hieroglyphics. Also, the most ancient civilization known was the Ancient Egyptian civilization. The proof of this lies in the ancient Egyptian Sphinx, as previously discussed. The original name given to these writings by the Ancient Egyptians is *Medtu Neter,* meaning "the writing of God" or *Neter Metu* or "Divine Speech." These writings were inscribed in temples, coffins and papyruses and contained the teachings in reference to the spiritual nature of the human being and the ways to promote spiritual emancipation, awakening or resurrection. The Ancient Egyptian proverbs presented in this text are translations from the original hieroglyphic scriptures. An example of hieroglyphic text is presented on the front cover.

Egyptian Philosophy may be summed up in the following proverbs, which clearly state that the soul is heavenly or divine and that the human being must awaken to the true reality, which is the Spirit, Self.

"Self-knowledge is the basis of true knowledge."

"Soul to heaven, body to earth."

"Man is to become God-like through a life of virtue and the cultivation of the spirit through scientific knowledge, practice and bodily discipline."

"Salvation is accomplished through the efforts of the individual. There is no mediator between man and {his/her} salvation."

"Salvation is the freeing of the soul from its bodily fetters, becoming a God through knowledge and wisdom, controlling the forces of the cosmos instead of being a slave to them, subduing the lower nature and through awakening the Higher Self, ending the cycle of rebirth and dwelling with the Neters who direct and control the Great Plan."

The Ancient Egyptian Symbols of Yoga

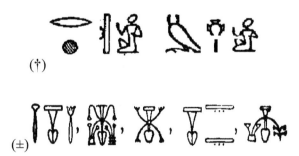

29

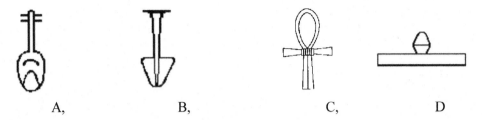

A,   B,   C,   D

The theme of the arrangement of the symbols above is based on the idea that in mythological and philosophic forms, Egyptian mythology and philosophy merge with world mythology, philosophy and religion. The hieroglyphic symbols at the very top (†) mean: *"Know Thyself," "Self-knowledge is the basis of all true knowledge"* and (±) abbreviated forms of *Smai taui,* signifies "Egyptian Yoga." The next four below represent the four words in Egyptian Philosophy, which mean *"YOGA."* They are: (A) *"Nefer"* (B) *"Sema"* (C) *"Ankh"* and (D) *"Hetep."*

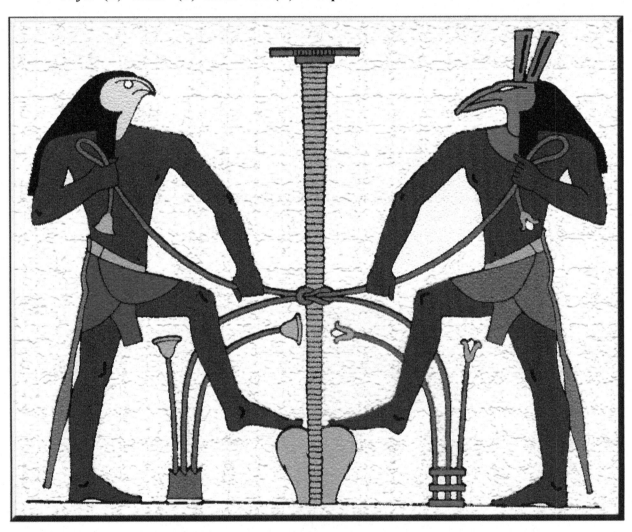

Figure 6: Above: Smai Heru-Set,

Heru and Set join forces to tie up the symbol of Union (Sema –see (B) above). The Sema symbol refers to the Union of Upper Egypt (Lotus) and Lower Egypt (Papyrus) under one ruler, but also at a more subtle level, it refers to the union of one's Higher Self and lower self (Heru and Set), as well as the control of one's breath (Life Force) through the union (control) of the lungs (breathing organs). The character of Heru and Set are an integral part of the *Pert Em Heru.*

The Study of Yoga

The study and practice of Yoga involves three distinct phases. These are: *Listening to the wisdom teachings, Reflecting on those wisdom teachings and making them an integral part of your life, and Meditation, the art of transcending ordinary human awareness and consciousness.* Since a complete treatise on the theory and practice of yoga would require several volumes, only a basic outline will be given here.[15]

When we look out upon the world, we are often baffled by the multiplicity, which constitutes the human experience. What do we really know about this experience? Many scientific disciplines have developed over the last two hundred years for the purpose of discovering the mysteries of nature, but this search has only engendered new questions about the nature of existence. Yoga is a discipline or way of life designed to promote the physical, mental and spiritual development of the human being. It leads a person to discover the answers to the most important questions of life such as Who am I?, Why am I here? and Where am I going?

As stated earlier, the literal meaning of the word *Yoga* is to *"Yoke"* or to *"Link"* back, the implication being to link the individual consciousness back to the original source, the original essence, that which transcends all mental and intellectual attempts at comprehension, but which is the essential nature of everything in Creation, termed "Universal Consciousness. While in the strict sense, Yoga may be seen as a separate discipline from religion, yoga and religion have been linked at many points throughout history and continue to be linked even today. In a manner of speaking, Yoga as a discipline may be seen as a non-sectarian transpersonal science or practice to promote spiritual development and harmony of mind and body thorough mental and physical disciplines including meditation, psycho-physical exercises, and performing action with the correct attitude.

The teachings which were practiced in the Ancient Egyptian temples were the same ones later intellectually defined into a literary form by the Indian Sages of Vedanta and Yoga. This was discussed in our book *Egyptian Yoga: The Philosophy of Enlightenment.* The Indian Mysteries of Yoga and Vedanta represent an unfolding and intellectual exposition of the Egyptian Mysteries. Also, the study of Gnostic Christianity or Christianity before Roman Catholicism will be useful to our study since Christianity originated in Ancient Egypt and was also based on the Ancient Egyptian Mysteries.

The question is how to accomplish these seemingly impossible tasks? How to transform yourself and realize the deepest mysteries of existence? How to discover "Who am I?" This is the mission of Yoga Philosophy and the purpose of yogic practices. Yoga does not seek to convert or impose religious beliefs on any one. Ancient Egypt was the source of civilization and the source of religion and Yoga. Therefore, all systems of mystical spirituality can coexist harmoniously within these teachings when they are correctly understood.

The goal of yoga is to promote integration of the mind-body-spirit complex in order to produce optimal health of the human being. This is accomplished through mental and physical exercises which promote the free flow of spiritual energy by reducing mental complexes caused by ignorance. There are two roads which human beings can follow, one of wisdom and the other of ignorance. The path of the masses is generally the path of ignorance which leads them into negative situations, thoughts and deeds. These in turn lead to ill health and sorrow in life. The other road is based on wisdom and it leads to health, true happiness and enlightenment.

Our mission is to extol the wisdom of yoga and mystical spirituality from the Ancient Egyptian perspective and to show the practice of the teachings through our books, videos and audio productions. You may find a complete listing of other books by the author, in the back of this volume.

---

[15] See the book *Egyptian Yoga: The Philosophy of Enlightenment* by Muata Ashby

The Discipline of the Yoga of Wisdom is imparted in three stages:

1-Listening to the wisdom teachings on the nature of reality (creation) and the nature of the Self.
2-Reflecting on those teachings and incorporating them into daily life.
3-Meditating on the meaning of the teachings.

Note: It is important to note here that the duplicate teaching which was practiced in the Ancient Egypt Temple of Aset[16] of **Listening** to, **Reflecting** upon, and **Meditating** upon the teachings is the same process used in Vedanta-Jnana Yoga of India of today. **The Yoga of Wisdom** is a form of Yoga based on insight into the nature of worldly existence and the transcendental Self, thereby transforming one's consciousness through development of the wisdom faculty.

The Egyptian Yoga Perspective on Death and its Influence on Gnostic Christianity

Egyptian Yoga is the philosophy and disciplines based on Ancient Egyptian mysticism which promote spiritual enlightenment. Spiritual enlightenment means a movement towards transcending death. In this context, death is not regarded as a miserable event, but a transition into a higher form of being if one's earthly life had been lived in accordance with the teachings of Maat. In ancient times, the Ancient Egyptians were often referred to by people in neighboring countries as "the most religious people of all the world" because they seemed to constantly affirm spiritual principles in every aspect of their lives. This is not to be considered as a fanatical existence, the way we would look at cults or obsessed fundamentalist religious groups of our time. The Ancient Egyptians recognized the fact that there is a higher reality beyond the physical. Since all living beings must die some day, and move into that other reality, it makes sense to seek to understand, and become comfortable with death, and to revere the Supreme Divinity which was discovered to be the author and sustainer of all creation. Therefore, death should not be viewed as a pathetic event, but as an inevitable occurrence for which one should be prepared, and can even look forward to.

The creators of Ancient Egyptian mythology and religion recognized that if people live their lives independent of spiritual acknowledgment, life will lose its focus and human beings will lose their way. They will get caught up in the pettiness of human life and their egoism will lead them to untold sufferings both in life on earth as well as beyond. Therefore, life should be a process of affirming the spiritual reality, and even a worship of the Divine. In this manner life itself becomes a spiritual movement towards enlightenment, a process of promoting prosperity and peace. For more insights into the nature of death in light of *Prt m Hru* philosophy, see the sections of this book entitled "Readings for the Guidance of the Dying Person and their Relatives" and "Readings for the Guidance of the Spiritual Aspirant."

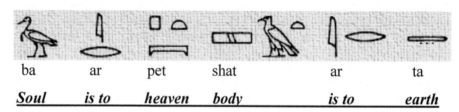

ba	ar	pet	shat	ar	ta
Soul	*is to*	*heaven*	*body*	*is to*	*earth*

From the Prt m Hru of the *Pyramid Texts* (3,200-2,575 B.C.E.)

The passage above shows that the fundamental teaching from the ancient period of Ancient Egyptian mystical philosophy never held a hope for a "physical resurrection." This understanding was carried over into Gnostic Christianity, which developed in Ancient Egypt during the Roman Period, and became a source for controversy between the Gnostic Christians and the Orthodox Christians. The main difference between Orthodox Christianity and other religions seems to have been the insistence on a physical resurrection from the dead. While other religions proclaimed a spiritual transformation of some kind, the Orthodox Christians fervently believed and still believe in a mysterious bodily resurrection from the grave. The Gnostic *Gospel of Philip* strongly refutes the Catholic view of a bodily resurrection, calling

---

[16] See the book *The Wisdom of* Aset by Dr. Muata Ashby

these notions ridiculous and misunderstood by the orthodox community. The following excerpt from the Gnostic *Gospel of Phillip* brings home this point.

"Those who say that the Lord died first and then rose up are in error, for he rose up and then died. We are to receive the resurrection while we live."

Many Egyptologists have suggested that the Ancient Egyptians embalmed their dead with the idea that the dead person would attain immortality, and that the Ancient Egyptians believed that the physical body, which was mummified, would rise up again someday. This idea spurred many Hollywood[17] movies. The statements above, from the early and late periods of Ancient Egyptian culture, clearly show that the Ancient Egyptians never sought a bodily resurrection or eternal life in the physical body. They understood death as a passageway to the next existence, and just as the physical body needs nourishment, the spiritual body was also provided for by means of the subtle essence of the solid food that was buried with the mummy.

The Catholic Christian Church Fathers gradually moved away from a mystical interpretation of Christianity and formed a religious doctrine based on a bodily resurrection from death, leading to one's existence in heaven at the right hand of the Father. The Gnostic Christian leaders disagreed with this view. The same predicament was experienced in Islamic countries during the years immediately following the death of Muhammad (also Mohammed).

The problem of human existence is the forgetfulness of the Divine essence of the Self and the identification with the body as the Self. Through concern with the body and its needs and desires, the true Self becomes identified with worldly concerns and the fulfillment of desires of the body, mind and senses. This is the development of the ego and individual soul. This identification with the desires of the body is what leads the soul to further ignorance of its true Self. It is the pursuit of desires that keeps the mind occupied with worldly thoughts such as the fear of disease and death of the body, the pursuit of pleasure and happiness, and the eradication of things which cause displeasure.

Gnosticism, Hinduism, Buddhism, Taoism and Ancient Egyptian Religion all emphasize the need to practice detachment and dispassion toward the body. These disciplines relieve the pressure of the lower desires, which impel a person to run after the illusions of life. These traditions hold that only through detachment is it possible to calm the mind enough for it to perceive the transcendental reality.

The constant preoccupation with the body is incessantly reinforced through many years of living with family and others in society. Such body consciousness leads to the conviction that the psychophysical complex (mind and body) is indeed the Self. It is this idea that is to be dispelled through the spiritual discipline of constantly turning towards the Divine (through the various disciplines of Yoga) instead of to the body and to the world of illusion.

This process becomes easier to understand through reflection on the fact that the body is composed of physical elements, which are themselves, transient. The body you have today is not the same as the one you had nine years ago. Every cell in your body has been regenerated. Even your bones are different. As surely as people are born, just as surely their body will someday cease to exist. Is it wise to hold onto something that you will definitely lose at some point in time? Impermanence is a given fact of life. Flowers grow, live and die. Insects grow, live and die. Yet people accept these changes. Why is it that people do not cry when the flower dies, or when a leaf falls from a tree and dies or for every creature in nature that has died? The fact is that it is not only death that causes fear, but attachment to that which died and has met the "unknown." So fear of death is due to ignorance of one's true nature.

Likewise, people hold on to life, no matter how miserable a situation they may be in, because they don't know any other way of thinking or acting, and also because they have the illusion that there is a chance they may find happiness someday or they may somehow come into some money. Wealth is a big

---

[17] Hollywood, Calif., area of greater Los Angeles known throughout the world as the home of the US movie industry.

illusion. You can read the papers and see how wealth destroys a person's peace of mind through the endless worries associated with acquiring, investing and protecting it.

Matthew 19
23. Then said Jesus to his disciples, Verily I say to you, That it is hard for a rich man to enter into the kingdom of heaven.
24 And again I say to you, It is easier for a camel to go through the eye of a needle, than for a rich man to enter into the Kingdom of God.

—Christian Bible

"Labor not after riches first, and think thou afterwards wilt enjoy them. He who neglects the present moment, throws away all that he hath. As the arrow passes through the heart, while the warrior knew not that it was coming; so shall his life be taken away before he knoweth that he hath it."

—Ancient Egyptian Proverb

An even greater illusion comes into play when a person tries to figure out which part of the body contains the soul. There is no body part which contains the soul or which can be considered to be the "Self." No body part can be called "me," yet somehow the conglomerate of thoughts, memories, physical body and senses is understood to be "me." This error or misunderstanding is the cause of human misery and pain because it involves the soul in the mishaps and troubles of the mind-body complex and its attending desires. If the mind and senses were transcended, these problems along with individual identification with the body-mind would cease, and the true Self would be discovered to be infinite and eternal. This is the discovery of the Saints and Sages. For this reason they have proclaimed that the soul has been overtaken by ignorance of its true Self, and due to this ignorance, it is subject to experience the pain of human existence.

A simple philosophical study of the body reveals the error in thinking that the body is the Self. If the senses fail to perceive, or a limb or organ ceases to operate, consciousness is still there. The awareness of being alive remains even if the perceptions of the senses or nerves fail. The practice of spirituality involves discovering that which transcends the body, as well as learning how to become attached to that transcendent reality as the truth, rather than remaining attached to the physical body and its desires and impulses, as well as to one's emotions throughout the ups and downs of human existence.

The world of unenlightened human existence is likened to being out in the middle of the ocean when there is a raging storm. The desires are the waves thrashing the mind about. Spiritual practice is the boat, which allows a person to weather the storm of the world with its ever-changing situations. It gives the power to move forward in life and not be disturbed by the choices, desires and unpredictability of the world-process.

The Stages of Human Spiritual Evolution and Aspiration

The Format of this Book

This book is written in a format which follows the manner prescribed for human spiritual evolution. Therefore, the following section will detail the ancient teachings of spiritual evolution and aspiration so that the reader may consciously be aware of the process which this book is striving to engender. The scribes of ancient times did not have a set order for the Utterances of the *Books of Coming Forth By Day*. They were prepared in accord with the needs, special inclinations and interests of those who requested that one be made for them. Many translators of the various Chapters or Utterances of Coming Forth By Day in modern times have also placed the utterances in accordance with their own understanding of the intent of the priests/priestesses. What follows is a compilation of the most important mystical utterances. It is a special sequence which is synchronous with the universal principles of spiritual evolution. The chapter numbers given by traditional Egyptologists will be provided as footnotes preceding each chapter for easy reference.

In Yoga philosophy, spiritual evolution is described as follows: Listening, Reflection and Meditation. All of the five major categories of yoga described before (Yoga of Wisdom, Yoga of Devotional Love, Yoga of Meditation, Tantric Yoga and Yoga of Selfless-Righteous Action.) can be found in the *Ru Prt m Hru*. A spiritual aspirant listens to the teachings, reflects upon their meaning and then enters into deep meditation on them.

Table 3: The Stages of Spiritual Evolution

The Stages of Spiritual Evolution	In the Shetaut Neter (Egyptian Yoga) system, there are three stages of spiritual evolution.
1- *Aspiration*- Students who are being instructed on a probationary status, and have not experienced inner vision. The important factor at this level is awakening of the Spiritual Self, that is, becoming conscious of the divine presence within one's self and the universe by having faith that there is a spiritual essence beyond ordinary human understanding.	*1-* **The Mortals:** *Students who were being instructed on a probationary status, but had not experienced inner vision.*
2- *Striving*- Students who have attained inner vision and have received a glimpse of Cosmic Consciousness. The important factor at this level is purgation of the self, that is, purification of mind and body through a spiritual discipline. The aspirant tries to totally surrender "personal" identity or ego to the divine inner Self which is the Universal Self of all Creation.	*2-* **The Intelligences:** *Students who had attained inner vision and had received a glimpse of Cosmic Consciousness.*
3- *Established*- Students who have become IDENTIFIED with or UNITED with GOD. The important factor at this level is illumination of the intellect, that is, experience and appreciation of the divine presence during reflection and meditation, Union with the Divine Self, the divine marriage of the individual with the universal.	*3-* **The Creators or Beings of Light:** *Students who had become IDENTIFIED with or UNITED with the light (GOD).*

The three steps of spiritual practice (myth, ritual and mystical philosophy and experience) which complete the practice of religion, follow the formats described above closely. Many students of Ancient Egyptian religion have focused on the religious stories of Ancient Egypt as mythical fables or superstitious rantings from a long lost civilization. In the Egyptian Yoga Book Series, we successfully show how the teachings of mystical spirituality were carefully woven into and throughout Ancient Egyptian Mythology. Ancient Egyptian Religion centers around the understanding that every human being has an immortal soul and a mortal body. Further, it holds that creation and the human soul have the same origin. How can this momentous teaching be proven and its reality experienced? This is the task of Mystical Spirituality (religion in its three phases and/or the practice of Yoga disciplines).

Thus, it is evident that the *Ru Prt m Hru* utilizes the universal principles of mystical spirituality and mystical religion. The *Prt m Hru* lays heavy emphasis on Ritual, Spiritual Wisdom and the Mystical Union with the Divine. One more subheading may be added, that is, Mythology. The spiritual wisdom is to be studied and deeply reflected upon, and this will lead to a transformation in one's personality. This process constitutes the journey that a spiritual aspirant must follow in order to go from mortality to immortality. However, in ancient times, the first level of religion, the myth, was well known by all people in Ancient Egyptian society. So the first Yogic step of listening to the teachings or the first step of religion, learning the myth, was more part of the socialization of the culture. A person would learn it as they were growing up and would not require an introduction such as has been presented in the first part of this book. Therefore, their practice would be more advanced than a present day aspirant. They would go right into the practice of the rituals, and begin to learn the mystical implications of these as they relate to the myth of Asar, Aset and Heru, which they already knew so well. Thus, we will combine the universal principles of mystical spirituality and mystical religion and arrange this volume in accordance with the following criteria. Part 1 will treat the following subjects: Presentation of the myth upon which the *Prt m Hru* is based, Gloss on the Myth, Gloss on the Philosophy behind the Myth and the *Prt m Hru*. Part 2 will present the translated scripture of *Prt m Hru* as follows: Awakening, Wisdom and Ritual, Transformation-affirmations for reflection and advancement, and Mystical Union.

The Evolution of The Book of Coming Forth By Day

Phases of Ancient Egyptian Literature

Myths
(Pre-Dynastic Period)
Shetaut Asar-Aset-Heru
The Myth of Asar, Aset and Heru

Shetaut Atum-Ra
The Myth of Creation

Pyramid Texts
(c. 5,000 B.C.E. or prior)

Pyramid of Unas
Pyramid of Teti,
Pyramid of Pepi I,
Pyramid of Mernere,
Pyramid of Pepi II

Wisdom Texts
(c. 3,000 B.C.E. – Ptolematic Period)
Precepts of Ptahotep
Instructions of Any
Instructions of Amenemope
Etc.

Coffin Texts

(c. 2040 B.C.E.-1786 B.C.E.)

Papyrus Texts
(c. 1570 B.C.E.-Roman Period)[18]
Books of Coming Forth By Day
Example of famous papyruses:

Papyrus of Any
Papyrus of Hunefer
Papyrus of Kenna
Greenfield Papyrus, Etc.

Monumental Inscriptions and
Theological Treatises

Example: Temple of Seti 1. Temple of Aset,
Temple of Hetheru, Shabaka Inscription,
Stele of Djehuty (Djehuty) Nefer, Hymns of Amun,
etc.

Hermetic Texts

---

[18] After 1570 BC they would evolve into a more unified text, the Egyptian Book of the Dead.

36

The Ancient Egyptian Scriptures

Coffin Texts 3,500 B.C.E.

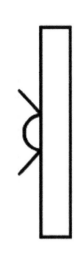

Pyramid Texts 5,000 B.C.E.

Papyrus Texts 2500 B.C.E.-300 A.C.E

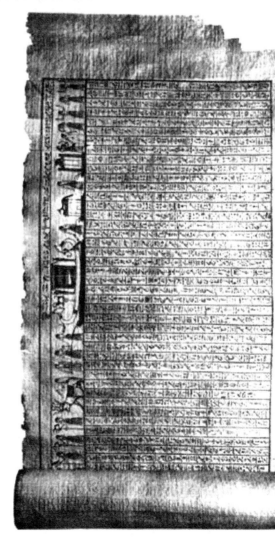

The Origins of the Scriptures of Prt m Hru

As mentioned earlier, the texts which comprise the *Rau nu Prt m Hru* originate in the far distant past. In the form of the *Pyramid Texts* they were codified as utterances which when understood and practiced could lead the practitioner to reach expanded levels of consciousness. This was symbolically referred to as gaining power over the gods and goddesses and becoming a Glorified Soul. The antiquity of the scriptures is attested to by some of the rubrics used on some chapters. For example, the rubrics for some of the versions of Chapters 31 and 36 state that they *were originally found* (not created) *by Hertataf at Khemenu, the city of the god Djehuty (Djehuty), while on a tour of inspection of the temples of Egypt.* Some variants assign the finding to *Semti,* who was a king in the first Dynasty. For this and other reasons it can be said that the scriptures originated in Pre-dynastic times, but were codified in Dynastic times.

The common view of the *Pyramid Texts* is that they are the earliest known versions of the "Book of the Dead." They seem to be compositions of scripture which refer to a king who is part of a ritual wherein offerings are given in the temple and spells are uttered or chanted for the purpose of attaining power or control over the spirits of the dead and over the gods and goddesses. This has been the traditional interpretation by Egyptologists and others who have not had the opportunity to study and practice the mystical teachings from around the world. If these studies are entered into with an open mind and if one is willing to read the texts within the context of mysticism, and an expanded belief in the potential of human experience, a much different understanding arises from the literal interpretations which have been provided thus far. From a mystical perspective, it must be understood that the utterances of the *"Prt m Hru"* were not only for individuals as they were approaching the time of death or who had already died, but they also incorporated rituals designed to engender a mystical experience in the participants. These initiates were not waiting or just preparing for the time of death to use the knowledge in the Netherworld. They were interested in discovering the mysteries of the other world even while still alive. Thus, the book is not for the dead, but for those who truly want to become alive. Therefore, earliest known versions of the texts are compositions of scripture which refer to an initiate who is part of a ritual wherein offerings are given and special words are recited, uttered or chanted for the purpose of transforming the consciousness of that individual, to attain power or control over the spirits of the demons (the egoistic tendencies) and over the gods and goddesses (virtuous qualities).

We will not attempt to provide a literal translation of the texts since this would lead to intellectual stagnation. It would be like reading a poem and trying to apply its meaning literally and critiquing it on its grammatical merits. Mystical literature should be understood as a grand metaphor which seeks to explain the origins of creation and humanity, along with providing an understanding of the transcendental modes of consciousness and the human experience. These modes may be termed as *Higher Consciousness, God, The Supreme Being, Universal Soul, Supreme Consciousness, etc.*

So a mystical teaching, while existing in an historical context, is in reality not concerned with history or ordinary human reality, since these are, in the end, transient, illusory and irrelevant to the attainment of higher consciousness. Therefore, while certain historical information is needed to set a context for our study in relation to world history, an emphasis will be placed on revealing the mystical meaning contained in it, because it is this meaning alone that will lead the spiritual aspirant to attain the goal of mysticism, that of transcending ordinary human consciousness and discovering the deeper realities that lie within the heart. In this sense the *Prt m Hru* is absolutely true and factual in every detail. Mystical teachings are primarily concerned with the here and now as well as the transcendental wisdom, and not specifically with any particular historical event. The use of mythological stories and ritual traditions should not be confused with history. Myths are used by Sages in order to convey mystical teachings about the human condition and the mysteries of the human heart. Thus, any study which does not affirm the transcendental nature of a myth is relegated to understanding only the superficial (exoteric) meaning of a teaching.

In the earlier times, the teachings of the Medtu Neter (Divine Speech- Egyptian Mysteries) and Shetaut Neter (The Secret Way of the Spirit) were inscribed in the mortuary pyramids of the wealthy nobles. These texts are called *Pyramid Texts.* Later, the texts were inscribed on the mortuary coffins themselves. These texts are referred to as *Coffin Texts.* The next evolution in the codification of the Ancient Egyptian teachings was the use of papyrus paper.

Figure 7: Coffin of Hent-Mehit, Singer (Chanter) of Amun, 21st dynasty showing anthropoid (human) features, texts and vignettes.

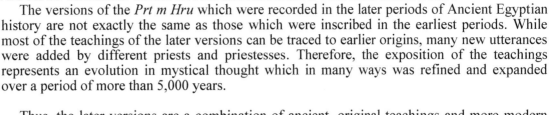

The versions of the *Prt m Hru* which were recorded in the later periods of Ancient Egyptian history are not exactly the same as those which were inscribed in the earliest periods. While most of the teachings of the later versions can be traced to earlier origins, many new utterances were added by different priests and priestesses. Therefore, the exposition of the teachings represents an evolution in mystical thought which in many ways was refined and expanded over a period of more than 5,000 years.

Thus, the later versions are a combination of ancient, original teachings and more modern expansions and additions to the teachings, which were not part of the original. The earlier texts did not include vignettes. The addition of vignettes is an important evolution in the transmission of the teaching since it adds a new dimension to the visual quality of the scripture. The vignettes first appear in the *Coffin Text* period.

Certain scriptures, such as Chapters 16 and 143, were always included in a vignette (illustrated, embellished with pictures) form, and never included text. Along with this, it should be understood that the teachings presented in the book itself are implicit, meaning that there is a certain amount of understanding which one must already have in order to fully understand the book even before picking it up for the first time. Also, once the book is picked up and studied it must be understood that its wisdom is not only transmitted by words, but also through the visual or pictorial nature of the scripture itself. The process of initiation serves to provide the student with information about the symbols and the subtle meanings or nuances of the philosophy. This is why, with the exception of Chapter 4[19], there are few explanations or glosses in the text itself. Certain Chapters, such as Chapter 33[20], are like compilations and refinements of earlier concepts. While containing their principles, there are no groupings of utterances in the earlier works which compile the *Negative Confessions* or *Precepts of MAAT* and the concepts or laws which must be followed in order to be pure of heart, as found in the later papyrus versions of the *Prt m Hru*. This aspect of the later versions does not represent a new concept or innovation, but a refinement and an expansion of that which was present at the inception of the teaching and first recorded in the form of the *Pyramid Texts*.

Figure 8: Coffin of Hent-Mehit, Singer (Chanter) of Amun, 21st dynasty showing anthropoid (human) features, texts and vignettes.

The Order of The Chapters

The collection of writings in the *Prt m Hru,* dedicated to spiritual enlightenment, are separate but complementary passages which may or may not relate directly to each other. The original format of the texts which are now referred to as the "Book of the Dead" was a collection of related texts which may be described as injunctions, admonitions or affirmations, hymns, litanies and chants related to promoting and bringing into reality the spiritual enlightenment of the individual initiate. These early texts are now known as the *Pyramid Texts.* These passages may be accurately referred to as "Chapters" or "Utterances." However, the ancient term was "Rw" (*roo* or *rau*, meaning "group of words to be spoken"). It is notable that the text and illustrations within the various papyri do not always coincide and that different scrolls contain the same utterances in different orders. This points to the fact that there is no correct order in which the utterances must be presented nor is there a prescribed number of utterances which must be included in a volume in order for it to be considered a complete book. Also, the hieroglyphic scripture could be written in either a vertical or horizontal form, from right to left or left to right, and some chapters have variants, making their length variable. Some chapters, like Chapter 10, even obtain special instructions expressing the need to copy the texts as it is found, when making new scrolls of the *Prt m Hru*. Thus, some chapters like 4 and 31, have a short and long version. Consequently, there was no set length for a papyrus scroll of the *Prt m Hru*. Its length could range from a few feet to 70 or 80 feet or more in length. In ancient times certain chapters would be chosen by individuals in accordance with their feeling or the direction of their spiritual preceptors (priests and priestesses).

---

[19] Generally referred to as Chapter 17
[20] Generally referred to as Chapter 125

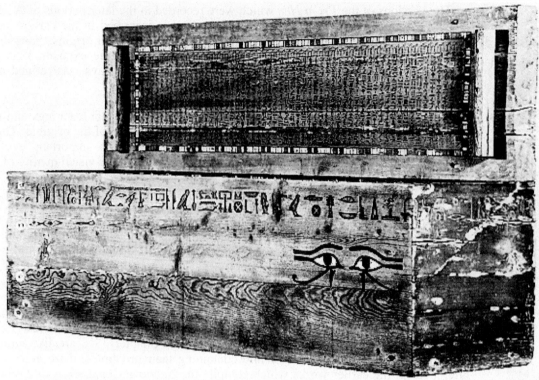

Figure 9: <u>Coffin of Ipi-Ha-Ishutef</u> Coffin texts version of Pyramid Texts that later appear in modified forms in the later papyrus *Prt m Hru*

Figure 10: Outer Coffin of Hapiankhtifi, 12th Dynasty, Middle Kingdom,

Pert-m-Heru from *Pyramid Texts* (3,200-2,575 B.C.E.):

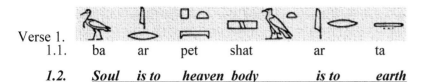

Verse 1.

1.1.	ba	ar	pet	shat	ar	ta

1.2. ***Soul   is to   heaven body   is to   earth***

1.3.   The soul belongs to heaven and the body belongs to the earth.

Pert-m-Heru from *Papyrus Texts* (332 B.C.E.- c. 30 B.C.E.):

Verse 1.

1.1.	pet	kher	ba	-	k	ta	khery	tutu	-	k

1.2. ***heaven under jurisdiction soul thine, earth jurisdiction of image - thine***

1.3.   heaven has control over the soul and is where your soul goes, earth has control over the physicality of the personality and is where the image of your soul, the physical body stays.

As the hieroglyphic scriptures above show, there are some concepts which existed in the earliest era of Kamitan/Kemetic culture which were maintained, over a period of thousands of years, down to the very late era. There are some utterances, chapters and concepts, which appear in most or all of the surviving copies. Some of these include Chapter 1, which pertains to coming forth by day, Chapter 9[21], which pertains to being triumphant over the enemies and understanding the deeper mystical wisdom about the nature of the Divine, and Chapter 36[22] which pertains to coming forth into the ultimate light, implying transformation from mortal human life into immortality and oneness with the Divine.

This presentation represents a new look at the *Prt m Hru,* the Ancient Egyptian compilation for scriptures dedicated to the purpose of attaining spiritual enlightenment, more fully translated: Ancient Egyptian Book of Coming Out of the World and Into Spiritual Enlightenment. It is the fruit many years of research into the mythology, mystical philosophy and culture of Yoga in Ancient Egypt. Also, it is the fruit of inner work by the author in the form of meditation on and spiritual practice of the teachings contained in the *Prt m Hru*. It is highly recommended that the reader should study the following volumes by the author first, before reading the *Prt m Hru* text in Part 2 of this volume. This advice is given because the teachings for coming into enlightenment which are contained in the *Prt m Hru* were not designed to be read by those who have not been initiated into the philosophy of Maat and Shetaut Neter. Therefore, it is suggested that the reader study the extensive introduction in Part 1 of this volume and also acquire the following volumes by the author as a further introduction to the mystical wisdom teachings of Ancient Egyptian Yoga Philosophy: *The Ausarian Resurrection, The Ancient Egyptian Bible* and *The Mystical Teachings of the Ausarian Resurrection.* The translation presented here is original, by the author, based on the original hieroglyphic texts. It is not intended as a literal, word for word treatise but as a prose translation in common English for better understanding. This format will better convey the meaning in terms that people in modern culture can more easily comprehend.

The *Rau nu Prt m Hru* is not a Bible, in the strict understanding of the term, from a religious-mythological point of view. As previously mentioned, religion has three levels of practice. First, there is the mythology upon which the religion is based. The text(s) that presents the story and basic beliefs of the religion is what constitutes the Bible of the particular religion. For example, in Christianity the religion is based on the myths related to the story of Jesus. This is what is presented in the Christian Bible, the myth. The words that are uttered in the church mass every Sunday are later developments of the tradition based on the myth. They represent the second stage of religion, the *Ritual* stage. In the same way, the myth that the *Ru Prt m Hru* is related to the story of Asar, his incarnation on earth, his death and resurrection but the myth is not told in the *Prt M Hru* texts themselves. The scripture which relates the story of Asar is the Bible, proper, of Ancient Egypt.[23] Therefore, the Bible of Ancient Egypt is the collection of scriptures containing the myth(s) related to

---

[21] Generally referred to as Chapter 17

[22] Generally referred to as Chapter 30

[23] See the book *The Ausarian Resurrection: The Ancient Egyptian Bible* by Muata Ashby.

the divinity. These were compiled in the book *The Ausarian Resurrection: The Ancient Egyptian Bible.* However, the utterances contained in the *Prt M Hru* book deal with the rituals related to the myth, i.e. the resurrecting Asar, the central teaching of the myth of Asar. This was explained in the books *The Ausarian Resurrection: The Ancient Egyptian Bible* and *The Mystical Teachings of the Ausarian Resurrection* also by the author. The *Prt m Hru* constitutes the utterances that are to be read, recited or chanted as a means of taking the teachings of the myth to the next level of practice, the ritual.

As occurs with the *Christian Bible, The Bhagavad Gita* and other texts, many people do not see the *Prt m Hru* as a book of spiritual principles and affirmations for transforming the mind. Rather, they insist that it is to be believed word for word. If this is the case, and if certain words, customs or ideas cannot be understood by theologians and scholars the *Prt m Hru,* it will become the object of many different interpretations and consequently, arguments. For this reason, the religious beliefs of the translator of the texts, which may or may not be in agreement with the original scriptural meaning, may influence the translation and therefore, the reader should exercise caution when choosing a translation to use for study. In the case of the *Prt m Hru*, scholars have consistently attempted to deny and downplay any mystical significance that may be found in the texts. This has served to minimize the understanding of the text and degrade the overall meaning of the spiritual philosophy behind it.

Another factor is that since languages change over time, it is necessary to update the translations on a regular basis. Present day English speaking people would not be able to understand the original King James Version of the Bible which was written only 387 years ago, much less scriptures that were written over 1,700 years ago. However, the essence of a teaching can be discerned and brought forth by those who are initiated into the correct understanding and practice of religious philosophy in its three steps[24]. This is why updates to the translations by qualified scholars are necessary. Another important factor is that there are new discoveries that arise from time to time which may alter the timelines of the *Prt m Hru*, the Christian Bible and other texts or elucidate a new meaning of the old text, which in turn may affect the meaning of the teachings. This has been a major task which this volume, ***Mysticism of the Prt m Hru: The Book of Enlightenment,*** has attempted to perform in reference to the scriptures presented.

The question and struggle is to determine how best to provide a translation without reinterpreting the text. Some translators provide a word-for-word translation which means that each word is translated individually, but this is often difficult to understand since the nuances of the culture, inflections and grammar of ancient times is pretty much alien to modern society. Some translators work individually, while others work in committees. It is thought that committees would do a better job since its individual members would be less susceptible to deviation from the original texts. Some translators work individually, but their work is checked by a committee. In contrast to the Christian Bible, the *Prt m Hru* has been translated relatively few times (a few dozen) in the last 175 years. However it faces some of the problems that the Biblical scriptures face. There are several thousand Christian Bibles produced for people in various languages. Unfortunately, some of these Bibles were produced by translators who were not checked by any committee. Others could not even read the original texts, but gave their rendition anyway, and still others were simply paraphrased by people who thought they were conveying a meaning, but instead deviated from the original texts substantially. Some may want to promote a conservative agenda or a liberal agenda. Others may want to highlight a particular doctrine or political view over another, etc. So under these circumstances, it is not surprising that in the days of slavery in America, when Christian slave owners wanted to justify their ownership of slaves, some Bibles were produced espousing interpretations of scriptures and commentaries on those scriptures which promoted sexist and racist ideas. Paraphrases can convey the meaning of certain texts more easily than the word for word translations, but can also more easily reflect the doctrinal viewpoints of the translators. Therefore, it is important to know who has produced the book and if they have or had any ulterior motives or hidden agendas in their work. Many people feel that when they pick up a Christian Bible, they are holding the "Word of God." This idea has been engrained in the minds of many people for so many years that most do not question the contents of the Bible they are reading, and even become hostile when their illusions are challenged. They brand anyone who deviates from the concepts they have accepted as blasphemers or worse. All the while they are filling themselves with ignorance which will hurt their own spiritual evolution and accordingly, humanity as a whole.

Like the Christian Bible translations, the the translations of the *Ancient Egyptian Book of Coming into Enlightenment* poses important problems because the meanings of some of the ancient symbols are not understood in part or at all by the scholars. This is due, in part, to the fact that the use of the hieroglyphic language died out in the middle of the first millennia of the common era (around 500 A.C.E.). This break in the initiatic tradition accounts for some of the loss in terms of the meanings of rare glyphs. However, just as modern language adopts new terms and allows others to fall out of usage, the Ancient Egyptian language as it is understood today can still convey the teachings with remarkable lucidity.

The third level of religion is mysticism. This level requires that the practitioner of the rituals understand the myth and its ultimate purpose. Thus, this volume contains a compendium of the myth. However, there is no substitute for the

---

[24] Myth, Ritual and metaphysical (Mysticism).

complete text with reproductions of the vignettes prepared by the Ancient Egyptian Sages themselves which have been compiled in the book *The Ausarian Resurrection: The Ancient Egyptian Bible*. Along with that volume it is recommended that the serious student study the detailed commentary of the myth in the book, *The Mystical Teachings of the Ausarian Resurrection* as well as the lecture series on the Ausarian Resurrection, available on audio tape by Dr. Muata Ashby.

The Versions of the Prt m Hru

The Ancient Egyptian scriptures today referred to as the "Book of the Dead" evolved through at least three phases, stages or editions. These are referred to by most Egyptologists as "recensions" or "versions" (editions). This classification generally follows a historical outline of the development of the central universities of Ancient Egypt. In ancient times there were four main centers of philosophical scholarship. These were the main Temple in the city of Anu (Greek-Heliopolis), the main Temple in the city of Waset (Greek-Thebes), the main Temple in the city of Hetkaptah (Greek-Memphis) and the Temple in the city of Abdu, the center of the worship of Asar. Anu, Waset and Hetkaptah were the capital cities of the country in different historical periods. These were the schools attended by the Greek students of philosophy, Pythagoras being one of the most famous. Abdu remained as the spiritual center of Ausarian worship throughout history.

The *Pyramid Texts* are regarded by Egyptologists as being the first versions of the *Prt m Hru*. This is known as the **Anunian Recension,** and it is regarded as containing 759 utterances (chapters). These are regarded as belonging to the *Old Kingdom Period*, (cultural period of development- Dynasties 1-5). The next grouping of writings of the *Prt m Hru are referred to as Coffin Texts*. They are regarded as belonging to the *Middle Kingdom Period* (Dynasties 11-12). They were inscribed on wooded coffins and include complete utterances from the *Pyramid Texts* along with completely new ones. These texts are regarded as containing 1,185 invocations (utterances, chapters). In the city of Waset the priests/priestesses created a new version of *Prt M Hru*. These are usually referred to as the **Wasetian (Theban) recension** of the *Prt m Hru*. The **Wasetian Recension** adopted several texts from the older recension but added many more new ones. This recension is found on papyrus scrolls and one of its principal features are the extensive vignettes. In the very late period (after 600 B.C.E.), most papyri included a possible total of 192 chapters. These are usually referred to as the **Saite Recension** (Greco-Roman Period). This edition was written in hieratic text, including vignettes and contained only a few Hymns and sections of Chapter 33 which concern the Great Judgment and the Confessions of Innocence (42 principles of Maat).

The entire panorama of Ancient Egyptian theology can be thought of as a university system. Within a university, many colleges may be found. Each may specialize in a particular aspect of a subject while working harmoniously with other subjects presented in the other colleges within the university system. Likewise, the theology of Ancient Egypt emerged all at once but aspects of it were developed in different periods, by different schools or colleges which emerged within Ancient Egyptian history with the purpose of emphasizing and espousing particular perspectives of the theology, thereby popularizing certain teachings and divinities at different times. The earlier edition of the *Prt m Hru* originated in the College of Anu and was based on the Supreme Being in the form of "Ra." The next important edition developed in Waset. It was based on the Supreme Being in the form of "Amun" or "Amun-Ra." Both the Anunian and Wasetian teachings are to be regarded as emphasizing more of a devotional aspect of spiritual practice. They are referred to as "Theban Theology." The College of Hetkaptah (Memphis) developed a tradition that was based on the Supreme Being in the form of "Ptah." The Memphite teachings are referred to independently as "Memphite Theology" and are to be regarded as emphasizing more of a philosophical and psychological aspect of spiritual practice and were not used in exactly the same manner as the writings now referred to as the collection of chapters known as "Book of the Dead." The teachings of the Temple in the city of Abdu are a direct extension of the Anunian teachings, as they deal with the mythology related to the grandson of Ra, i.e. Asar. The later editions will be discussed at length in the following sections, as well as in the glosses and notes throughout this book.

The **Anunian edition** was inscribed in the pyramids of the early kings of Ancient Egypt in hieroglyphics. It is thus known as the *Pyramid Texts*. Some parts of it were inscribed in coffins, papyri, tombs, and steles. It should be noted that while this period roughly corresponds to 5,000 B.C.E.- 3,000 B.C.E., this is only the period in which the writings were codified (set down in hieroglyphic text). There are archeological and anthropological indications that the teachings existed prior to this period, in the vast reaches of so called "pre-history" referred to as the "Pre-dynastic" period.

The **Wasetian edition** (Theban-cultural period of development- Dynasties 18-20) can be found on papyri in hieroglyphics. The writings were partitioned into chapters with titles, but were still not given any definite order in the collection. These texts can be found after the cultural period of the 20th dynasty in hieroglyphic text as well as hieratic text.

Another version is recognized, called **Saite** or **Ptolemaic edition.** The Ptolemies were the Greek descendents of one of Alexander the Great's generals who took control of Egypt after Alexander had died. It is the latest cultural period of

Ancient Egyptian history in which the country was besieged by outside conquering nations (Persians, Greeks, and especially the Romans) as well as internal social disintegration due to wars, breakdowns in social order and periods of civil unrest, martial law or the absence of government order altogether. In this edition, the chapters were arranged in a definite order and were written in hieroglyphics as well as hieratic text. However, this order was not absolutely rigid, nor did all the papyri follow what might be considered a sequential pattern for reading and studying purposes. It was considered sufficient that the chapters be present in the scroll (Ancient Egyptian book form).

The texts used for this present translation rely on the older versions (*Pyramid Texts* and *Coffin Texts*) in reference to the general themes of Kemetic spirituality content and as a method of determining the proper order of the collection of writings. Since the papyrus versions are summaries of the writings of the *Coffin Texts*, which are themselves expansions on the *Pyramid Texts,* the later versions (papyrus versions) are good sources in reference to the titles and format of separation of the chapters as well as the presentation of vignettes and the conciseness of writing in the presentation of certain concepts, for in the later versions, there is to be found a refinement of the verses which appeared in the earlier texts. The collection presented in this volume represent the most mystical chapters taken from all versions of the *Prt m Hru*. In this volume, when discussing writings from the *Pyramid Texts,* they will be referred to as "utterances." When discussing writings from the *Coffin Texts,* they will be referred to as "invocations," and when discussing the Papyrus Texts they will be referred to as "chapters." It should be noted that the use of the words *invocations, utterances*, or *chapters* can be confusing since in the *Pyramid Text* and *Coffin Text* writings, utterances can be as short as one sentence or as long as a long essay akin to the chapters of the later texts.

Due to the lack of diligence in transcribing the texts in ancient times, some of the chapters were duplicated within the same scroll, sometimes exactly the same way and at other times with grammatical errors, errors in meaning or minor changes that are inconsequential to the overall mystical importance of the teaching. In later papyruses, many innovations and expansions and sometimes even embellishments on the scripture can be found. These are not always in keeping with the intent of the original scriptures, those at the inception of the teaching. In these cases the errors, duplications or concepts not in keeping with the original scriptures and which may even be considered degradations in the philosophy, such as the *ushabti*[25] (*Coffin Text* 472) teachings or the predilection to remain in the Sekhet Hetep (enjoying heavenly pleasures) as opposed to moving forward into the Sekhet Yaru and on to discover and become one with Asar, have been either repaired, incorporated into one chapter or omitted altogether. Some of these discrepancies can also be accounted for by the vast periods of time since the scriptures were created, and also the intervening periods of social disturbances which have occurred. Keeping this in mind, it is remarkable that despite the minor discrepancies, the scriptures of Coming Forth from the early period of the *Pyramid Texts* to the Late period of the *Papyrus Texts* in the Ptolemaic and Roman Conquest Periods, display a faultless concordance of mythology and yogic mystical philosophy.

The occurrence of errors in the *Prt m Hru* should not be surprising to the student of Ancient Egyptian scripture. In fact, all scriptures from around the world including the Bible, the Koran, Bhagavad Gita, The Tao, and others, in themselves or their related scriptures, contain errors, both grammatical and/or contradictions in meaning. This is due to the vast amount of writing as well as the vast intervening periods of time between the writings, the versions, compilations etc., of the same scripture. The refinement of any scripture, as any book, depends on not writing, but rewriting. Those scriptures written independently and by different personalities at different times are bound to display inconsistencies. These should not be a basis for viewing that scripture in a negative light, but should promote understanding and a keen eye which knows how to sift truth from untruth. Added to these issues is the fanatical reverence of some aspirants. Some people have developed the opinion that simply because a text is ancient, that it must necessarily be correct in every detail. Further, many people believe that if a text is not ancient, it cannot be authentic or correct. This of course translates to the implication that modern day Sages are not to be revered as the Sages in ancient times. These are of course, misconceived ideas of the ignorant. In fact, the teachings are to be imparted by living spiritual teachers and authentic spiritual teachers have always updated and interpreted the teachings. This was true in ancient times and continues to be true today.

A true spiritual aspirant is not like an orthodox, narrow-minded personality who must believe that every single word in a particular scripture is "exactly" correct, or otherwise wrong and must be discarded altogether. An Ancient Egyptian proverb admonishes that true spiritual aspirant goes to the "essence of the meaning" without being distracted by minor concerns in grammar or correspondences of unimportant aspects of the scripture which have little bearing on the essence of the teachings.

"Strive to see with the inner eye, the heart. It sees the reality not subject to emotional or personal error; it sees the essence. Intuition then is the most important quality to develop."

"Never forget: the words are not the reality, only reality is reality;

---

[25] See the section of this book entitled "The choice of chapters" in Part II of this volume.

picture symbols are the idea, words are confusion."

"It takes a strong disciple to rule over the mountainous thoughts
and constantly go to the essence of the meaning; as mental complexity increases,
thus will the depth of your decadence and challenge both be revealed."

—Ancient Egyptian Proverbs

Language, Pronunciation, Spelling and Meaning

The authors of all of the world's scriptures were divinely inspired, however, they worked with the limited instrument of the human personality, which is in itself prone to error. This was true in ancient times as it continues to be true in modern times. The pursuit of perfection in life is not found in a perfectly written scripture. In any case, none exist, for one person's perfection can be another person's garbage. What is good for one person is not necessarily good for another. People have different tastes, opinions, etc., because they come from different walks of life, and not because one thing is intrinsically better than the other. Therefore, while one person likes one scripture over another, this does not mean that one is better than another. It simply means that one scripture appeals to one person's sensibilities, based on their cultural background, personality inclinations, etc. Further, just as it is impossible to know the exact pronunciations of words in old English, and yet it is possible to understand what writers like Chaucer and Shakespeare meant, it is unnecessary to know the exact pronunciations of Ancient Egyptian words where the meaning is well established. The teaching of the Ancient Egyptian *Myth of Ra and Aset*[26] bears out the importance of the essence of meaning as opposed to the spoken words. Further, since Ancient Egyptian language experienced at least three major periods of evolution (Old Kingdom, Middle Kingdom and New Kingdom), when determining pronunciations, like the spellings, we are faced with period differences, regional differences and personality differences. Some texts have different spellings for the same word within the same papyrus. Add to this the differences between colloquy[27] and script, the ever-changing regional accents and expressions, and the question then becomes which pronunciations are we talking about, the ancient or late ones, the ones of the north or those of the west, etc? Remarkably, the hieroglyphic texts underwent less changes than one might expect given the excessively long period of time for its usage, the longest in the world at over 5,000 years! Consider that it has only been since the beginning of the eighteenth century that western culture "standardized" language. Were it not for this, modern English speaking people might not understand the English speeches and writings of George Washington. Pronunciations can be approximated in many ways: correlating to Greek words, which correspond to the Ancient Egyptian, correlating to Coptic words derived from Ancient Egyptian, extrapolating from known words, etc. However, these will always be approximations and a spiritual aspirant should not spend too much time with this issue, but rather on understanding the philosophy behind the words, for no matter how they are pronounced or spelled, the essence remains intact and effective, and the essence is the meaning. The following Hermetic[28] proverbs give insight into the feelings of the Ancient Egyptian Sages on the question of pronunciation and meaning.

"Keep this teaching from translation in order that such mighty Mysteries might not come to the Greeks
and to the disdainful speech of Greece, with all its *looseness and its surface beauty*, taking all the
strength out of the solemn and the strong - the energetic speech of Names."

Ancient Egyptian literature has its own style and feeling, and the *usage* of the Kemetic language is exhorted above other languages because it is precise and more importantly, concise in its descriptions and terms, with a minimum of flowery language (*looseness and surface beauty*) while achieving a certain poetic sentiment. The absence of superfluous parts of speech in a language will consequently allow the language to be more direct and concise and thus, less subject to misinterpretation. This injunction is relating the idea that Kemetic grammar, the system of inflections, syntax, and word formation of the language, is simple, containing a minimum of prepositions[29] and adjectives to embellish a subject. Many Greeks who came to Ancient Egypt were not interested in changing their ways to suit the teaching, but rather wanted to suit the teachings to their lifestyles without making the fundamental changes that are necessary to attain enlightenment. In modern times, many people use Kemetic symbols and may even utter certain Ancient Egyptian words, but do so without true feeling or insight because they do not *live* the culture. In essence, they continue to be worldly people while appearing to adopt some spiritual philosophy, and therefore, their efforts fall far short of what is necessary to make the teachings

---

[26] See the book Mysticism of the Goddess by Dr. Muata Ashby
[27] **col·lo·quy** (kŏl'ə-kwē) *n.*, *pl.* **col·lo·quies. 1.** A conversation, especially a formal one. **2.** A written dialogue.
[28] Ancient Egyptian philosophy in the Greek-Roman period.
[29] In some languages, a word placed before a substantive and indicating the relation of that substantive to a verb, an adjective, or another substantive, as English *at, by, in, to, from,* and *with.* (American her. Dic.)

effective. Thus, it is all right to translate the word *Asar* (Kemetic) into *Osiris* (Greek), as long as the meaning remains intact. However, this can only occur if one is deeply involved in the culture and if one is led by an authentic spiritual teacher. The objection above is not on the basis of pronunciation, but that in translating it the Greeks apparently wanted to make the terms into something other than what they were supposed to be. Thus, just as it is virtually impossible for a twentieth century English speaking person to communicate with a ninth century English speaking person, it would be more than likely that an Egyptologist of our time could not communicate verbally with an Ancient Egyptian person, but could communicate by writing hieroglyphs back and forth. The meaning, which transcends words and their time period of usage, is higher than the words themselves.

This is emphasized in the second proverb below where the objection is raised, because when the translation is made into Greek, the meaning is often lost. The language is taken but not the teaching (*the teachings keepeth clear the meaning of the words*). The meaning gives value to the words and thus, any words are useful in describing the transcendental essence. For example, the word "Neberdjer" from Ancient Egypt, "Brahman" from India, "Tao" from China, etc., have the same meaning, the Transcendental Absolute. A Chinese person using the word "Tao" will discover the same truth as the person who follows Kemetic Philosophy using the word "Neberdjer." Thus, meaning is more important than grammar or pronunciation since the mind assigns meaning first and pronunciation afterwards. Further, the medium of words cannot fully capture the perfection of thought because it is a limited medium. The fullness of the true essence of the Divine cannot be captured by any concept and words cannot capture the totality of any idea. However, sound and pronunciation do have legitimate purposes and uses in spiritual study and especially in the study of the Kemetic language.

The Language of Names

"Unto those who come across these words, their composition will seem most simple and clear; but on the contrary, as this is unclear, and has the true meaning of its words concealed, it will be still unclear, when, afterwards, the Greeks will want to turn our tongue into their own - for this will be a very great *distorting and obscuring* of even what has heretofore been written. Turned into our own native tongue, *the teachings keepeth clear the meaning of the words*. For that its very *quality of sound, the very power of Egyptian names*, have in themselves the bringing into act of what is said."

The Kemetic language is special in many ways because it reflects many universal cosmic principles of sound. An example of this is the Ancient Egyptian word "*mut.*" Mut means mother and it is reflected in "mata" of the Hindu language, "madre' of Spanish, "mother" in English, etc. The "m" sound is a universal "seed sound" principle of motherhood. However, this is not an absolute rule because other words are used as well. The use of names in the Kemetic language is important because they act as keys to unlocking the mysteries of life, but this is true only for those initiated into the philosophy. In Kemetic philosophy, words are seen as abstract representatives of phenomenal reality. Since the mind is the only reality and the external world only reflects a conceptualized form based on an idea in God's mind, words are a higher reality when compared to the physical world and all Kemetic words are names for objects and/or concepts. In fact, Creation is a concept given a name and not an absolute, abiding reality in and of itself.

By studying the phonetic and pictorial (Kemetic language is not only phonetic, but also illustrative) etymology (the origin and development of a linguistic form) and etiology (the study of causes or origins) of names and applying the initiatic science, it is possible to decipher the mysteries of Creation by discovering the teachings embedded in the language by the Sages of Ancient Egypt.

For example, the Kemetic word "Pa" is central to understanding the deeper essence of nature, divinity and the gods and goddesses of the *Prt m Hru*. In the study of the word "Pa," philosophy as well as pictorial and phonetic associations must be considered. Along with this, the variations in spellings act to expand the possible associations and thereby also the appropriate meaning in the given usage. Sometimes the very same words may be used, but its usage in different texts denotes a slight difference in the nuance of the meaning in accordance with the usage. This aspect of assigning the proper meaning of a word which is used even with the same spelling but in different contexts in different or even the same Kemetic scriptures, is an artistic development which comes to a translator with time. Thus, there is no right or wrong interpretation, but there is greater and greater approximation to the higher intended truth behind the teaching as research moves forward. Also, it should be remembered that research here implies not only studying books, but also meditation and introspection, as well as living in accordance with the philosophy.

Table 4: Study of the Kemetic Word "Pa"

The Etymological, Etiological, Phonetic and Pictorial Study of the Kemetic word "Pa"	Meaning
A-	A- **Pa**- demonstrative, this, the, to exist
B-	B- **Pau** - Primeval Divinity- The Existing One
C-	C- **Paut**- Primeval time - remote ages- beginning time
D-	D- **Paut**- stuff, matter, substance, components which make something up.
E-	E- **Pauti**- The Primeval God; Primeval Divinity who is self-Created; Dual form relates to rulership of Upper and Lower Egypt
F-	F- **Pauti-u**- Primeval Divinity with male or female determinative - source of all multiplicity in Creation.
G-	G- **Pat** (paut) **n Neteru**- Company of gods and goddesses
H-	H- **Pauti**- Company of nine gods and goddesses
I-	I- **Pau** or **Paut** -human beings, me, women

The Ancient Egyptian words and symbols related to the Company of Gods and Goddesses (Pauti) indicate several important mystical teachings. The root of the Ancient Egyptian word Pauti is **Pa** (Figure A). Pa means "to exist." Thus, Creation is endowed with the quality of existence as opposed to non-existence. **Pau** (Figure B) is the next progression in the word. It means the *Primeval Divinity*, the source of Creation. **Paut** (Figure C and D) is the next evolution of the word, Pau, meaning *primeval time* and *the very substance out of which everything is created is the one and the same*. **Pauti** is the next expression of **Pa** and it has two major meanings. It refers to the *Primeval Divinity* or Divine Self (God) (Figure E). **Pautiu** refers to **Pauti** but in plural, as well as being a gender specific term implying, *the Divinity as the source of the multiplicity in creation*. In the Ancient Egyptian language, like Spanish for example, all objects are assigned gender. Also, Pauti refers to the deities who comprise the *Company of Gods and Goddesses* (Figure G and H). **Paut** (men) or **Pautet** (women) also refers to *living beings*, especially *human beings* (Figure I).

Pa ➔ Pau ➔ Paut ➔ Pauti ➔ Pautiu ➔ Paut and Pautet

Therefore, the most important teaching relating to the nature of Creation is being given here. The gods and goddesses of the creation are not separate principles or entities. They are in reality one and the same as the Primeval Divinity. They are expressions of that Divine Self. However, they are not transformations of or evolutions from the Divine Self, but the very same Divine Self-expressing as Creation. So even though God is referred to as a primordial deity who did something a long time ago or set into motion various things, in reality God and Creation are one and the same. Ra is the "God of the primeval time" as well as the gods and goddesses of Creation which sustain it all the time. With this understanding, it is clear to see that God is not distant and aloof, observing Creation from afar. The Divine Self is the very basis of Creation and is in every part of it at all times. This is why the terms *Pa-Neter* and *neteru* are also used to describe the Divine. Pa-Neter means "The Supreme Being" and neteru means "the gods and goddesses." Also, the word "neteru" refers to creation itself. So neter-u emanates from Neter. Creation is nothing but God who has assumed various forms or neteru: trees, cake, bread, human beings, metal, air, fire, water, animals, planets, space, electricity, etc. This is a profound teaching which should be reflected upon constantly so that the mind may become enlightened to its deeper meaning and thereby discover the Divinity in nature.

The Divine Self is not only in Creation but is the very essence of every human being as well. Therefore, the substratum of every human being is in reality God as well. The task of spiritual practice and Yoga is to discover this essential nature within your own heart. This can occur if one reflects upon this teaching and realizes its meaning by discovering its reality in the deepest recesses of one's own experience. When this occurs, the person who has attained this level of self-discovery is referred to as having become enlightened. They have discovered their true, divine nature. They have discovered their oneness with the Divine Self.

In conclusion, it must be understood that Kemetic language is synonymous with Kemetic philosophy. As such, when speaking, one must adhere to truth. The ultimate truth is, that when we speak of objects, we are in reality speaking about principles, deeper basis of which is the Divine Self. When words are spoken, they immediately take on the first level of reality as they engender an image in the mind of the listener. When a listener acts upon what has been heard, the speech takes on a reality in the physical plane. Therefore, the speech is a reflection of an idea, a concept, and the physical reality is a reflection of speech. The cause underlying the concept is the real name of a thing, its higher reality, and this essence has no name or form in its potentiality, but only in its relative manifestation. This relative manifestation is the world of time and space and all living and non-living objects in it. Therefore, we have three levels of reality, the thought, the word and the actual object existing in the physical world. However, these are only relative realities since they are all ephemeral in nature and not abiding. The creative essence (God-transcendental consciousness) which gave power to the thought, the concept, is the source and substratum which lends temporary reality to the projection (thought, the word and the actual object).

Flowery and imprecise language as well as language that praises worldliness as opposed to the Divine (ex. language that promotes arrogance, pride and the illusion that human existence is abiding) distracts the mind away from this great practice. Thus, it becomes an agent of ignorance and confusion, fostering and sustaining a deluded notion of reality. This is the higher teaching which is otherwise espoused as *Maakheru* –"Truth of Speech." Therefore, truth is a higher reality in relation to words, language or symbols, etc. Thus, while one should endeavor to be as accurate as possible, understanding the meaning of the words and their teaching is more important than their pronunciation or spelling. The following Ancient Egyptian proverbs extol the ideals just introduced.

"If you are in authority, then you should do perfect things, those which will be remembered by posterity. Never listen to the words of flatterers or words that fill you with pride and vanity."

"Words cannot give wisdom if they stray from the truth."

"Words are not the reality, only reality is reality;
picture symbols are the idea,
words are confusion."

As one can imagine, studying the phonetic and pictorial etymology of names can be an extensive discipline and learning the Kemetic language entails much more than it would appear on the surface. Exploring this aspect of Kemetic culture could take an entire lifetime and would fill several volumes. In fact, the Egyptian Yoga Book Series is the fruit of such researches, exploring the essential basis and practice of Kemetic mysticism, and more will come in future years. In this sense it is like no other language. It is a world in and of itself, apart from the spoken verbalizations used to communicate in ordinary human situations. It is a language of the soul and of the cosmos, mystical philosophy and spiritual enlightenment. It is a language designed to take the mind beyond words.

New Terms

This volume will introduce new terminology to describe certain aspects of the writings contained in the *Prt m Hru*. The reason for this is, the terms that have been used by traditional Egyptologist have become outdated, and in order to have a clearer understanding, we must now progress to the use of terms and definitions which more closely approximate the meaning for our modern understanding. This is necessary because many of the terms which have been used are merely conventions devised by Egyptologists to account for Ancient Egyptian words and ideas, which have no direct translation in other languages. Therefore we must begin to study the terms and gain a new understanding and feel for these in their own language.

The pursuit of perfection in life does not come from discovering a grammatically perfect scripture, for there is none. It is gaining understanding from a scripture that speaks to us based on our karmic makeup (personality inclinations) as to the essence of our human existence, the Higher Self. In this sense, all the world's spiritual scriptures are perfectly capable of promoting spiritual enlightenment, for those to whom they appeal, if they are correctly understood and if allowances are made for human frailties. This is why a spiritual preceptor is so important on the spiritual path. That person can steer the mind when it is caught up in the petty issues of spiritual practice. That person is a guide to let the aspirant know how to deal with issues that on the surface seem like insurmountable contradictions or obstacles, which can bring an aspirant's spiritual evolution to a halt, but which are in reality insignificant misunderstandings to be out-stepped.

As stated earlier, in some cases, later versions of the *Prt m Hru* were refined or expanded and sometimes modified by the priests/priestesses or scribes of the later time. An example of this is the refinement of the concept of the neteru or gods and goddesses and their relationship to the initiate. In Utterances 273-274 of the *Pyramid Texts*, the concept of assimilating the neteru is put forth using the metaphor of eating the gods and goddesses and even cooking them as well. In Chapter 27 of the papyrus versions, the concept is refined to direct statements affirming knowledge of the true nature of the neteru and thus, the idea of becoming those same gods and goddesses by self-discovery. This concept is related to the original Kemetic concept of the consecration[30] idea (receiving and consuming the eye of Heru) which is contained in both the earlier texts (*Pyramid Texts*) as well as the later texts (papyrus versions) of the *Prt m Hru*. Where these additions and changes were in harmony with the earlier, original texts and added to the spiritual importance and understanding of the text, they were retained.

---

[30] This is the prototype for the Christian Eucharist ritual of consecrating items such as bread and wine in the Mass Ritual..

Ancient Kemetic Terms and Ancient Greek Terms

In keeping with the spirit of the culture of Kemetic Spirituality, in this volume we will use the Kemetic names for the divinities through which we will bring forth the Philosophy of the Prt M Hru. Therefore, the Greek name Osiris will be converted back to the Kemetic (Ancient Egyptian) Asar (Ausar), the Greek Isis to Aset (Auset), the Greek Nephthys to Nebthet, Anubis to Anpu or Apuat, Hathor to Hetheru, Thoth or Hermes to Djehuty (Djehuty), etc. (see the table below) Further, the term Ancient Egypt will be used interchangeably with "Kemit" ("Kamit"), or "Ta-Meri," as these are the terms used by the Ancient Egyptians to refer to their land and culture.

Table 5: Kemetic Names of the main Gods and Goddesses of Ancient Egypt and the Greek translation in common use.

Kemetic (Ancient Egyptian) Names	Greek Names
Amun	Zeus
Ra	Helios
Ptah	Hephastos
Nut	Rhea
Geb	Kronos
Net	Athena
Khonsu	Heracles
Set	Ares or Typhon
Bast	Artemis
Uadjit	Leto
Asar (Ausar)	Osiris or Hades
Aset (Auset)	Isis or Demeter
Nebthet	Nephthys
Anpu or Apuat	Anubis
Hetheru	Hathor (Aphrodite)
Heru	Horus or Apollo
Djehuty (Djehuty)	Thoth or Hermes
Maat	Astraea or Themis

How To Study The Mystical Teachings Of The Prt m Hru

The Papyrus of Ani, as it has come to be known, is an excellent example of the *Prt m Hru* text as it existed in the New Kingdom Dynastic period of Ancient Egypt. The hieroglyphic texts of Ancient Egypt, the teachings of Egyptian mystical spirituality are called "Khu" or "Hekau," meaning *utterances* or *words of power,* and are collectively known as "Medtu Neter," Words of The God or Neter Medtu - Divine Speech. Modern Egyptology, the scholarly study of Ancient Egyptian civilization from the early nineteenth century to the present, has labeled these *utterances* as *spells* or *incantations.* In a way this assessment is correct because these utterances are to be understood as words which, when spoken with meaning and feeling, can have a transforming effect on the mind, allowing expansion of consciousness. However, the Hekau should not to be understood in the context of Western magic or witches spells or voodoo, etc. To do so would be a grievous error of intellectual laziness and cultural egoism, trying to make simple correlations to lower forms of spiritual practice. This form of treatment would yield the conclusion that the Ancient Egyptian religion is merely a myriad of conflicting stories and the presumption that Ancient Egyptian spirituality is a conglomerate of idol worshipping and occult nonsense.

In ancient times, Ancient Egyptian spirituality drew followers from all corners of the world. Those who came from far away recognized the greatness of Egypt, which was the fruit of the Temple system of education. The Temple was a formidable power for human mental, physical and spiritual development, healthcare and social government.

Any study of mystical spirituality needs to be carried out from the perspective of the present. This means that the teachings need to be understood in the context of today and how it affects one's life right here and right now. What good would it do to know all about the history of what a Sage, such as Ptahotep, did and taught 5,000 years ago if it is not understood in the context of a teaching which can be used in the present? As the reader, whether or not you believe and practice the teachings or are simply interested in understanding them, you should look upon them from the perspective of something which is alive and viable for today. The following instructions are included for those who wish to seriously integrate the teachings into their lives for the purpose of discovering their deeper meaning and their power to transform the human mind.

Before undertaking this study, we need to establish the parameters by which we will explore the teachings. Many people do not realize that mystical spirituality is like an advanced form of psychotherapy, incorporating not only a keen understanding of psychology, human emotion, and social relationships, but also the relationship between individual human consciousness and Cosmic Consciousness. Unlike the discipline of Western psychotherapy or the psychological treatment of mental, emotional, and nervous disorders, mystical spirituality or psychology is not just concerned with the mentally insane and how to bring them back into the mainstream of society or normal human life. This is because this so called "normal" social structure cannot be so normal if it turns out psychotics or those who suffer from any of a class of serious mental disorders in which the mind cannot function normally and the ability to deal with reality is impaired or lost. These mental illnesses and psychoses include: anger, hatred, greed, lust, envy, jealousy, depression, schizophrenia, sadism, manic depressive psychosis, and paranoia. The structure of modern society is conducive to the development of social stresses, based on passion, greed and lust, as well as both physical and mental disease, due to pollution of the environment and the mind. The ordinary practice of religion does not incorporate a mystical aspect. This shortcoming is the source of strife and dysfunction in family relations, social relations and spiritual relations of in modern culture. Mystical spirituality integrates and develops not only the intellect, but also the emotions to deal with practical life and the will power capacity of the personality, all the while leading the soul to ultimate spiritual self-discovery. It promotes harmony in society, harmony with nature and harmony between humanity and the Divine. Therefore, mystical psycho-spiritual counseling is more powerful than ordinary psychoanalysis.

Mystical teachings should be studied in the context of a transpersonal discipline which not only seeks to promote the ordinary standards of "normalcy," but also to transcend these in order to achieve a supernormal mental, physical and spiritual level of health. This element is what differentiates ordinary thinking in psychology, sociology and medical science from the ideals of mystical teaching. The ordinary discipline seeks to settle for a worldly reward in the form of what is commonly accepted as peace and joy, but which is in reality, limited, ephemeral, fragile and illusory. Mystical psychology seeks to go beyond the ordinary and to discover the that which is to be known and which upon knowing, all is known, the Absolute, which transcends time and space. This idea is extremely important because ordinary human life cannot satisfy the inner need of the heart of a human being since it is transient, ephemeral and unpredictable. So no matter how well integrated ordinary psychology may help a person to become, they will be missing the spiritual dimension wherein lies the abiding fulfillment of the human being.

Figure 11: Above left: Forms of the God Djehuty (Djehuty)/Djehuty

The Creator of Hieroglyphic Text and Author of Medu Neter (Divine Words-Speech)

Figure 12: Above right: Forms of the Goddess Maat/Maati

The embodiment of truth, justice, regularity and harmony.
She is the bestower of Maak-heru (Spiritual Enlightenment)

The Elements of the Human Personality

In order to properly understand the perspective of the Pert-mHeru Egyptian Book of Coming Forth By Day [Enlightenment] it is necessary to have a foundation in the wisdom of the Parts or Elements of the Human Personality. It is important to understand the architecture of the human constitution. The *Prt m Hru* makes a distinction between these because the human personality is a conglomerate or composite of several aspects or levels of existence. These elements are not readily discernible to the ordinary person due to the lack of spiritual sensitivity. Further, one element may not be effective in all planes of existence. For example, the Ka may not be discernible in the Ta or Physical Plane, while the Khat may not be discernible in the Pet or Heavenly Plane. It is necessary to know about these, because in knowing them, one gains greater insight into the higher planes of existence and the teachings of the *Prt m Hru*. This section will concentrate on the subtle human anatomy and the anatomy of all existence. It will discuss the Physical, Astral and Causal planes of existence and their inner workings as they relate to the elements that compose the human personality. First we will review the themes and essential wisdom developed in the book *Egyptian Yoga: The Philosophy of Enlightenment*. Then we will proceed to look into the nature of the subtle spiritual Self with more detail and depth. The Ancient Egyptian concept of the spiritual constitution recognized nine separate but interrelated parts that constitute the personality of every human being.

Thus, the Sage looks on the body as a marionette, created with thoughts by the Self, or as a projection as in a dream. Having awoken from the dream, when the physical body dies, the Sage who has discovered {his/her} oneness with the Self remains as the Self and does not create any more bodies to further incarnate. This is because {he/she} has discovered {his/her} essential nature and there are no more desires for experiences as a human being. Thus, there is no cause for the creation of a new ego-personality. This is the state that Sages experience with respect to the waking world of ordinary human beings. They are no longer caught up in the illusion of the world. This is called Liberation, Salvation, Heruhood, Waking up, Meeting Asar, Resurrection, Nirvana, etc. This is the loftiest goal of human life.

"Knowledge derived from the senses is illusory. True knowledge can only come from the understanding of the union of opposites."

–Ancient Egyptian Proverb

If you look at yourself objectively, you will realize that every cell in your body is changing from moment to moment, and that you are never the same as you were a moment ago. Even solid objects are changing and decaying, albeit at a slower rate, but eventually they will decompose into their constituent elements. In much the same way, the human body is changing and constantly moving towards extinction. But is this real? Is this change a quality of your inner Self? Upon closer examination, the real you is not changeable; the real you is Pure Consciousness and one with the Supreme Being who is eternal. Remember the teaching: ***"The Great God inside the common folk"*** from Chapter 17 of the *"Prt m Hru."* This is what it means. Your inner Self is one with the Divine Self. Initiatic science shows that the real you, the innermost Self, is unchanging.

What is it that is constantly moving, constantly restless from the time you wake up until the time you go to bed again? This is the thinking mind with all of the worries, all of the desires, all the beliefs, all of the ambitions and all of the regrets. These thoughts, worries, desires, beliefs, ambitions and regrets constitute your mental conditioning, your personality, and your ego-self-concept. Through the process of your human experience in the world, your mind has become conditioned to expect to see reality in a certain way and therefore, it perceives life according to its conditioning. This conditioning, your ego, is what is holding you back from being able to realize your innermost Self, which is all encompassing, all-knowing, and all-blissful contentment and peace.

Your ego-personality is like a movie character that emerges at the beginning of a movie and fades away at the end. The movie screen remains in order to receive images from other movies. In the same way your personality emerged out of your mental conditioning at the time of your birth and since then, it has never stopped changing, moving, craving and searching for fulfillment. Egoism is the feeling of separation from the Self and attachment to an illusory personality that arises out of the dream quality of consciousness. It is intensified by the distractions of the mind due to the pursuit of fulfillment of sensual desires. At the time of your death, the gross aspects of your personality (Khat and Ren) will cease to exist, but the impressions created through these in the unconscious will leave you still craving for the unfulfilled desires. This is because the deep unconscious mind with its conditioned impressions of desire, survives death and follows you into the Duat (astral plane) until you finally are born again in the earth plane to once again continue seeking fulfillment.

"Get thyself ready and make the thought in you a stranger to the world-illusion"
–Ancient Egyptian Proverb

The concept of relativity of time is expressed in the hieroglyphic text entitled, *The Songs of The Harper*. In one verse, the relativity of the passage of time is explained as follows:

"The whole period of things done on the earth is but a period of a dream."

This formula of the Harper, when put together with the *Coffin Text* formula given previously about the nature of Atum Ra (*after the millions of years of differentiated creation, the chaos that existed before creation will return; only the primeval god [31] and Asar will remain steadfast-no longer separated in space and time*) form an exceedingly powerful combination which should act as a fuse to ignite the mind's deeper insight into the nature of Self. The "period of millions of years" mentioned in the *Coffin Texts* is in reality the same as the period of a dream, and as you know, a long period of time can be experienced in a dream, but in reality nothing has happened, except that your consciousness has emanated a dream world. But as you also know, the dream world comes to an end and dissolves back into consciousness. In the same manner, God has emanated this world and will someday dissolve it back into the Primeval Ocean of potential consciousness. Consider your dreams. They may seem to occur over a period of hours. You may even experience the passage of years within your dream, and yet upon waking up you realize that the entire time you were in bed asleep for a few hours. In the same way, the entire period of the existence of the universe is nothing but the span of a short dream in the mind of God.

From an advanced perspective, neither time nor space can be said to exist as something that is real, just as time, space, matter or physical objects within a dream cannot be called "real." The entire dream world exists in the mind and does not require real time or space. The phenomenal world, which is experienced in the Waking State of consciousness, is also not real and does not exist except in the mind of God. This teaching is not only confirmed by the *Hymns of Amun*,[32] but it is also a primary teaching of Memphite Theology that is presented in the *Shabaka Inscription*.[33] In reality only eternity is real, and God is eternity. Since all matter is in reality constituted of the thought energy of God, and the changes in matter are called time, it must be clearly understood that God is the only reality that exists.

God is eternity itself. The limited perceptions of the unenlightened human mind and senses are what human beings refer to as "time" and "space" awareness. However, the perception of time and space is due to the limitations and conditioning of the human mind and body. If it were possible to perceive the entire universe, then you would discover that there is only oneness, an eternal view that is not restricted to time and space. This is the view that God has towards Creation. The task of the spiritual aspirant is to grow out of the limitations of the mind and body and discover the Cosmic Vision that lies within. When this is accomplished, there is a new perception of the universe. This represents the death of the human being and the birth of the spiritual life in the human being.

God has assumed the form of the neteru or Pautti. These "neteru" are cosmic forces, energies that sustain the universe and which constitute "physical matter." Therefore, this "physical" universe is in reality the body of God and everything in it is Divine, from the smallest atom to the largest celestial bodies in the heavens. It must be emphasized that in this process, *The Universal Ba*[34] itself becomes the individual Ba of every human being, due to its association and identification with the feelings of the emotional body, *Ka,* and the cravings of the Physical body, *Khat.*

By practicing the disciplines of Maat, the initiate is able to curb the wanton desires of the ego and thereby strengthen the will of the intellect. The science of practicing virtue in life will serve to assist the aspirant to purify the heart (mind), to cultivate peace of mind, and thereby to develop insight into the innermost Self. At this stage, the movement or vibration in the Primeval Waters which caused the world to be, subsides. Just as a calm lake reflects a pure image, the purified mind will reflect the clarity of the Cosmic Soul. The waves, caused by movements of the mind, would once again become just as the waves in the Primeval Ocean before creation, silent, at rest, at peace.

Your innermost Self, the Cosmic Soul, is constantly interacting with the world through the mind. If you had yellow sunglasses on, when you look at anything you would see a yellow tinge. In the same way, when you look at the world

---

[31] Referring to the Supreme Being in the form of Atum-Ra
[32] See the book *Egyptian Yoga Volume II* by Dr. Muata Ashby
[33] See also Egyptian Yoga: The Philosophy of Enlightenment (Egyptian Yoga Volume I)
[34] The terms: The Universal, World Ba, Pa Neter, Amun, Nebertcher are to be understood as being synonymous.

through your conditioned mind and senses, your vision reflects the tinge of egoism and divergent thoughts, but most of all, ignorance of your true Self which causes body identification. If you were to eradicate your mental conditioning, you would see a different reality. This is the goal of the various disciplines of mystical spirituality, to purify the intellect, **Saa**. By developing your higher intellectual ability to cut through the illusions of life with the ax of wisdom, you purify your subconscious mind from all of the conditioning. It is this purification of Saa which can lead you to awareness of the Higher Self.

The philosophy of the four states of consciousness (waking, dream, dreamless sleep, undifferentiated (transcendental) consciousness) is of paramount importance for the spiritual aspirant. A profound understanding of this teaching will lead you to develop subtlety of intellect in discerning the reality of the thoughts in your own mind as well as that which is real around you. In the book *The Cycles of Time,* we explored in depth, the practices of how this teaching is applied in everyday life in order to realize its significance at the deepest levels of the mind through virtuous living, the practice of Maat.

Maat philosophy provides us with a guideline for determining what is real and what is not. This is crucial to the correct operation of the mind because the mind supports whatever reality it believes to be true. You experience the world through your mind and senses. You have learned that these are valid criteria to determine the validity of the world and of your inner experience. Everything must be known through your rationalizing mind once it has been perceived by your senses. However, as we showed in the books *Egyptian Yoga: The Philosophy of Enlightenment* and *The Hidden properties of Matter*, what is normally considered to be real and abiding, solid matter, is nothing more than energy in its grosser states of being. It must be clearly understood that mental perceptions are not direct perceptions of matter. Your hand which you use to hold an object is itself a swirling mass of energy which is connected to other masses of energy conduits that lead to the brain. Sensual stimulus is an interaction between different forms of energy that registers in the brain centers in a specific manner. The mind perceives these stimuli by reacting to the centers and then acknowledges a perception. Therefore, perception occurs in the brain itself and not in the hand. Consider for a moment the situation of a paralyzed person or your own experience if a limb has fallen "asleep." In these eventualities, there is still a limb, but there is no perception. Why? Because the perception media, the senses, are incapacitated. Consider the possibility of the paralyzed limb coming into contact with an object. Did any interaction occur? From the standpoint of the observation yes there was some sort of interaction between two objects, but not from the standpoint of the person with the disability.

Now consider the Dream State of consciousness. When you have dreams you perceive various objects, you touch them and you may even feel you own them. They appear to be real and "feel" very solid and true. However, upon waking you realize that they did not exist and never did. They were simply energy forms, which you created out of the subtle astral matter and perceived through the deluded mind. They were fleeting masses of subtle energy that arose out of your own mind and were perceived by your own mind. You developed an illusory triad of consciousness during your Dream State and from this arose an entire world. Your waking ego self-concept dissolved and you became a new subject. This "new" you used the subtle senses to perceive objects which you yourself imagined to exist. This is the triad of *seer, seen and sight.* When you woke up, this triad dissolved into your waking consciousness as if it never existed. However, upon waking up, you did not wake up into a reality, but rather you moved into another form of triad.

The *triad* of human consciousness arises out of your inability to perceive reality without the mind and senses. The mind and senses along with your soul form the three elements of the triad. If you were to transcend the mind and senses, you would perceive reality directly through your soul. Only through direct perception is it possible to know the truth or reality. The teaching of the triad is expressed in the symbolism of the Divine Trinity, which arises out of the Primeval Ocean.

The whole idea here is that the world you perceive as real is illusory. The senses, which you use to perceive the world are illusory, and the mind which you use to perceive the world is also illusory. Therefore, there is only one factor left which qualifies as real. That factor is the *witnessing consciousness* that perceives all of the different states. Through spiritual practices (yoga of wisdom, yoga of action, yoga of devotion and yoga of meditation) you can gradually lead your mind to deeper and deeper levels of perception of the truth until you discover the Absolute Truth beyond all of the illusory layers of the mind.

This essay has been presented so that the practitioner may begin to understand the visualization that is desired by the *Prt m Hru* texts, when it is written that the initiate is to say statements such as the following ones in part tow of this volume as well as understand what part of the personality is being referenced in the ancient text and how that relates to the quest for immortality and enlightenment. They are mystic formulas designed to awaken the innermost memory of one's true and ultimate identity as one with the Divinity who has brought all into existence and who will also dissolve it.

This is the ultimate discovery, coveted by all mystics of the world. In other words, the temporary mortal existence is not the ultimate reality.

Figure 13: A two dimensional depiction of the elements of the personality.

The diagram above shows the Kemetic concept of the elements of the personality (bodies) with the grossest (human body) at the center, and the subtlest (Spirit, God) at the outer edge.

The human personality has aspects or elements or parts that are derived from a source. Each element derives from a universal source lime a drop from an ocean. That source is the Divine Self or Universal God/Goddess. The following illustration provides a visual representation of this Ancient Egyptian concept. Therefore, the Individual derives from and remains supported by and connected to the Universal.

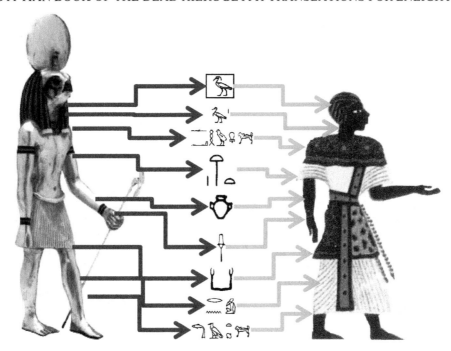

Figure 14: The elements of the Individual human personality are derived from the Universal God Ra

(1) THE KHU or AKHU:

The Khu or Akhu

The hieroglyph of the word Khu is the "crested ibis." The ibis is representative symbol of Djehuti, the god of reason and knowledge. As such it relates to the pure spiritual essence of a human being that is purified by lucidity of mind. The Khu or Akhu is the spirit, which is immortal; it is associated with the Ba and is an Ethereal Being. The Khu is also referred to as the "being of light" or "luminous being." The Khu illumines the personality and without this light, the personality and the mind cannot function. It is the light of consciousness itself.

(2) THE BA:

The Ba

The hieroglyphic symbol of the Ba is the Jabiru bird. The Jabiru is a stork. It symbolizes the nature of the soul to spread its wings and take flight, and exist apart from the body. The Ba is the heart or soul which dwells in the Ka with the power of metamorphosis. Sometimes described as the "Soul" and "Higher Self," it is seen as a spark from the Universal Ba (God). The Ba may be dialogued with and can be a spiritual guide to the developing individual. It is the equivalent of the Hindu "Atman." It is the indestructible, eternal and immortal spark of life. It is not affected by anything that may happen to the senses, body, mind or intellect (higher mind).

Through the mind, the Ba (soul-consciousness) "projects" and keeps together an aggregate of physical elements (earth, air, water, fire) in a conglomerate that is called the psycho-physical personality. When the soul has no more use for the physical body, it discards it and returns to the Universal Ba if it is enlightened. If it is not enlightened, it will tune into another aggregate of elements to make another body (reincarnation).

(3) THE SAHU:

The Sahu

The hieroglyphs of the word Sahu are the door bolt, meaning consonant "s" or "z," the arm, meaning the guttural sound "ain," the intertwined flax - consonant "h," the chick is the vowel "u," the determinative cylinder seal, meaning "treasure" or "precious," and the determinative of the "corpse" or "body." The Sahu is therefore sometimes referred to as the "glorious" spiritual body in which the Khu and Ba dwells. When the elements of a person are integrated (i.e., person moves towards or reaches enlightenment), the spiritual and mental attributes of the natural body are united and deified. The Sahu is the goal of all aspiration. It is the reason for human existence – to become Godlike while still alive by spiritualizing one's physical aspects and thereby allowing these to become proper vessels for the higher aspects of the personality to unfold.

(4) THE KHAIBIT:

The Khaibit

The hieroglyphs of the word Khaibit are the "sunshade" and the consonant "t." The sunshade produces a shadow when the light is reflecting on it. Similarly, the shadow of a person, their personality, is produced when the light of their true essence (Akhu) is shining on the aspects of the personality. The Khaibit is therefore, an outline of the soul that is illumined by the light of the Spirit, which reflects in the mind as a subtle image of self (ego). In Chapter 31 of the *Prt M Hru,* it is stated *I* (as the sundisk) *fly away to illuminate the shades* (in the Duat). The shades are the subtle reflection of the soul, which are not self-illuminating and which therefore exist only due to the presence of light and an object. In this case, the object is the Soul. The Khaibit is a subtle manifestation of the elements of the personality that acts somewhat as the resistor in an electronic component. A resistor causes a shadow in a manner of speaking, when it is placed in an electric circuit. In the same manner, the Khaibit and the other elements of the personality consume spiritual energy from the spirit and produce a particular image thereafter referred to as the individual personality of a human being. The Khaibit or Shadow is associated with the Ba from which it receives nourishment. It has the power of locomotion and omnipresence.

(5) THE AB:

The Ab
"The conscience (Ab) of a man is his own God."

The Ab or conscience is the source of Meskhenet (Ari, Karma) and the mother of reincarnation. The Ab represents the heart. It is the symbol of the deep unconscious mind, the conscience and also the repository of unconscious impressions gathered in past experiences from the present life and previous lives. As desires can never be fulfilled by experiences or from objects in the world of time and space, at death, the ignorant soul will harbor impressions of unfulfilled desires which will lead to further incarnations in search of fulfillment. This point is described in Chapter 36, from the *Egyptian Book of Coming Forth by Day:* ***"My heart, the mother of my coming into being."*** The mind is seen as the source of incarnation (coming into being) because it contains the desires and illusions which compel a human being to be born to pursue the fulfillment of those desires. In the judgment scene from the *Book of Coming Forth By Day,* the Ab undergoes examination by Djehuti, the god of reason. In other words, one's own reasoning faculty will be the judge as well as that which is being judged. The heart (mind) itself metes out its own judgment based on its own contents. It is one's own heart which will fashion (*mother*) one's own fate (*come into being*) according to one's will and desires, which are based on one's understanding (wisdom) about one's true Self. Thus, the new embodiment is fashioned in accordance with what a person has done during previous lives and what they desire for the future. A desire for worldly experience will cause embodiment. A desire to go to the west and join with God will bring spiritual enlightenment.

(6) THE SEKHEM:

The Sekhem

Sekhem is the Life Force or Power that exists in the universe. The symbol of Sekhem is the hand held staff pictured above. When used in worldly terms it refers to a scepter that means physical power, authority and strength. In spiritual terms, the Sekhem is the power or spiritual personification of the vital Life Force in humans. Its dwelling place is in the heavens with the Khus, but all life draws upon this force in order to exist. Sekhem also denotes the potency, the erectile power or force used in fashioning one's own glorious new body for resurrection.

(7) The KA:

The Ka

The hieroglyph of two upraised arms that are joined is the Ka. It is the abstract personality or ego-self. It is the source from which subconscious desires emerge. It is also considered to be the ethereal body possessing the power of locomotion. It survives the death of the physical body. It is the ethereal double containing the other parts of the personality. The concept of the Ka was known in India, and the word was also known. The Indian God Brahma had a Ka (soul-twin). This teaching of the Ka in Ancient Egypt and in India shows that there is a keen understanding of the reflective quality of the personality. In reality the physical personality is a reflection or more accurately, a projection of the astral body. The Ka is associated with the Sekhem in that it is the dynamic aspect of a person's personality in the Astral Plane. It is the dynamic aspect of the vital force in the body of a human being.

(8) THE REN:

The Ren

The Ancient Egyptian word Ren means "name." The name is an essential attribute to the personification of a being. You cannot exist without a name. Everything that comes into existence receives a name. This is an essential quality of that which comes into the realm of time and space. The Ancient Egyptian symbols that signify name are the "mouth" and "water." The name is sometimes found encircled by a rope of light called a cartouche, which is associated with the Shen (a symbol of eternity), the top part of the Ankh Symbol. The cartouche represents a rope of sunlight or Life Force harnessed into the form of a circle. It is the most impregnable structure to protect one's name against attack. The ⬭, means mouth.

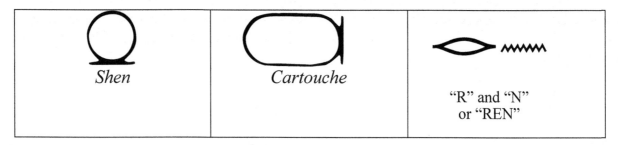

Shen	*Cartouche*	"R" and "N" or "REN"

The symbol of the mouth is of paramount importance in Ancient Egyptian Mystical wisdom. The symbol of the mouth refers to the consonant sound "r," and it is a symbol of consciousness. It is the mouth which is used in two of the most important mystical teachings of Ancient Egyptian Yoga, *The Creation* and the *Opening of the Mouth Ceremony* of the *Book of Coming Forth By Day.* God created the universe by means of the utterance of his own name. In the *Book of Coming Forth By Day,* the mouth is manipulated so as to promote enlightenment. Why is the mouth so important to this mystical symbolism? This issue is discussed in more detail in the following section entitled "More Mystical Implications of the Name"

(9) THE KHAT:

The Khat

The hieroglyphs of the word Khat are the fish meaning "dead body" and the consonant "k," the vulture meaning the vowel "a," the symbol of "bread" and the consonant "t," the egg-like determinative symbol of "embalming" and the determinative symbol of the "mummy," "corpse" or "body." The Khat is the concrete personality, the physical body. It refers to the solid aspect of a human being (bones, skin, blood, sense organs, etc.) which is transient and mortal.

More Mystical Implications of the Name

Consider the following. When you think of anything, you attach words to your thoughts. In fact, it is difficult to think without words. Therefore, words are the symbols that the human mind uses to group thoughts and which constitute intellectual forms of understanding. However, thoughts are conditioning instruments. This means that when you think, you are actually differentiating. The differentiation process allows the mind to be conscious or aware of differences in matter. It labels these differences with different names based on the form or function of the object or the relationship it has to it. The mind learns to call objects by names. For example, a chair is an aggregate of matter just like a rock. However, the mind has learned to call it a particular name and associate the name "chair" with a particular kind of object which looks in a particular way and serves a particular function that is different from the rock.

When the mind goes beyond words, it goes beyond thoughts and thereby experiences undifferentiated consciousness. This is the deeper implication of the opening of the mouth ceremony. It signifies opening the consciousness and memory of the undifferentiated state of existence. At a lower state of spiritual evolution, consciousness appears to be differentiated, even though the underlying essence is undifferentiated. However, when intuitional realization or spiritual enlightenment dawns in the human mind, words are no longer viewed as differentiating instruments, but merely as practical instruments for the spirit to operate and interact with the world through a human personality. This is the difference between a human being who is spiritually enlightened and one who is caught in the state of ignorance and egoism.

The vocal capacity in a human being is intimately related to the unconscious level of the mind. This is why those who do not practice introspection and self-control often blurt out things they do not wish to say, and later regret. For this reason, the teachings enjoin that a spiritual aspirant should practice the disciplines of virtue which lead to self-control through right action and righteous living. In this manner, one's speech becomes *maakheru,* the highest truth. When one's speech becomes truth, one's consciousness is truth. When one's consciousness is truth, it is in harmony with the transcendental truth of the universe which is symbolized by the Ancient Egyptian goddess Maat. Thus, becoming true of speech is a primary goal for every spiritual aspirant. It is synonymous with coming into harmony with the universe and thus, refers to spiritual enlightenment itself.[35]

The symbol of the water recalls the image of the Primordial Ocean of Consciousness. Thus, Ren relates to consciousness manifesting through names, words and sound itself.

The Importance of the Spiritual Name

Figure 15: (right) Queen Nefertari as initiate Asar.

The hieroglyphic inscription reads *"Asar Nefertari, the great queen, beloved of goddess Mut and Maakheru (spiritually victorious) is in the presence of Asar, the Great God"*

In Ancient Egyptian Asarian mysticism, all initiates were given the spiritual name *"Asar"* regardless of if they were male or female. Thus, in the Papyrus of Ani, Ani, who was a man, was renamed Asar Ani. Likewise, Nefertari, who was a woman, also received the name Asar Nefertari. Thus, in the same manner, other papyruses of the *Prt m Hru* prepared for other initiates, were not prepared for the man or woman, but for the spiritual aspirant. While Asar is usually seen as a male divinity his higher attributes include those which relate him as an androgynous, transcendental Spirit. The term "ren" relating to the aspect of the personality of a human being therefore refers to the ego and not to the Higher Self. So every human being has a Divine Name and an ego name.

What is the deeper implication of this? This is a very important mystical teaching relating that the deeper Self within Ani is Asar, the Divine Self. That is, his true identity is not the birth name, but the Divinity which transcends mortal existence. In modern times, John would be Asar John, Cynthia would be Asar Cynthia, etc. It is an affirmation and

---

[35] For a detailed examination of the principles embodied in the neteru or cosmic forces of the company of gods and goddesses, the reader is referred to the books *The Hidden Properties of Matter, The Ausarian Resurrection* and *The Mystical Teachings of The Ausarian Resurrection* by Dr. Muata Ashby.

acceptance of one's Divine true essential nature not only as an expression of God, but as God in fact. Thus the entire journey of self-discovery revolves around your discovering that the deeper reality within you is God. This does not contradict other religions. In Buddhism, the deeper reality a Buddhist is looking for is Buddha Consciousness. Thus, in Ancient Egyptian terms as related in the *Book of Coming Forth By Day*, the deeper reality to be sought is Asar. So as you live your life, see your existence as a journey of discovery. Feel that you have come from a divine source and that as you practice the teachings, you are drawing ever closer to discovering that source. See your entire life as a ritual. When you wake up in the morning reflect on the majesty of the Sun (Divine) just as Ani does with his prayer. When you eat, see this as an offering to the Divine Self within you.

There are essentially three important elements being imparted in the *Prt m Hru*. The first is the message that righteousness leads to spiritual realization. The second is that the process of purification is acting with righteousness. The third message of the text is the wisdom about the Divine. By learning about the nature of the Divine, acting, feeling and thinking as the Divine, it is finally possible to become one with the Divine. The spiritual name is an essential and powerful force linking the initiate to that spiritual source as well as a constant reminder of the true glory of the Higher Self.

The Mystical and Cosmic Implications of the Elements of the Personality

This section will provide a more detailed classification of the human being in an attempt to understand the underlying origin and cause of human existence. Also, it will seek to bring forth a deeper understanding of how the Cosmic Forces operate through the human constitution at gross and subtle levels.

As discussed earlier, the Universal Soul, God, Pure Consciousness, emanates Creation and all that is within it, all that is. The human being is like a ray of that emanation which refracts into several parts composing all of the levels of existence. Human consciousness may be compared to a reflection of the sun in a pool of water. Human consciousness is a reflection of divine consciousness in the pool of the mind which operates through the brain and nervous system. This idea is also reflected in the relationship between the parts of the spirit called BA and AB.

BA ⇔ AB

The Ab is the heart or seat of the mind, and it is in the mind where the soul, Ba, reflects. So the mind has no independent existence without the soul's sustaining life force and consciousness, and the individual human soul has no independent existence without the Universal Soul.

Universal Ba ⇨ Individual Ba ⇨ Individual Ab[36]

These levels of existence transfer into the four states of consciousness and various levels of psycho-spiritual psychology related to the Uraeus-Serpent Power system.[37]

Table 6: The Three Bodies of Men and Women and of God

The three basic parts of the human being are the Causal Body, the Astral Body and the Physical Body. They may be viewed in a increasing order of density as follows. These bodies also relate to the bodies of the universe:

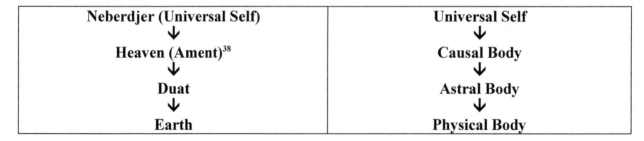

Neberdjer (Universal Self)	Universal Self
↓	↓
Heaven (Ament)[38]	Causal Body
↓	↓
Duat	Astral Body
↓	↓
Earth	Physical Body

---

[36] Human heart and mind.
[37] See the book *The Serpent Power* by Dr. Muata Ashby
[38] In Kemetic Philosophy there are two heavens, a lower physical heaven wherein the lower aspects of the personality (Khat, Ren, Sekhem, Ab) reside and a higher heaven wherein the higher aspects of the personality such as the Akhu, Sahu, and Ba reside.

The Universal Ba or Soul, or in other words, the consciousness of the Supreme Being, emanates and sustains each individual human being through the various parts of the human spirit. There are three basic parts to the human being. These are further broken down into more specific parts.

Sages of ancient times who were able to discern, through their intuitional vision (spiritual eye), the different levels of vibration and psychology within all human beings, have set forth this teaching about the constitution of the human being. An important point to note is that each of the lower three states involves duality while the highest state involves non-duality. The human soul is a projection of the divine into the realm of duality (causal -astral- physical planes). The human soul forgets its divine origin and believes itself to be a creature among other creatures; hence, the idea of duality arises. The ignorant human being is not aware that {he/she} is at all times most intimately connected to the Universal Self, as are all objects and all other human beings. Just as each wave in the ocean is essentially the same as the ocean, each wave-like human personality and all the objects in Creation are essentially the Primeval Ocean, the Self. Ignorance of this then gives rise to the various egoistic feelings. The ignorant human being, not aware of {his/her} storehouse of innate potential to experience fullness and peace within, goes on seeking for fulfillment in the worlds of duality instead of seeking to know and experience the only source of true fulfillment, the Universal Self, which encompasses all other realms. Non-duality is experienced as absolute oneness and interconnectedness with all that exists. There is no feeling of you and me, here and there, male or female; there is no desire for objects because all objects are one with the Self. There is only the experience of awareness of the Self. Human words and concepts are not capable of describing the actual experience of oneness with the Self, therefore, all mystical descriptions are transcended in the actual experience. They are like a map, but you must take the journey and arrive at the destination by your own will and self-effort. Thus, they serve as guides, to lead the mind toward the understanding of yogic philosophy. --

The nine major elements or parts of the human personality espoused by the Ancient Egyptian Sages may be classified as follows within the three basic bodies for the purpose of study and understanding, as illustrated below. God is also understood to have three bodies: Universal Causal Body, Universal Astral Body, Universal Physical Body, the three aspects of universe or planes of existence. Within these bodies are the constituent elements, totaling nine in number. God also has nine elements. However, unlike those of the human being which are limited and characterized by their individuality, the divine elements are universal and all pervading in their respective level of existence. Thus we are told in the Ancient Egyptian scriptures that God has a Universal Ba, a Universal Sahu, a Universal Khu (Akhu), a Universal Khaibit, a Universal Ka, a Universal Sekhem, a Universal Ab, a Universal Khat, and a Universal Ren. Thus, the individual elements that compose the personality of each individual human being emanate from the same Supreme Being.

Table 7: The Nine Aspects of the Human personality and of God.

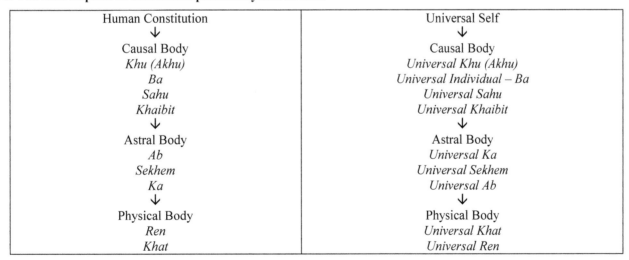

Human Constitution	Universal Self
↓	↓
Causal Body	Causal Body
Khu (Akhu)	Universal Khu (Akhu)
Ba	Universal Individual – Ba
Sahu	Universal Sahu
Khaibit	Universal Khaibit
↓	↓
Astral Body	Astral Body
Ab	Universal Ka
Sekhem	Universal Sekhem
Ka	Universal Ab
↓	↓
Physical Body	Physical Body
Ren	Universal Khat
Khat	Universal Ren

Ren = Name
Khat = Form

(Name and form are the basis of physical existence on the earth plane.)

It should be noted that while the gross elements of the ego-personality are evident at the level of the physical body, the original cause of the existence of the individual and {his/her} separation from the Divine occurs at the level of the Causal Body. Many people erroneously think of their soul as existing within their physical body. However, the opposite is true. The soul emanates from the Self. It in turn creates the other parts of the personality. All of this creation occurs within the Divine Self and not the body. The Causal Body is where the slightest tendency towards thought and desire occurs. It is here where the deep unconscious impressions cause the other parts of the body to emerge. When the physical body of an un-enlightened person dies, the gross elements of the ego (name and personality used in a particular lifetime) also die. The Astral and Causal bodies survive with the unconscious impressions collected from that lifetime. Through these bodies the soul continues the pursuit of fulfillment of desire (unconscious impressions lodged in the Astral-Causal mental subtle matter). The pursuit of fulfillment of desires may continue in the Astral plane (Duat-Netherworld) for a time, where the individual experiences of pain or pleasure (heaven or hell) according to {his/her} Meskhenet (karmic basis composed of impressions gathered from feelings, actions and desires of many lifetimes).

The task of an aspirant is to cleanse the Physical, Astral and Causal planes of the mind so as to regain conscious perception of the Universal Self. Since the Universal Self is non-dual, immortal, eternal and the source of all planes and all objects within those planes, the union with the Universal Self bestows omniscience and a boundless vision of infinity, immortality and a feeling of non-duality and connectedness to all things great and small. The correct practice of the various yogic disciplines are designed to accomplish this cleansing process. If successful, the soul comes into communion with the Self (Universal Ba, Asar, Ra, Aset, etc.) while still alive, and after death the soul of the enlightened person dissolves in the ocean of pure consciousness from whence it came originally. This is the meaning behind the teaching of *merging with the maker* presented in the Ancient Egyptian story known as *The Story of Sinuhe*.[39]

Earlier we discussed the fact that in the process of embodiment, the Universal Ba itself becomes the individual Ba of every human being due to its association and identification with the feelings of the emotional body, *Ka,* and the cravings of the physical body, *Khat.* If this is true, then how is it possible that the Universal Self (*Ba*) is also non-dual, meaning without a second, one and alone, all-encompassing as well as transcendental? At this more advanced level you must understand that all of the parts of the body are merely emanations from that same divine Self, just as you emanate a dream in your sleep or an idea in your Waking State, out of the depths of your consciousness.

In the same way this entire universe and everything in it is nothing but the emanation of God's consciousness. All that exists is ethereal, subtle matter, the Self. The process of thought has the effect of coagulating matter in a form as directed by the thought. In this way you have created your body and mind along with all of the other parts of your individual existence. In reality these parts are nothing more than subtle energy held together by your thoughts and ultimately, every one of those parts are not yours, but are parts of the Self. Thus, nothing exists outside of the Self, God. Therefore, even though there appears to be many objects, colors and differences in creation, the underlying essence of it all is the Self. Think about it. If there was something other than the Self, then the Self could not be all-pervasive, all-encompassing and all-powerful. Its movements would be restricted. The idea that there is a devil or some evil being who is the nemesis of God is erroneous because there can be no other being outside of the Self. The Self is the soul or substratum of all that is.

The idea of a "devil" who is a counterpart or nemesis of God who is "all good" was a development out a dualistic way of understanding life and mythology. This dualistic view is contrary to the teachings of mystical spirituality. It is the basis for egoism and misunderstanding in the practice of true religion. True religion means that you look for a connection, a oneness between yourself and God. For this to be possible you need to discover that your ego-personality is only a superficial expression of your deeper reality which is God. When you discover the depths of your own being, you realize that you are not an individual, separate from the universe and God. You discover that underneath the apparent separation there is oneness. A dualistic view looks for differences and affirms that there is a separation between God, creation and humankind. Thus, a practitioner of dualism prays to God, looks to God for salvation and believes he exists as an individual while the non-dualist practices the teachings that lead to the understanding that the innermost reality in the heart is God. God is in all things everywhere, and nothing exists besides God.

If you were to let go of your thoughts related to your body consciousness, you would discover that you are separate from your body. In the advanced stages, you could dematerialize and materialize it at will as well as perform other feats that are considered as miracles or psychic powers. The parts of the spiritual body are in reality like layers of clothing on your true Self. Therefore, in the *Gospel of Thomas,* Jesus exhorts his disciples to strip without being ashamed and on that day they will see him (Christhood, Enlightenment).

42. His disciples say to him: "On what day wilt thou appear to us, and what day shall we see thee?" Jesus says: "When you strip yourselves without being ashamed, when you take off your clothes and lay them at your feet like little children and trample them! Then {you will become} children of Him who is living, and you will have no more fear."

---

[39] See Egyptian Yoga: The Philosophy of Enlightenment (Egyptian Yoga Volume I)

All of the elements of the personality come together and create a conglomerate which collectively makes up likes and dislikes, opinions, feelings, thoughts, and desires of an individual. All of them constitute a conditioning[40] of the individual consciousness. This conditioning is referred to as egoism. The ego must be dismantled and stripped from the mind. When this occurs you will discover that what seemed so real and concrete (astral body, physical body) is nothing more than condensed thoughts. This discovery will free you from them as a bird is freed from a cage. When you take them off, what is left is the true Absolute you. All Creation has that same Absolute Self at its core. Therefore, you must seek to transcend all of the layers of ethereal matter so as to discover your true Self. This is accomplished by the practice of all of the disciplines of yoga presented here and in the Egyptian Yoga Book Series.

When we speak of "conditioning" we are referring to the conditioning of consciousness into the forms of the parts of the spirit in the same way that consciousness becomes conditioned into various forms (subjects, objects and interactions) in a dream. What is holding it all together? Desire born of ignorance of the Higher Self, which is transcendental and independent of concepts, and is whole, or free from fragmentation. The subtlest parts of the body: *Khaibit, Individual - Ba, Sahu,* and *Khu or Akhu,* are the deepest levels of the unconscious mind. Contained in them is the cause of separation between the individual soul and God. This individuation principle is called *ignorance.* Therefore, ignorance, based in the causal body, is the primary "cause" of the astral and physical bodies (ego) coming into being. This is why it is called the causal body. It causes the other bodies to come into existence. When this ignorance is removed, all of the bodies become as if transparent, as when you wake up in a dream even when you are still asleep. The dream continues, but you "know" it is a dream, so you witness it as a dream and not as reality. Upon waking from a dream you discover that even while things seemed to be so real, they were not. You were not even moving; you were placidly lying on the bed. In the same way, a Sage discovers that the Self is not moving; only the thoughts, senses and body controlled by those thoughts can be said to be moving. Does a dream move? No. In the same way, the real you is not located in the body and is not moving. Therefore, you are the "Unmoved Mover." You are Atum, the creator who causes movement but itself does not move.

Thus, the Sage looks on the body as a marionette, created with thoughts by the Self, or as a projection as in a dream. Having awoken from the dream, when the physical body dies, the Sage who has discovered {his/her} oneness with the Self remains as the Self and does not create any more bodies to further incarnate. This is because {he/she} has discovered {his/her} essential nature and there are no more desires for experiences as a human being. Thus, there is no cause for the creation of a new ego-personality. This is the state that Sages experience with respect to the waking world of ordinary human beings. They are no longer caught up in the illusion of the world. This is called Liberation, Salvation, Heruhood, Waking up, Meeting Asar, Resurrection, Nirvana, etc. This is the loftiest goal of human life.

> "Knowledge derived from the senses is illusory. True knowledge can only come from the understanding of the union of opposites."
>
> –Ancient Egyptian Proverb

If you look at yourself objectively, you will realize that every cell in your body is changing from moment to moment, and that you are never the same as you were a moment ago. Even solid objects are changing and decaying, albeit at a slower rate, but eventually they will decompose into their constituent elements. In much the same way, the human body is changing and constantly moving towards extinction. But is this real? Is this change a quality of your inner Self? Upon closer examination, the real you is not changeable; the real you is Pure Consciousness and one with the Supreme Being who is eternal. Remember the teaching: ***The Great God inside the common folk*** from Chapter 17 of the *"Prt m Hru."* This is what it means. Your inner Self is one with the Divine Self. Initiatic science shows that the real you, the innermost Self, is unchanging.

What is it that is constantly moving, constantly restless from the time you wake up until the time you go to bed again? This is the thinking mind with all of the worries, all of the desires, all the beliefs, all of the ambitions and all of the regrets. These thoughts, worries, desires, beliefs, ambitions and regrets constitute your mental conditioning, your personality, and your ego-self concept. Through the process of your human experience in the world, your mind has become conditioned to expect to see reality in a certain way and therefore, it perceives life according to its conditioning. This conditioning, your ego, is what is holding you back from being able to realize your innermost Self, which is all encompassing, all-knowing, and all-blissful contentment and peace.

Your ego-personality is like a movie character that emerges at the beginning of a movie and fades away at the end. The movie screen remains in order to receive images from other movies. In the same way your personality emerged out of your mental conditioning at the time of your birth and since then, it has never stopped changing, moving, craving and searching for fulfillment. Egoism is the feeling of separation from the Self and attachment to an illusory personality that

---

[40] See also Egyptian Yoga: The Philosophy of Enlightenment (Egyptian Yoga Volume I)

arises out of the dream quality of consciousness. It is intensified by the distractions of the mind due to the pursuit of fulfillment of sensual desires. At the time of your death, the gross aspects of your personality (Khat and Ren) will cease to exist, but the impressions created through these in the unconscious will leave you still craving for the unfulfilled desires. This is because the deep unconscious mind with its conditioned impressions of desire, survives death and follows you into the Duat (astral plane) until you finally are born again in the earth plane to once again continue seeking fulfillment.

"Get thyself ready and make the thought in you a stranger to the world-illusion"

–Ancient Egyptian Proverb

The concept of relativity of time is expressed in the hieroglyphic text entitled, *The Songs of The Harper*. In one verse, the relativity of the passage of time is explained as follows:

"The whole period of things done on the earth is but a period of a dream."

This formula of the Harper, when put together with the *Coffin Text* formula given previously about the nature of Atum Ra (*after the millions of years of differentiated creation, the chaos that existed before creation will return; only the primeval god [41] and Asar will remain steadfast-no longer separated in space and time*) form an exceedingly powerful combination which should act as a fuse to ignite the mind's deeper insight into the nature of Self. The "period of millions of years" mentioned in the *Coffin Texts* is in reality the same as the period of a dream, and as you know, a long period of time can be experienced in a dream, but in reality nothing has happened, except that your consciousness has emanated a dream world. But as you also know, the dream world comes to an end and dissolves back into consciousness. In the same manner, God has emanated this world and will some day dissolve it back into the Primeval Ocean of potential consciousness. Consider your dreams. They may seem to occur over a period of hours. You may even experience the passage of years within your dream, and yet upon waking up you realize that the entire time you were in bed asleep for a few hours. In the same way, the entire period of the existence of the universe is nothing but the span of a short dream in the mind of God.

From an advanced perspective, neither time nor space can be said to exist as something that is real, just as time, space, matter or physical objects within a dream cannot be called "real." The entire dream world exists in the mind and does not require real time or space. The phenomenal world, which is experienced in the Waking State of consciousness, is also not real and does not exist except in the mind of God. This teaching is not only confirmed by the *Hymns of Amun*, [42] but it is also a primary teaching of Memphite Theology that is presented in the *Shabaka Inscription*. [43] In reality only eternity is real, and God is eternity. Since all matter is in reality constituted of the thought energy of God, and the changes in matter are called time, it must be clearly understood that God is the only reality that exists.

God is eternity itself. The limited perceptions of the unenlightened human mind and senses are what human beings refer to as "time" and "space" awareness. However, the perception of time and space is due to the limitations and conditioning of the human mind and body. If it were possible to perceive the entire universe, then you would discover that there is only oneness, an eternal view that is not restricted to time and space. This is the view that God has towards Creation. The task of the spiritual aspirant is to grow out of the limitations of the mind and body and discover the Cosmic Vision that lies within. When this is accomplished, there is a new perception of the universe. This represents the death of the human being and the birth of the spiritual life in the human being.

God has assumed the form of the neteru or Pautti. These "neteru" are cosmic forces, energies that sustain the universe and which constitute "physical matter." Therefore, this "physical" universe is in reality the body of God and everything in it is Divine, from the smallest atom to the largest celestial bodies in the heavens. It must be emphasized that in this process, *The Universal Ba* [44] itself becomes the individual Ba of every human being, due to its association and identification with the feelings of the emotional body, *Ka,* and the cravings of the Physical body, *Khat.*

By practicing the disciplines of Maat, the initiate is able to curb the wanton desires of the ego and thereby strengthen the will of the intellect. The science of practicing virtue in life will serve to assist the aspirant to purify the heart (mind), to cultivate peace of mind, and thereby to develop insight into the innermost Self. At this stage, the movement or vibration in the Primeval Waters which caused the world to be, subsides. Just as a calm lake reflects a pure image, the purified mind will reflect the clarity of the Cosmic Soul. The waves, caused by movements of the mind, would once again become just as the waves in the Primeval Ocean before creation, silent, at rest, at peace.

---

[41] Referring to the Supreme Being in the form of Atum-Ra
[42] See the book *Egyptian Yoga Volume II* by Dr. Muata Ashby
[43] See also Egyptian Yoga: The Philosophy of Enlightenment (Egyptian Yoga Volume I)
[44] The terms: The Universal, World Ba, Pa Neter, Amun, Nebertcher are to be understood as being synonymous.

Your innermost Self, the Cosmic Soul, is constantly interacting with the world through the mind. If you had yellow sunglasses on, when you look at anything you would see a yellow tinge. In the same way, when you look at the world through your conditioned mind and senses, your vision reflects the tinge of egoism and divergent thoughts, but most of all, ignorance of your true Self which causes body identification. If you were to eradicate your mental conditioning, you would see a different reality. This is the goal of the various disciplines of mystical spirituality, to purify the intellect, *Saa*. By developing your higher intellectual ability to cut through the illusions of life with the ax of wisdom, you purify your subconscious mind from all of the conditioning. It is this purification of Saa which can lead you to awareness of the Higher Self.

The philosophy of the four states of consciousness (waking, dream, dreamless sleep, undifferentiated (transcendental consciousness) is of paramount importance for the spiritual aspirant. A profound understanding of this teaching will lead you to develop subtlety of intellect in discerning the reality of the thoughts in your own mind as well as that which is real around you. In the book *The Cycles of Time,* we explored in depth, the practices of how this teaching is applied in everyday life in order to realize its significance at the deepest levels of the mind through virtuous living, the practice of Maat.

Maat philosophy provides us with a guideline for determining what is real and what is not. This is crucial to the correct operation of the mind because the mind supports whatever reality it believes to be true. You experience the world through your mind and senses. You have learned that these are valid criteria to determine the validity of the world and of your inner experience. Everything must be known through your rationalizing mind once it has been perceived by your senses. However, as we showed in the books *Egyptian Yoga: The Philosophy of Enlightenment* and *The Hidden properties of Matter,* what is normally considered to be real and abiding, solid matter, is nothing more than energy in its grosser states of being. It must be clearly understood that mental perceptions are not direct perceptions of matter. Your hand which you use to hold an object is itself a swirling mass of energy which is connected to other masses of energy conduits that lead to the brain. Sensual stimulus is an interaction between different forms of energy that registers in the brain centers in a specific manner. The mind perceives these stimuli by reacting to the centers and then acknowledges a perception. Therefore, perception occurs in the brain itself and not in the hand. Consider for a moment the situation of a paralyzed person or your own experience if a limb has fallen "asleep." In these eventualities, there is still a limb, but there is no perception. Why? Because the perception media, the senses, are incapacitated. Consider the possibility of the paralyzed limb coming into contact with an object. Did any interaction occur? From the standpoint of the observation yes there was some sort of interaction between two objects, but not from the standpoint of the person with the disability.

Now consider the Dream State of consciousness. When you have dreams you perceive various objects, you touch them and you may even feel you own them. They appear to be real and "feel" very solid and true. However, upon waking you realize that they did not exist and never did. They were simply energy forms, which you created out of the subtle astral matter and perceived through the deluded mind. They were fleeting masses of subtle energy that arose out of your own mind and were perceived by your own mind. You developed an illusory triad of consciousness during your Dream State and from this arose an entire world. Your waking ego self-concept dissolved and you became a new subject. This "new" you used the subtle senses to perceive objects which you yourself imagined to exist. This is the triad of *seer, seen and sight.* When you woke up, this triad dissolved into your waking consciousness as if it never existed. However, upon waking up, you did not wake up into a reality, but rather you moved into another form of triad.

The *triad* of human consciousness arises out of your inability to perceive reality without the mind and senses. The mind and senses along with your soul form the three elements of the triad. If you were to transcend the mind and senses, you would perceive reality directly through your soul. Only through direct perception is it possible to know the truth or reality. The teaching of the triad is expressed in the symbolism of the Divine Trinity, which arises out of the Primeval Ocean.

The whole idea here is that the world you perceive as real is illusory. The senses, which you use to perceive the world are illusory, and the mind which you use to perceive the world is also illusory. Therefore, there is only one factor left which qualifies as real. That factor is the *witnessing consciousness* that perceives all of the different states. Through spiritual practices (yoga of wisdom, yoga of action, yoga of devotion and yoga of meditation) you can gradually lead your mind to deeper and deeper levels of perception of the truth until you discover the Absolute Truth beyond all of the illusory layers of the mind.

This essay has been presented so that the practitioner may begin to understand the visualization that is desired by the *Prt m Hru* texts, when it is written that the initiate is to say statements such as the following ones below. They are mystic formulas designed to awaken the innermost memory of one's true and ultimate identity as one with the Divinity who has brought all into existence and who will also dissolve it. This is the ultimate discovery, coveted by all mystics of the world. In other words, the temporary mortal existence is not the ultimate reality.

PART TWO: TRANSLATED SELECTED CHAPTERS OF THE PERMHERU

TRANSLATION FORMATS USED FOR PRESENTING THE TRANSLATIONS

Conventional Interlinear Format

The conventional or regular interlinear format of translating Ancient Egyptian hieroglyphic texts presents a phonetic transliteration of the Ancient Egyptian hieroglyphs and transposes the hieroglyphs into the characters of the language they are being translated into. The second line presents a word for word translation. This level of translation can sometimes result in a limited, choppy and less intelligible presentation of the original intent of the script. When the translation is between languages of dissimilar structure and cultural references such as the difference between the Ancient Egyptian language, which is rich in metaphor and iconographical implied wisdom versus the European languages which are based on a stricter alphabetic matrix, the structural differences along with differences of culture mean that a strict word for word translation can be insufficient to convey a full understanding of the intended meaning. So, while the conventional interlinear format is useful to a certain extent, a more comprehensive translation matrix is needed to gain the deeper richness of the meaning and import of the original hieroglyphic text.

Example of the Regular Interlinear Format:

Verse 1.   *ORIGINAL TEXT*
    1.1.   Transliteration into the phonetic letters of the language of the reader

    1.2.   Translation in to the words of the language of the reader

Ex:

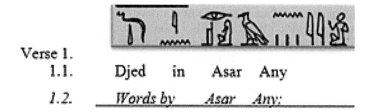

Verse 1.
    1.1.   Djed   in   Asar   Any

    1.2.   *Words by   Asar   Any:*

Trilinear Contextual Format

The Trilinear Format for translating the Ancient Egyptian writing is a method as well as, to some degree, also a decipherment protocol that allows a layout for viewing the meaning from its source through layers of meaning extraction to the final rendition. The term "decipherment" is used because to the modern mind, whose concerns are often far removed from the world and philosophy of the Ancient Egyptians, the contexts and philosophy of the ancients is akin to more than a mystery, but also as an scarcely fathomable idea that is like a code or formula to be discovered so as to unlock the secrets of life, death and the afterlife. Over the years, Dr. Muata Ashby has developed a format of translating Ancient Egyptian hieroglyphs into the native language of the reader that incorporates three levels of translation instead of the two levels of the ordinary conventional interlinear format. In a few cases the conventional interlinear format is used in this volume. However, in most other cases a Ternary System will be used. The Ternary System devised by Dr. Muata Ashby adds a third layer of translation to the work that includes a contextual translation beyond the word for word translation. This added layer of translation may be termed "Contextual Translation" and all together constitutes the ***Trilinear Contextual format***.

The Trilinear Form (which is a ternary system) of translations is a format developed by Dr. Muata Ashby for translating the Ancient Egyptian Hieroglyphic texts. It contains a *tripartite* arrangement composed of three translation sections or layers/levels. The <u>first level</u> is a phonetic transliteration. The <u>second level</u> is a direct word for word translation from hieroglyphic to the native language of the reader. These two levels generally constitute the "Conventional Interlinear Format" of translation. The Trilinear Format adds a new level of translation. The <u>third level</u> of translation is a contextual translation bringing out the meaning in an informal colloquial context in prose style incorporating: A- the Ancient Egyptian Sebait (philosophical) tenets along with B- the Ancient Egyptian Matnu (mythic) references and Ancient Egyptian "Maut" (morals or takeaways of the myth to which the text appertains) contained in the text in order to better reveal the intended meaning for the reader's language and culture.

Example of the Trilinear Format:

Verse 1.   *ORIGINAL TEXT*
    1.1.   Transliteration into the phonetic letters of the language of the reader

    1.2.   Translation in to the words of the of the language of the reader

    1.3.   Translation with contextual insights which may include philosophical and or mythological and/or historical background insights with colloquial references.

Ex:

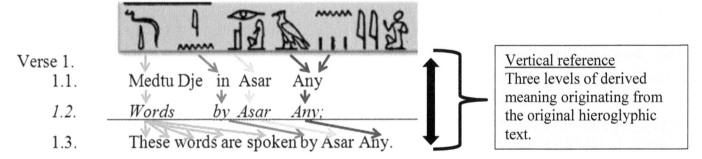

Verse 1.
    1.1.   Medtu Dje in Asar Any
    1.2.   *Words   by Asar   Any;*
    1.3.   These words are spoken by Asar Any.

Vertical reference
Three levels of derived meaning originating from the original hieroglyphic text.

NOTE: Each level of translation is designed to be both a reference to the other levels (vertically) but also to the previous and next statement in each level; so for example: Verse translation Level 2.1 relates to 2.2 and 2.3 (vertical) but 2.2 also relates to 1.2 and 3.2 (horizontal). Therefore, if all the Level 2 translations are read by themselves or Level 3 translations are read by themselves one after the other, there will be a continuous and coherent rendering of the text

Example

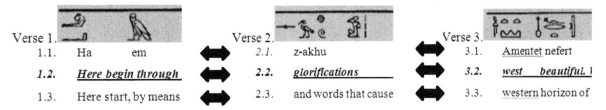

Verse 1.
    1.1.   Ha   em
    1.2.   ***Here begin through***
    1.3.   Here start, by means

Verse 2.
    2.1.   z-akhu
    2.2.   *glorifications*
    2.3.   and words that cause

Verse 3.
    3.1.   Amentet nefert
    3.2.   *west   beautiful.*
    3.3.   western horizon of

In this way, the readings of Verse 1.2 followed by Verse 2.2, followed by Verse 3.2, translations, one after the other (ignoring .1 and .3 levels), horizontally, provide a continuous and coherent word for word narative of the translation.

Also, the readings of Verse 1.3 followed by Verse 2.3, followed by Verse 3.3, translations, one after the other (ignoring .1 and .2 levels), horizontally, provide a continuous and coherent prose narative of the translation.

Reading the Philosophy Embedded in Ancient Egyptian Hieroglyphic Writings

Here I will provide two examples, using two of the most important hieroglyphs to demonstrate why and how the philosophy of the Ancient Egyptian Mysteries is determined in the texts to be read. As stated earlier, reading the Ancient Egyptian texts in a literal way, ascribing meanings that relate to the culture of the reader is a disservice to the ancient culture and also it is a distortion of the meaning of the texts and the legacy of the original priests and priestesses who created them.

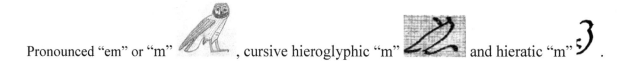

Pronounced "em" or "m" , cursive hieroglyphic "m" and hieratic "m" .

The first glyph is the owl. Perhaps one of the most important glyphs, unlike determinatives, which do not convey phonetic aspects to the word, the owl has phonetic and philosophical meaning. Whenever the owl appears the meaning can range from "in, within, inside, through, as, in the form of. This means that it is a pivotal term especially when it relates the person for whom the text has been created to any particular or general Divinity [god or goddess]. It therefore means that such a person is being identified with that divinity or with an aspect of divinity or they are being recognized as "becoming, or appearing or manifesting as". This of course signifies a movement of transformation either in progress or already attained. This glyph is seldom interpreted in such a manner and thus the overall outcomes of such neglectful translations will render a mundane and or erroneous insight into the Ancient Egyptian hieroglyphic writings.

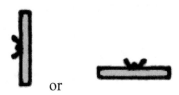

or

Another important glyph is the scroll.

Generally, the Ancient Egyptian language is composed of phonetic, ideographic and determinative glyphs. The determinative glyphs do not contribute a phonetic aspect to the word but rather contributes a reference and or philosophical implication to be inferred by the reader. The scroll is a determinative glyph that, when appears, forces the application of a perspective abstractness that allows a vision of a meaning that transcends a strictly mundane or specific application. This is a reading that incorporates a philosophical and or conceptual basis to the meaning of the particular word. An example of how to apply the scroll in reading a word or sentence or passage is that its conceptual abstractness is to be applied to the regular meaning of the world; and the abstractness relates to the Ancient Egyptian philosophy of the spiritual mysteries that affirms a transcendental nature of life that goes beyond physical reality.

As a group, determinatives provide a similar function and constitute an integral and essential means of understanding the deeper wisdom and intent of the Ancient Egyptian written language. Below are some of the most important determinatives.

Simple determinatives that appear most frequently.

Determinatives are symbols that convey a general or specific meaning to a word. They are un-vocalized and are only to be read; they are placed at the end of a word, so they also act as word dividers. Very rarely some texts have been found using a small dot to separate units of thought. They occur less frequently in the older texts and more frequently in later texts. Thus, there is an indication that the classical form of the language is not the "original" form but a development of it. The earlier form, as depicted in Pre-Dynastic inscriptions, is more of an ideographic and phonetic (alphabetic) system. Determinatives are an advantage because they determine what type of word is being read, and they also separate words. The use of determinatives becomes more important the more ideograms are used, when there are less vowels used, and when there is less phonetic complementation in a word. In any case, to revive the language, it would be advantageous to create a standard for the spelling of words. This could be accomplished by spelling out words, and using phonetic complements and vowels. Then there would be less need for determinatives. The ancient Egyptian language has within itself the capacity to support a range of options for its usage, as the evidences for these forms can be found in varied texts or in varied periods of ancient Egyptian history. The usage of any of these forms does not affect the orthography (letters and their sequences in words) or syntax (the grammatical arrangement of words in sentences i.e. sentence structure**.**

Some determinatives can be associated with one word. Others can be associated with a class of words. For example, the seated robed man with long beard ![glyph] lets us know that all the words it appears with are about a God. These kinds of determinatives are referred to by scholars as *Generic Determinatives*. A list of common generic determinatives is below:

✓ Many ancient Egyptian words have the same apparent consonant spelling which is differentiated only by the determinative (as explained earlier, which would not be necessary of there was more use of the vowels). However, the determinative can provide a more precise feeling for the genre of a word and its relation to contexts that go beyond the strictly phonetic values. So there can be many dimensions of meaning depending on the particular choice of spelling of the word and the particular determinative used.

The word *rek* ![glyph] can have different meanings depending on the determinative used to assign a reference meaning to the word:

Ex. 1: ![glyph] *rek* = time - determinative used ![glyph] (sundisk)

Ex. 2: ![glyph] *rekh* = burn - determinative used ![glyph] (fire)

In the written language, determinatives allow a great range of words to sound alike and yet have different meanings - determined by the determinatives. Of course this would lead to confusion if the script were to be read out loud unless the context were understood; but some of the written language is designed primarily to be read instead of written. The examples below illustrate this aspect of the "determinization" in ancient Egyptian writing.

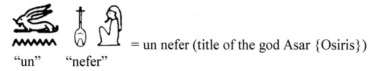

= un nefer (title of the god Asar {Osiris})

"un"   "nefer"

= open – determinative is the *top of a door* (door open)

"un"

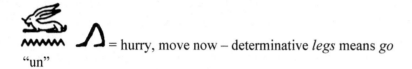

= hurry, move now – determinative *legs* means *go*

"un"

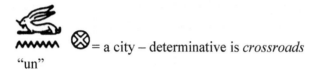

= a city – determinative is *crossroads*

"un"

Important Points

✓ Because there are many similar spellings, the language lends itself to a great capacity for punning and poetic literature.

✓ Many of the ancient Egyptian words have meanings that do not need to be memorized because the determinative helps the interpretation of the meaning when it is encountered.

✓ In Hieratic script, the scribes tended to use more determinatives than the carved monuments and hieroglyphic inscriptions. However, a modern effort to revive the language could benefit from adopting a set number of determinatives as in order to facilitate the learning and reading process.

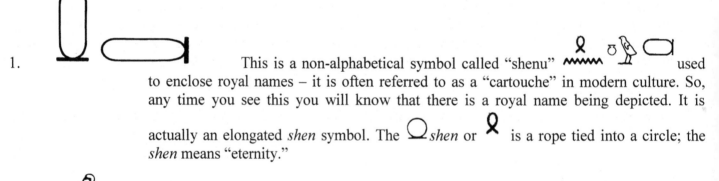

1.   This is a non-alphabetical symbol called "shenu" used to enclose royal names – it is often referred to as a "cartouche" in modern culture. So, any time you see this you will know that there is a royal name being depicted. It is actually an elongated *shen* symbol. The *shen* or is a rope tied into a circle; the *shen* means "eternity."

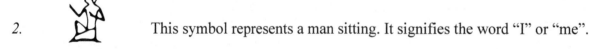

2.   This symbol represents a man sitting. It signifies the word "I" or "me".

3.   This symbol represents a woman sitting. It signifies that the person is female.

4.   calling, hail

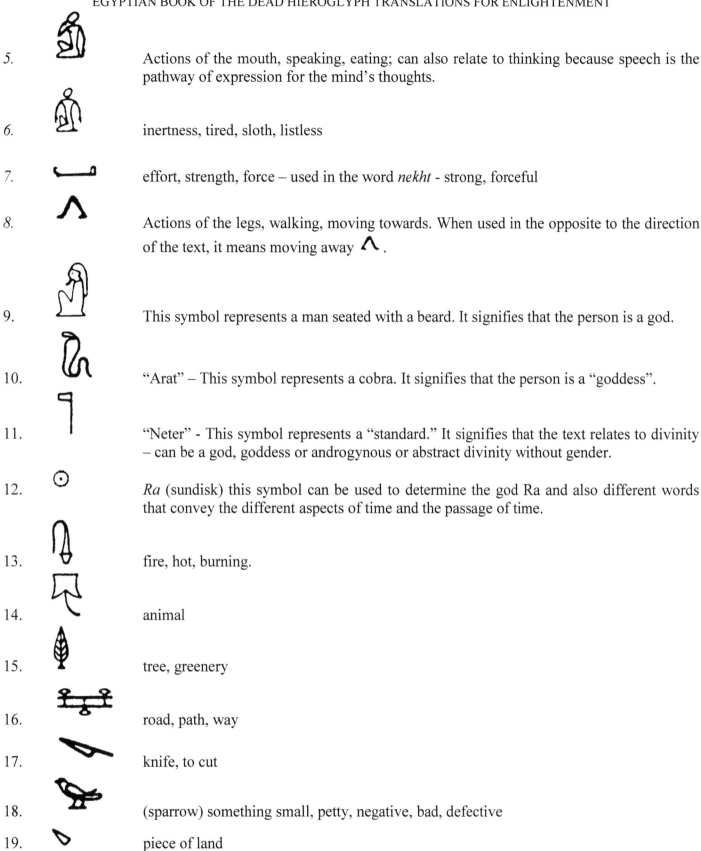

5. Actions of the mouth, speaking, eating; can also relate to thinking because speech is the pathway of expression for the mind's thoughts.

6. inertness, tired, sloth, listless

7. effort, strength, force – used in the word *nekht* - strong, forceful

8. Actions of the legs, walking, moving towards. When used in the opposite to the direction of the text, it means moving away ∧ .

9. This symbol represents a man seated with a beard. It signifies that the person is a god.

10. "Arat" – This symbol represents a cobra. It signifies that the person is a "goddess".

11. "Neter" - This symbol represents a "standard." It signifies that the text relates to divinity – can be a god, goddess or androgynous or abstract divinity without gender.

12. *Ra* (sundisk) this symbol can be used to determine the god Ra and also different words that convey the different aspects of time and the passage of time.

13. fire, hot, burning.

14. animal

15. tree, greenery

16. road, path, way

17. knife, to cut

18. (sparrow) something small, petty, negative, bad, defective

19. piece of land

20. "ta" land

21. "ta" land

22.   flesh, skin

23.   This symbol represents a crossroads. It signifies that the word it appears in is a town.

24.   " " *mdjat* {medjat} - This symbol represents a "scroll," or a "book" and can generally symbolize wisdom as in the wisdom that is contained in a scroll written by a sage containing wisdom teachings or philosophy. It also means that the meaning of the word it appears in is not exactly the mundane meaning suggested by the words themselves but goes beyond that –so it is an abstract rendition of the mundane meaning.

25.   This symbol represents the "sky" or in some cases "heaven" and is called "pet".

For more on the Ancient Egyptian Hieroglyphic Writing see the book *Ancient Egyptian Hieroglyphs for Beginners* by Muata Ashby

Spoken Offering Invocation Used Before Studying The Ancient Scriptures

SPOKEN OFFERING: Invocatory prayer for peace and success on the spiritual journey-to be read prior to engaging a study of the Pert-m-Heru

Verse 1.

   1.1.   *Hotep*   *di nesu*   *Neter aah Anpu*   *Wep- wat*

   1.2.   <u>*"Offering is given to Supreme Divinity Anubis,*   *Upwat*</u>

   1.3.   "Offering is given to the Supreme Divinity, the source of all Creation, and to Anpu, the divinity who prepares the aspirant for the journey and Wepwat the one who leads the aspirant on the journey and opens the spiritual paths and makes them free of obstructions,

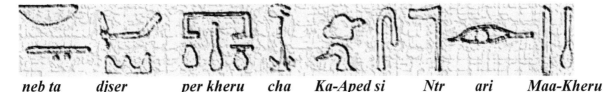

Verse 2.

   2.1.   *neb ta*   *djser*   *per kheru*   *cha*   *Ka-Aped si*   *Ntr*   *ari*   *Maa-Kheru*

   2.2.   <u>*lord of the sacred land, spoken offering 1000 beef 1000 geese. Doing this True of Speech"*</u>

   2.3.   and to the lord of the sacred land, this spoken offering is 1000 beef (maleness) and 1000 geese (femaleness), supreme peace and union of opposites. Doing this spoken offering causes the Divine to make one True of Speech, that is, successful on the spiritual journey by discovering spiritual victory and enlightenment."

Opening Hymns from the Pert-m-Heru Ancient Egyptian Book of the Dead

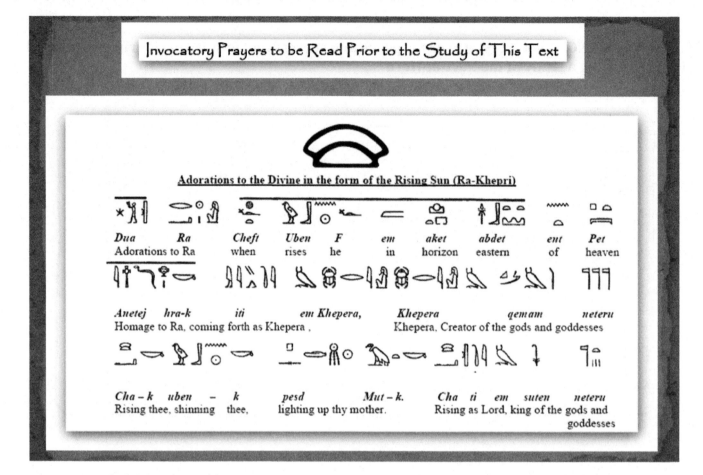

Invocatory Prayers to be Read Prior to the Study of This Text

Adorations to the Divine in the form of the Rising Sun (Ra-Khepri)

Dua	Ra	Cheft	Uben	F	em	aket	abdet	ent	Pet
Adorations to Ra		when	rises	he	in	horizon	eastern	of	heaven

Anetej	hra-k	iti	em Khepera,	Khepera	qemam	neteru
Homage to Ra, coming forth as Khepera ,				Khepera, Creator of the gods and goddesses		

Cha – k	uben	–	k	pesd	Mut – k.	Cha	ti	em	suten	neteru
Rising thee, shinning		thee,		lighting up thy mother.		Rising as Lord, king of the gods and goddesses				

Plate 1: The Crescent Moon, symbol of the divinities Asar, Djehuti and Khonsu.

Adorations to the Divine in the Form of the Moon (Asar)

Dua	Asar	Un-Nefer	Neter	Aah	Her	Ab	Abdu	Suten	Heh	Neb Djetah	Sebeby	Heh
Adorations to Asar		Un-Nefer	Divinity	Great,	personality	(in) heart	(of) Abdu	King	eternity,	Lord of Forever	travelling (for)	eternities,

M	aha	-f	sa	dep	n	chat	Nut	utet	n	Geb	rpat	neb
(in) form	raised	he.	Son	primary	of	body	(of) Nut,	engendered	by	Geb	master	lord (of the),

Ureret	qai	hed	ity	neteru	rmteg
Ureret crown	exalted	white crown	prince	(of) gods and goddesses	(and) people

Chapter 1: Beginning the Words by Which a Person Can Become Enlightened –Originally Presented in the Book "THE EGYPTIAN BOOK OF THE DEAD ©2000. Translation by Dr. Muata Ashby Translation Level 3 ©2016

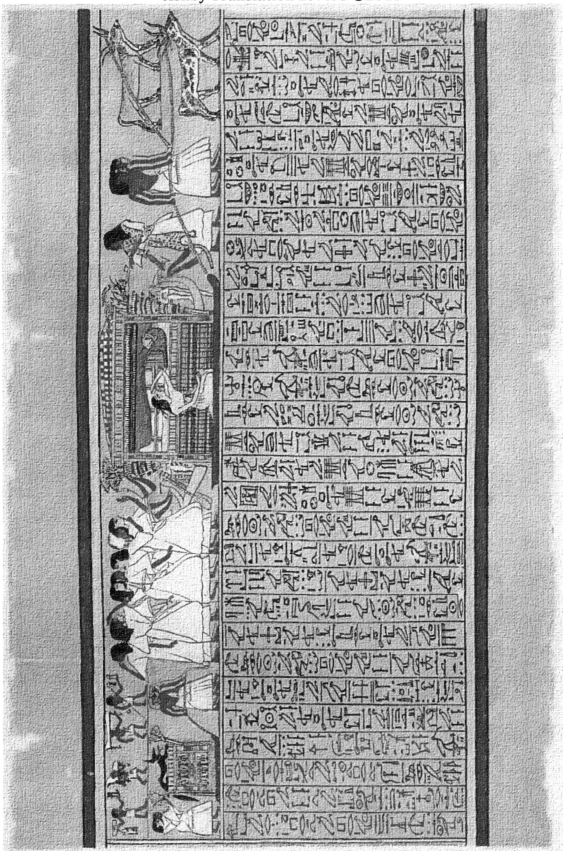

Chapter 1: Beginning of the Words By Which a Person Can Go Into The Coffin and Come Out as Light (Enlightened Spirit)

From Papyrus Ani Levels 1 and 2 translations ©2000, Level 3 translations ©2016 Sema Institute Translation by Dr. Muata Ashby

Verse 1.

1.1.   Ha   em   rau   nu   pert   em   heru   zetjezu

1.2.   *Here begin through words   for   coming forth as   light,   praisings*

1.3.   Here start, by means of words and chapters, the teachings for becoming light itself, the light of spirit, with enlightend consciousness. These praisings

Verse 2.

2.1.   z-akhu   pert   hayt   em   neter-khert akhu   em

2.2.   *cause glorification   coming out   going in   through Lower-astral-plane glorious   in*

2.3.   and words that cause one to become a glorious being are for coming out after going into the cemetery, which is the lower part of the astral plane via the

Verse 3.

3.1.   Amentet nefert   djedtu   heru   n   qeres   aq   em   chet   pert

3.2.   *west   beautiful.   Words to say   day   of   burial   going   in   cocoon   coming out.*

3.3.   western horizon, the beautiful west, the entrance to the further Netherworld. These words are to be said on the day of the burial, the going in of the body in a mummified form, like an insect in the form of a cocoon that later comes out as a fully transformed being.

Verse 4.

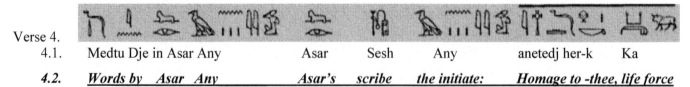

4.1.   Medtu Dje in Asar Any   Asar   Sesh   Any   anetedj her-k   Ka

4.2.   *Words by   Asar   Any   Asar's   scribe   the initiate: Homage to -thee, life force*

4.3.   These words now are to be spoken by the Asar Any, the recently deceased spiritual aspirant: "I praise you oh divine Bull, oh you paragon of male generative life force

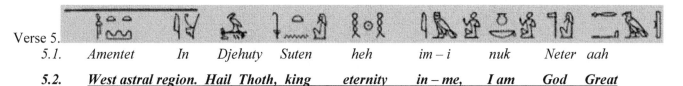

Verse 5.

5.1. *Amentet   In   Djehuty   Suten   heh   im – i   nuk   Neter   aah*

5.2. **West astral region. Hail Thoth, king   eternity   in – me,   I am   God   Great**

5.3. of the beautiful west, the abode of blessed beings after death. Hail Oh Thoth (Lord Djehuty), god of eternity and divinity of intellect and cosmic mind, who are within me, I see myself now not as a human but as a great god

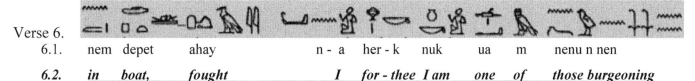

Verse 6.

6.1. nem depet   ahay   n - a   her - k   nuk   ua   m   nenu n nen

6.2. **in   boat,   fought   I   for - thee I am   one   of   those burgeoning**

6.3. who sails in a boat, like many other divinities such as Ra, Aset and Heru.   I am worthy to see myself in that way because I stood up for the right values when it was time to do so, when I was alive on earth; I am one of those flourishing

Verse 7.

7.1. Neteru udjaudjau   se-maak-heru   Asar   er   cheftau-f   heru

7.2. **Gods   magistrates   allow to become spiritually victorious Asar   as to enemies- his   day**

goddesses

7.3. gods and goddesses who are judicial officers that review the souls of Asar aspirants and permit those who are found to be righteous to be spiritually victorious against their enemies, the vices, worldly desires, negative thoughts, negative feelings and ignorance, on the day

Verse 8.

8.1. puy   n   udjad   medutu   Nua   imtu   -k   Asar! Nuk   ua

8.2. **that of weighing   words.   I am   advocate – yours   Asar! I am   one**

8.3. of weighing the words, the judgment of Maat wherein the sum-total of a person's experiences and spiritual maturity gained and lived by while on earth are assessed. I declare to you, Asar, the Supreme Divinity, that I am your advocate, your supporter and I do not support what is unrighteous or impure. I am one

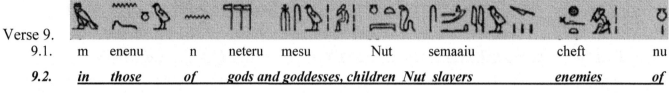

Verse 9.

9.1.	m	enenu	n	neteru	mesu	Nut	semaaiu	cheft	nu
9.2.	**in**	**those**	**of**	**gods and goddesses, children**		**Nut**	**slayers**	**enemies**	**of**

9.3.   of those who recognizes himself as among the gods and goddesses, the children of Nut, the fighters who

destroy the enemies of

Verse 10.

10.1.	Asar	chnra	sebiu	her	f	nu	imtu	k	Heru
10.2.	**Asar**	**restrain**	**fiends**	**person his**		**I am**	**advocate**	**yours**	**Heru**

10.3.   Asar and who restrain the fiends, the evil cosmic forces from within and from outside, that try to obstruct his

personality. Also I say to Heru that just as Lord Djehuty was his advocate, I am also his advocate and I

support his quest of spiritual aspiration, to be successful against the unrighteousness of Set, the ego aspect of

the personality and I support his taking his rightful seat at the throne of the world and as the sovereign of my

life.

Hymn to Amun-Ra from Pert-m-Heru Papyrus HUNEFER. Hieroglyphic translation by Muata Ashby ©2016

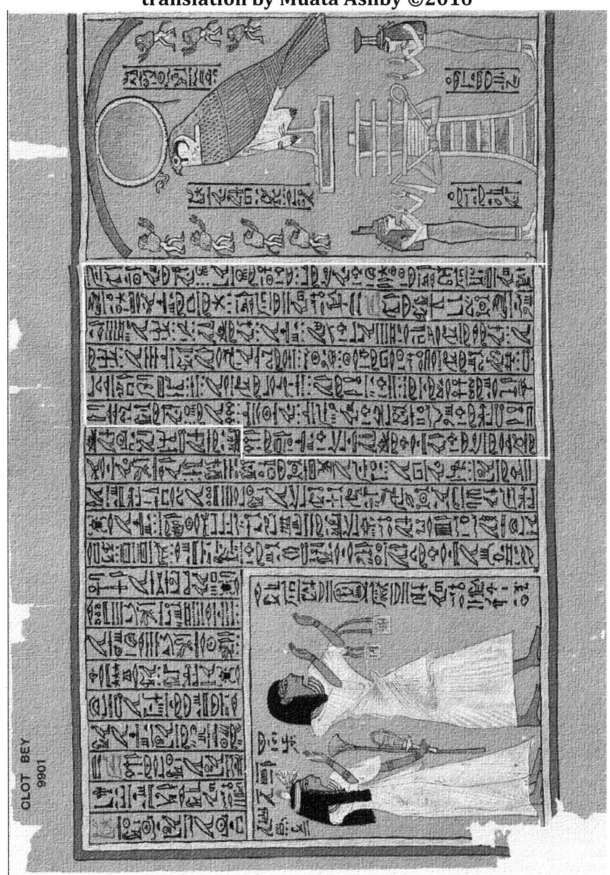

The Papyrus Hunefer is a version of the Ancient Egyptian Book of the Dead (Egyptian Book of Enlightenment) that was written for a national supervisor of facilities under the Pharaoh Seti I This section is the Hymn to Amun-Ra

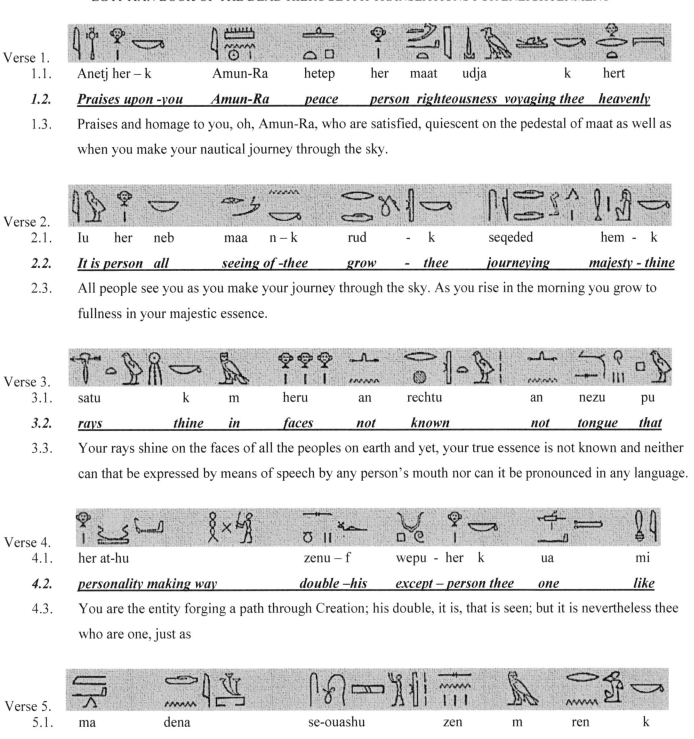

Verse 1.

1.1. Anetj her – k   Amun-Ra   hetep   her   maat   udja   k   hert

1.2. ***Praises upon -you   Amun-Ra   peace   person righteousness voyaging thee   heavenly***

1.3. Praises and homage to you, oh, Amun-Ra, who are satisfied, quiescent on the pedestal of maat as well as when you make your nautical journey through the sky.

Verse 2.

2.1. Iu   her   neb   maa   n – k   rud   - k   seqeded   hem - k

2.2. ***It is person all   seeing of -thee   grow   - thee   journeying   majesty - thine***

2.3. All people see you as you make your journey through the sky. As you rise in the morning you grow to fullness in your majestic essence.

Verse 3.

3.1. satu   k   m   heru   an   rechtu   an   nezu   pu

3.2. ***rays   thine   in   faces   not   known   not   tongue   that***

3.3. Your rays shine on the faces of all the peoples on earth and yet, your true essence is not known and neither can that be expressed by means of speech by any person's mouth nor can it be pronounced in any language.

Verse 4.

4.1. her at-hu   zenu – f   wepu - her   k   ua   mi

4.2. ***personality making way   double –his   except – person thee   one   like***

4.3. You are the entity forging a path through Creation; his double, it is, that is seen; but it is nevertheless thee who are one, just as

Verse 5.

5.1. ma   dena   se-ouashu   zen   m   ren   k

5.2. ***brings   vegetation chamber   causing worship   they   through   name   thine***

5.3. one who brings vegetable growth to the chamber of growing vegetation and with it food sustenance, an act causing them (faces, people) to worship you by means of uttering your name.

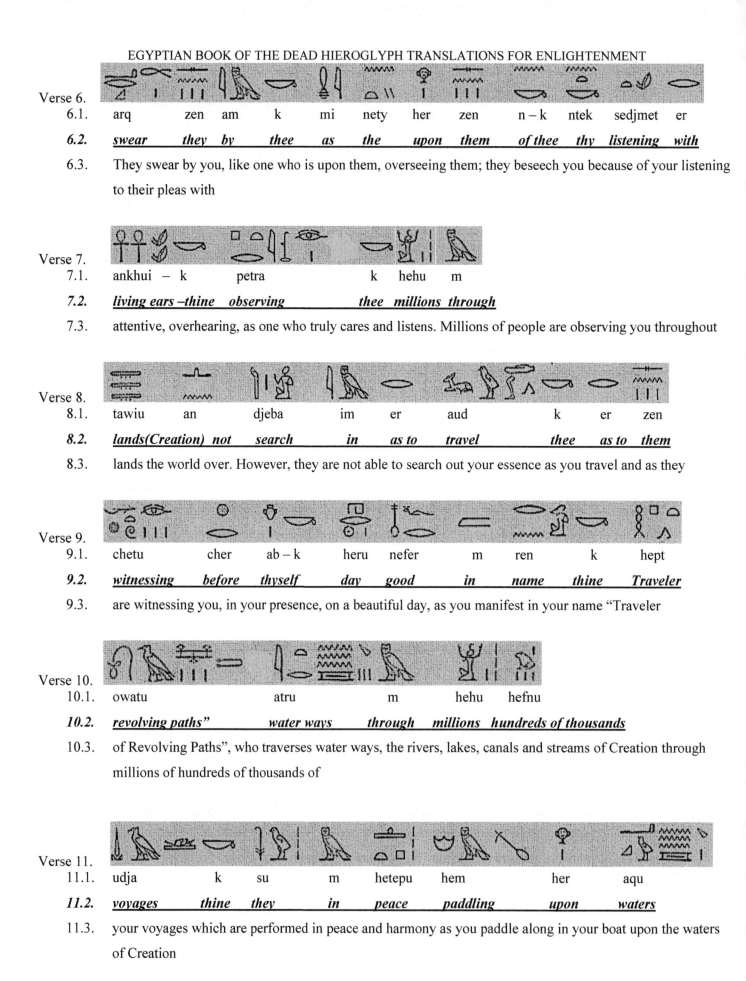

Verse 6.

6.1. arq zen am k mi nety her zen n – k ntek sedjmet er

6.2. swear they by thee as the upon them of thee thy listening with

6.3. They swear by you, like one who is upon them, overseeing them; they beseech you because of your listening to their pleas with

Verse 7.

7.1. ankhui – k petra k hehu m

7.2. living ears –thine observing thee millions through

7.3. attentive, overhearing, as one who truly cares and listens. Millions of people are observing you throughout

Verse 8.

8.1. tawiu an djeba im er aud k er zen

8.2. lands(Creation) not search in as to travel thee as to them

8.3. lands the world over. However, they are not able to search out your essence as you travel and as they

Verse 9.

9.1. chetu cher ab – k heru nefer m ren k hept

9.2. witnessing before thyself day good in name thine Traveler

9.3. are witnessing you, in your presence, on a beautiful day, as you manifest in your name "Traveler

Verse 10.

10.1. owatu atru m hehu hefnu

10.2. revolving paths" water ways through millions hundreds of thousands

10.3. of Revolving Paths", who traverses water ways, the rivers, lakes, canals and streams of Creation through millions of hundreds of thousands of

Verse 11.

11.1. udja k su m hetepu hem her aqu

11.2. voyages thine they in peace paddling upon waters

11.3. your voyages which are performed in peace and harmony as you paddle along in your boat upon the waters of Creation

Verse 12.

12.1.	er	aset		mer	n – k	ari – k	su	m	unnut
12.2.	**as to**	**abode**		**loved**	**by – thee**	**maker – thee**	**them**	**in**	**moment**

12.3. so as to reach the dwelling place that is desired by you. You make those voyages, which occur in a moment of time

Verse 13.

13.1.	sherat	hetep	k	kam	n – k	unnut	in	Asar	mer	per
13.2.	**small**	**peace**	**thee**	**ending**	**by thee**	**time**	**by**	**Osiris**	**overseer**	**buildings**

13.3. that is small. You do this even as you are in that peaceful state that neutralizes duality and you bring to an end time itself. Now these words are spoken by the initiate Osiris, who served as overseer of buildings,

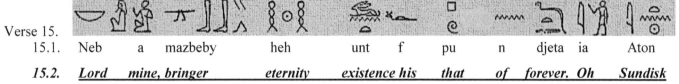

Verse 14.

14.1.	n	neb	tawy	"HUNEFER"	maa-kheru	djed	f	ia
14.2.	**of**	**all**	**two lands**	**"One of Good Spiritual Taste"**	**true of speech**	**says**	**he:**	**"Oh**

14.3. all of them in the two lands of Upper and Lower Egypt. "HUNEFER" ["One of Good Spiritual Taste"] who is true of speech [spiritually victorious] and therefore recognized as victorious on the spiritual journey of life and the goal of spiritual enlightenment. He says: "Oh

Verse 15.

15.1.	Neb	a	mazbeby	heh	unt	f	pu	n	djeta	ia	Aton
15.2.	**Lord**	**mine,**	**bringer**	**eternity**	**existence**	**his**	**that**	**of**	**forever.**	**Oh**	**Sundisk**

15.3. my Lord, you who are the bringer of eternity, whose very existence is that of eternity and of forever. Oh, sundisk who is the face of your deeper essence,

Verse 16.

16.1.	pu	neb	satut	uben	k	ankh	her nebu	di	k
16.2.	**that**	**all**	**sunrays**	**shine**	**thee**	**life**	**persons all**	**give**	**thee**

16.3. from which all sunrays shine forth, out of thee, and which afford life to all people. You give

85

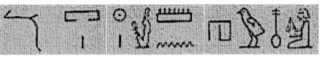

Verse 17.

17.1.	maa	tu	her dep	duaty	heru	neb	in	Asar	sesh
17.2.	**see**	**you**	**person captain**	**morning**	**day**	**every**	**by**	**Osiris**	**scribe**

17.3. the glory of the sight of thee, who are the first and foremost being, leader of the morning, each day." These words were spoken by the Osiris initiate, the scribe,

Verse 18.

18.1. mer per Men Maat Ra HUNEFER

18.2. **overseer buildings Stability in Righteousness Order and Truth in the Spirit, Hunefer.**

18.3. who served as overseer of buildings for the king/pharaoh, whose spiritual name (of the king) is [*MenMaatRa*] *–One Who is Firm in Righteousness Order and Truth in Spirit*, also known as *Seti Ua* (Seti the First); thus these words were spoken by the initiate HUNEFER as adoration of Amun-Ra and declaration of devotion, wisdom and enlightenment afforded by the majesty, Amun-Ra.

Painting From The Tomb of Queen Nefertary With Adoration and Revelation of Amun Ra

The following translation is included here as an adjunct to the Hymn to Amu-Ra presented above since it offers insights into the integral teaching about the nature of Amun, Ra, and Asar. It is a relief from the Tomb of Queen Nefertary based on the same scriptural tradition of the Pert-m-Heru. It is important because it unequivocally harmonizes and integrates all three of the main male divinities of Ancient Egyptian religion into a balanced whole that at once allows us to understand how a spiritual aspirant can be at the same time be referred to as "an Asar" and also Ra as well-at the same time; It is because all three divinities reside and "rest" in each other so there is no conflict or contradiction. In fact any of the three can be worshipped and their wisdom studied since either leads to a harmonization of all their representative principles into a non-dual and transcendental unity that gives rise to supreme peace and enlightenment, the goal of spiritual life.

Figure 16: Painting From The Tomb of Queen Nefertary

Dua Hetheru. Medtu dje in Asar su hemt urt Nefertary merit Mut Maa kheru

Adorations to Hathor. Words spoken by she who is an Osiris and First Wife and Queen, Nefertary, the beautiful beloved of Goddess Mut, and true of speech (spiritually victorious).

Translation of Panel Image from the Tomb of Nefertary with adoration to Amun-Ra

Verse 1		1.1	Amun	1.2-God Amun 1.3-Amun represents hidden witnessing consciousness behind all Creation.
Verse 2		2.1	Ra	2.2-God Ra 2.3-Ra represents dynamic mind which allows the witnessing consciousness to be aware of and express its spiritual light in time and space.
Verse 3		3.1	Nebethet	3.2-Goddess Nebethet (Nephthys) 3.3-Nephthys represents physicality and one half of the aspect of duality in time and space.
Verse 4		4.1	Aset	4.2-Goddess Aset (Isis) 4.3-Isis represents Spiritual intuitional wisdom, the other half of the aspect of duality in time and space. Together with Nebethet they are also the Dual Maat goddesses and the dual serpent power life force goddesses.
Verse 5		5.1	Was	5.2-Was 5.3- The was scepter (represents the capacity to project power of god)

Verse 6		6.1	Asar Hetep M R A	6.2-Asar (Osiris) in peace as Ra. 6.3-When Asar is in non-dual inner peace he rests in his inner nature as Ra and together they manifest as Amun-Ra
Verse 7		7.1	Ma'at	7.2- Righteousness order and truth 7.3- Amun-Ra stands on the pedestal of Ma'at, which is the foundation of all inner peace and non-dual spiritual enlightenment and thus the foundation for experiencing Amun-Ra higher consciousness.
Verse 8		8.1	Ra Pu Hetep M Asar	8.2-Ra this (is) in peace as Ra. 8.3-When Ra is in non-dual inner peace he rests in his inner nature as Asar and together they manifest as Amun-Ra So, together with Verse #6, Asar and Ra together are Amun-Ra and Amun-Ra is Asar and Ra and all one and the same.

Verse 9		9.1	saa	9.2-a protection,
			Ankh	providing life,
			Djed	stability
			Was	and power,
			Senab	health,
			Neb	all
				9.3-The performance of this adoration of the image of Amun-Ra in this manner and with this wisdom and understanding, along with righteous character, order and truth in body mind and soul, is a protection against what is unrighteous and detrimental to spiritual evolution: confusion and ignorance. It leads to experiencing Amun-Ra and attaining spiritual enlightenment.

Chapter 21: Proceedings from the 2014 Neterian Conference and Festival Pert-m-Heru Lecture on Highlights of Chapter 21 of the Ancient Egyptian Book of the Dead

From Papyrus Auf Ankh[45]

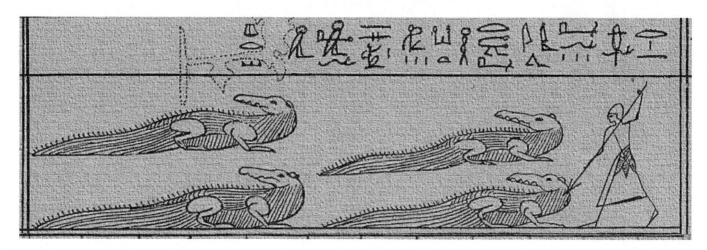

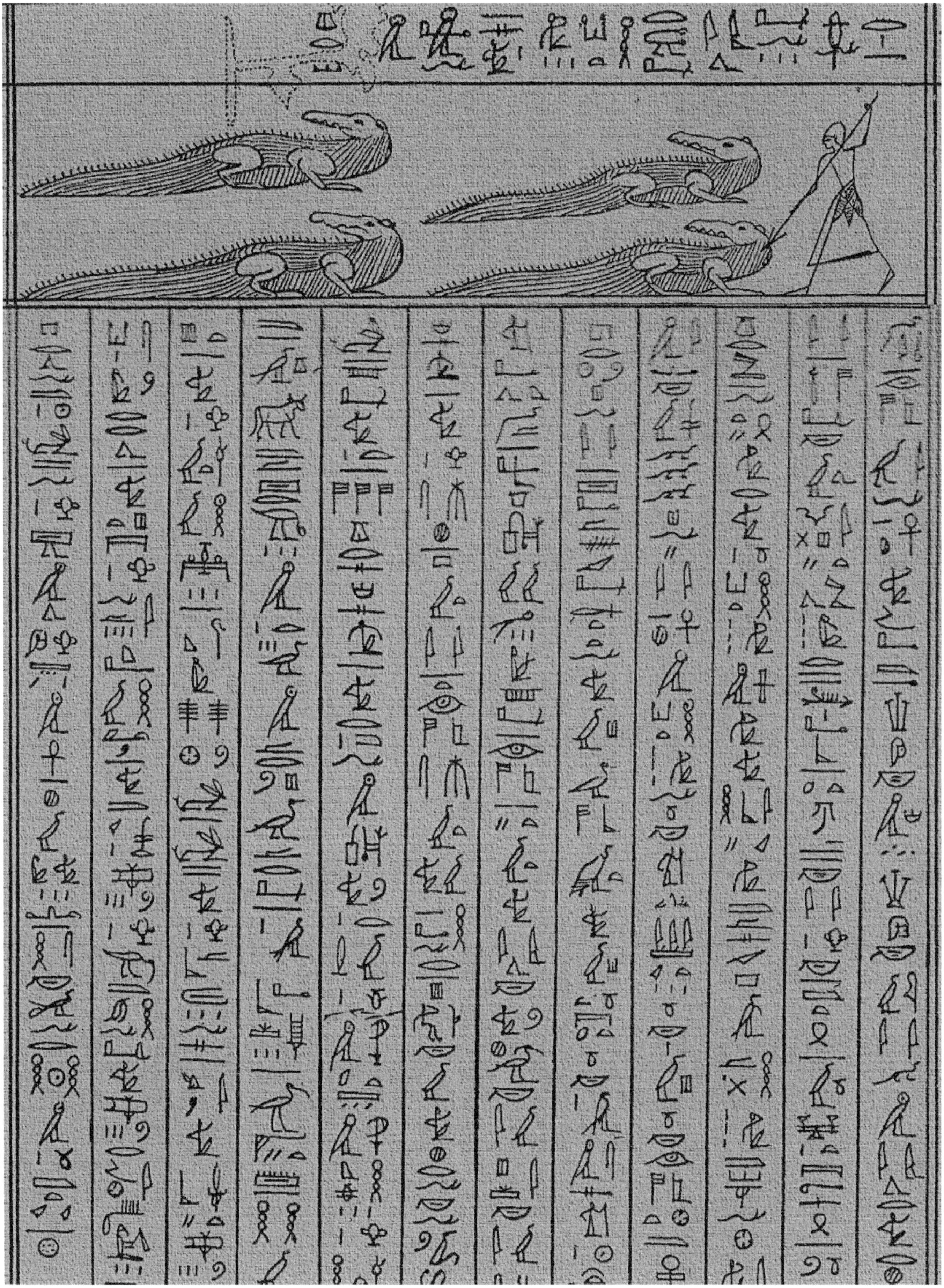

CHAPTER TITLE

Verse 0

0.1 Ra chesefu Ii er tjet Hekau nz–a ma f m Neterkhert

0.1	0.2	0.3
Ra chesefu Ii er tjet Hekau nz–a ma f m Neterkhert	Chapter repulsing oncoming who want to seize and carry off the person's words of power of theirs coming he in the Lower Region of Heaven (i.e. cemetery)	This chapter of the Ancient Egyptian Book of Enlightenment is about the period after death when one's personality comes to the cemetery and trying to make the transition from the living state to the after death state and trying to move on from there to the Netherworld to go on and discover the Supreme Spirit and spiritual enlightenment. If one's life on earth had been one of ignorance and vice then devouring forces that consume the personality can appear and cause great pain to and destroy the personality. However, for those who are equipped with special words of power born of self-knowledge and spiritual insight, they can resist and repel those cosmic and unconscious forces that would otherwise accost the personality during the period of the cemetery and then they can move freely on to the netherworld where they can discover and become one with the higher Self in the form of the Supreme Soul, recognized as the god Osiris.

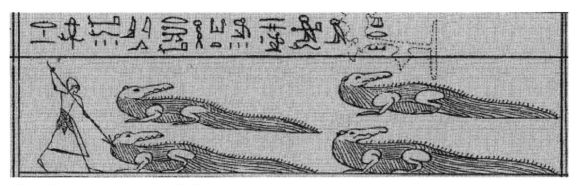

Verse 1	1.1	1.2
	Medtu dje	Words spoken
	in	by
	Asar	Asar
	Auf	Auf
	Ankh	Ankh
	Maa	True of
	Kheru	Speech (victorious)
	Ha	Get back!!
	K	You!
	hem	Run off, shoo! shoo!
	Ha	Get back!!
	K	You!
	Shuy	Crocodile
	m	(stop) movement
	Ii	coming
	Er	towards me
	a	I
	Rech	Know
	a	Within
	m	myself
	hekau	Words of power!

1.3-

These words are spoken by the aspirant by the name of Osiris Living In The Flesh {Living Flesh Of Osiris} who is true of speech, spiritually victorious.

"Get back you, shoo, shoo! Get back you crocodile who are trying to devour me as if I was a weak and ignorant person. Stop coming towards me because I know my power; I have power because I know who I am! So I have words of power!

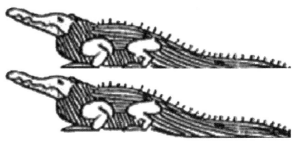

1

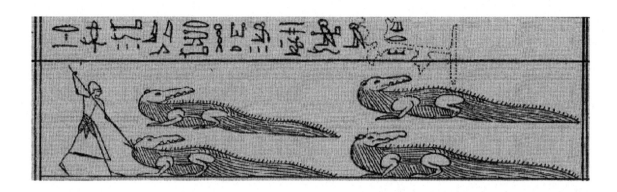

Verse 3c 3c.1   3c.2

Arit-f   Action/deed
m   by means of
Hekau   Words of power
pen   these

> 3c.3/4c.3 **By means of these effective words of power I command you to get back and not harm me in any way: "I am that I am Osiris". I am bonded with my father and mother, Geb the god of earth and Nut, the goddess of heaven; so I am a divine being, one with Osiris and therefore a powerful and free spirit, beyond your reach.**

Verse 4c 4c.1   4c.2

Nuk   I am
Pu   that
Nuk   I am
Asar   Asar

Chetm   Sealed
n-f   to he (who is)
tef -f   father his
Geb   Geb
hna   with
mut   mother
f   his
Nut   Nut

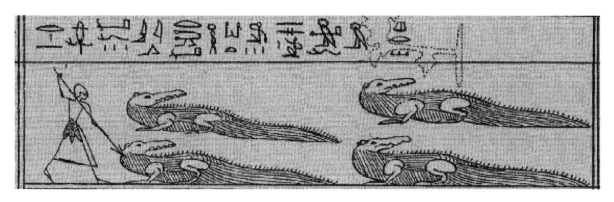

Verse 5c, 5c.1   5c.2

Nuk	I am
Heru	Heru
semz	Eldest son / heir / prince
ra cha	(on the) day (of) risings
Nuk	I am
Anpu	Anubis
ra	(on that) day
ap	(of) reckoning
Nuk	I am
pu	that
Nuk	I am
Asar	Asar

5c.3

I am not a weak mortal; I am Horus the eldest son of Osiris and Isis and I am therefore, a prince, an heir to divine glories and eternal existence. On the day of death, when there is a reckoning of the deeds done while one was alive on earth, I am Anubis the Lord of the Balance Scales of Maat. So I judge myself and so I am master of my fate. On that day I say: "I am that I am Osiris!" Therefore, on that day I am protected and I will not suffer the fate of being eaten by crocodiles.

Heru/(Horus)

5c

Verse 6bc	6bc.1	6bc.2
	Nuk	I am
	una	open
	n	to
	Asar	Osiris
	nty	that is
	tu	of
	a	me
	li	coming
	kua	(to) thee
	ach	(as) shining spirit
	kua	(to) thee
	ap	reckoning
	kua	(for) thee
	user	Strong and Mighty
	kua	(for) thee
	li	coming
	n - a	(to) thee
	Anetedj	as protector,
	nu her	advocate
	n – a	to me
	nz - a	for myself

6bc.3

My personality is open to God. My shining spirit comes to me and I am strong and mighty thereby. Osiris, my inner higher Self, is coming, as a Shining Spirit, as a protector. So with this wisdom and glory coming from my higher self, my enlightened being, protects me; I am the protector of my very self.

6bc

Verse 7ab	7ab.1	7ab.2
	hemz	resting
	n – a	of my
	her	personality (in)
	meschen	place of birth
	tuy	this
	nt	of
	Asar	Osiris
	mes	birth
	tu	(is) to
	au	me
	hna - ſ	with -him
	renpt	Years of youth (when)
	ku-a	you in
	cher	presence
	ſ	his

Verse 10b	10b.1	10b.2
	Un	Existence
	Un n	Being
	n	to
	a her	my personality
	debenu	reciprocally
	ſ	he

7ab/10b.3
My personality is resting in the place of birth of Osiris. It is to me as it is to him. My time of youth was with him as he grew up. So my growing up was in his presence as he grew up; therefore my existence is his same existence. Therefore we are one i.e. he is I and I am he.

7ab,10b

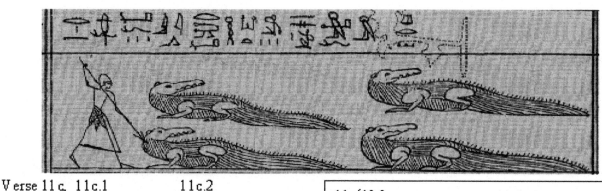

Verse 11 c,	11c.1	11c.2
	ar	As to
	rech	knowing
	ra	chapter
	pen	this
	iu – f	for sure it is
Verse 12	12.1	12.2
	Per	Going forth
	-f	he
	m	in
	ra un-n	the day existence
	f	to him
	her	personality
	shemt	can move (freely)
	her dep	captain
	ta	earth
	m	with
	ankhu	abundance of life
	an	not
	sehk	iniquity
		For that person
	f - er	this is about
	heh	eternity
	m	within
	shes	locked / tied
	m	are
	tawi	two lands /fields

11c/12.3

Anyone who knows this chapter, its devotion and identification with Osiris, its special words of power and its mystic wisdom, for those persons, it will mean going forth into the daylight, that is, the capacity to attain spiritual enlightenment, immortality and oneness with the Supreme Spirit. This is assured.

This means freedom from spiritual obstructions, as one who is the captain of their life and not a slave to the frailties of life or the vicissitudes of society or the world of natural phenomena and being able to live abundantly before and after death, during the time of physical existence while on earth and beyond. Let's make the meaning here unambiguous: this means freedom from any negative taint in the personality, body mind and soul, and an unbreakable bonding with Spirit and union of the lower self with the higher Self (Egyptian Yoga).

11c, 12

100

MAP OF THE EARTH, THE NETERCHERT (CEMETERY) AND THE NETHERWORLD

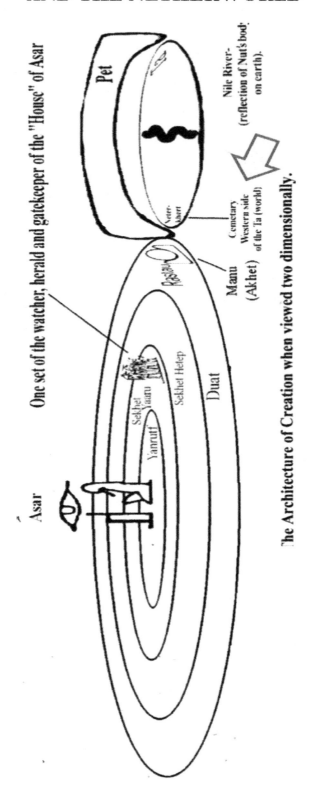

Pet

One set of the watcher, herald and gatekeeper of the "House" of Asar

Nile River- (reflection of Nut's body on earth).

Rastau

Manu (Akhet)

Neter-chert

(Cemetary Western side of the Ta (world)

Sekhet Hetep

Sekhet Yaaru

Yanrutf

Duat

Asar

The Architecture of Creation when viewed two dimensionally.

EGYPTIAN BOOK OF THE DEAD HIEROGLYPH TRANSLATIONS FOR ENLIGHTENMENT

Chapter 175 PMH Pertemheru Chapter Section: Conversation with Temu -Presented at the 2015 Neterian
Conference. Translation by Dr. Muata Ashby

Papyrus Any

EGYPTIAN BOOK OF THE DEAD HIEROGLYPH TRANSLATIONS FOR ENLIGHTENMENT

Pert-M-Heru
Chap. 175

Chapter 175 PMH
Perumheru
chapter
conversation with
hieroglyphic
text translation by
Dr. Muata Ashby
©2015

Verse 1.

1.1.
| Medtu Dje | in | Asar | Any | | Aa | Temu | ashest | pu |

1.2.
Words *by* *Asar* *Any;* | | | *Any* | | *Exclaims! Hey Temu! What* | | | *this*

1.3.
These words are spoken by Asar Any.   Any exclaims: "Hey Lord Temu. What is going on here? What is…

Verse 2.

2.1.
| shaz | a | er | zet | Iu | gert | an | mu | zet | an | nafu | zet | metchti |

2.2.
come | *I* | *to* | *this* | *It is* | *however* | *not* | *water* | *it* | *not* | *air* | *it* | *deep*

2.3.
this place that I have come to ? I arrived here but I don't see any water or air and the depth of this place

Verse 3.

3.1.
| sep sen kektuti | sep sen hyhti | sep sen | ankhti | im | z | m |

3.2.
twofold darkness | *twofold boundless* | *twofold.* | *Living* | *in* | *this through*

3.3.
is twice the depth I expected, seems vast. Temu Responds: Living in this place is not like the physical realm

where you came from; being here is sustained by means of

Verse 4.

4.1.
| hetep ab | an | iu | gert | an | aritu | nedjemmytu | im | - | z |

4.2.
peace of heart | *not* | *is* | *though* | *not* | *making* | *pleasure sexuality* | *in* | *- | it*

4.3.
contentment. Also, here, in this realm, there are no sexual pleasures in it.

103

Verse 5.

5.1.

Erdi – na	akhu	m	asuy	mu	nafu	hena
Given to me	*spirit being*	*in*	*exchange*	*water*	*air*	*with*

5.3. Any speaks: To be given to me is becoming an Akh (spirit/enlightened being) instead of food and drink with

Verse 6.

6.1.

nedjemmytu	hetep	ab	m	asuy	ta	heqt	nefery	su
Sex pleasures	*peace*	*heart*	*in*	*exchange*	*bread*	*beer*	*good*	*that*

6.3. Sexuality. Instead of those things I get inner peace; instead of food and drink I get inner peace; and this is a good thing, in fact I will be better off.

Verse 7.

7.1.

Temu	m	maa	her – k	an	gert	uchedu	- a	gau	- k
Temu	*in*	*eyes*	*face-thine*	*not*	*though*	*sick*	*- I*	*deprived*	*- thee*

7.3. Lord Temu's eyes, his spiritual vision, are in your face and you will not be a sickly person and you will not be deprived. You will not feel as if you are missing out on anything because the fullness of spirit will be in your perspective as opposed to being afflicted by the limited vision of individuality and myopic self-regard based on egocentricity.

Verse 8.

8.1.

lu	neter	neb	hab	-nef	nest	f	m	khenty	hehu	iu
It is	*divinity*	*every*	*convey*	*to he*	*throne*	*his*	*in*	*foremost*	*millions*	*it is*

8.3. Every god and goddess will transmit their thrones to him (Osiris Any) and he will be the foremost being existing for millions of years. It is

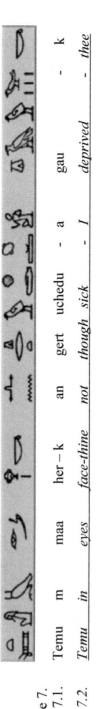

104

Verse 9.

9.1.

| Nest – k | n | sa | k | Heru | nefery | Temu | unen | gert | hab | - | f |

9.2. *Throne yours of son yours Horus good Temu existence though conveys - he*

9.3. the thrones of your son Horus. This is good and has said it Temu that there will be beautiful existence as he gives to the

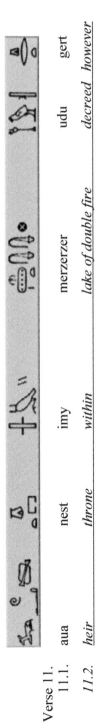

Verse 10.

10.1.

| uru | | iu | - f | gert | heqa | - f | nest – k | iu | f | er |

10.2. *prince/noble. It is - he though rulership - he throne thine It is he as to*

10.3. princes/nobles. It is he who, however, will rule your thrones (because you are Osiris and you rule in heaven and your son rules on earth for you).

It is he who

Verse 11.

11.1.

| aua | nest | imy | merzerzer | udu | gert |

11.2. *heir throne within lake of double fire decreed however*

11.3. is heir to the throne within the lake of double fire, located in the Duat, where one can bask in the rays of Ra in his presence and become purified

thereby as decreed; however

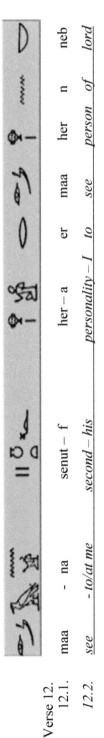

Verse 12.

12.1.

| maa | - na | senut – f | her – a | er | maa | her | n | neb |

12.2. *see - to/at me second – his personality – I to see person of lord*

12.3. he may see me as his second and so that my personality may see his personality, he being the lord

Verse 13.

13.1.   Temu   ashzet   pu   aha   m   ankh   nefery   iu - k   er

13.2.   Temu.   What   the   time   in   life   goodly?   It is   thee   about

13.3.   Temu.   What is the duration of life in this form of good existence? Answer: For you it will be

Verse 14.

14.1.   hehu   n   hehu   aha   n   hehu   iu   erdi – na

14.2.   millions   of   millions   durations   of   millions.   It is   giving -to you

14.3.   a duration of millions of millions of years. This is a granting to you

Verse 15.

15.1.   hab   - f   uru   iu – a   gert   er   hedj   arit   na   nebt

15.2.   the conveying - he   greatness.   It is - I   though, about dismantling   created for me all

15.3.   the status of Greatness of God who is Great. It is also about how I dismantle what was created for me, my illusory time and space existence, all of it.

Verse 16.

16.1.   iu   ta   pen   er   ay   m   Nunu   m   huhu   mi   tepy – f

16.2.   It is   earth   this   about   coming   as   primordial being   through   primordial waters   like   chief -he

16.3.   It is like when the earth, this one we stand on, came forth by means of Nunu, the primordial being/God who existed in the all-pervading undifferentiated ocean/consciousness that gave rise to Creation and like unto himself

Verse 17.

17.1.

| a | nuk | zep | hena | Asar |

17.2. *condition. I am fated with Osiris*

17.3. in that former condition, the way he was before he emerged. I am fated with the God Osiris since I am also Osiris; so I share his fate and his being chief of all beings and also with enlightenment, the return to how he was in the beginning before the Creation emerged, that original condition of his, when he was pure and without taint or dismemberment, that condition is mine too.

HYMN TO RA BY HUNEFER. Presented at the 2015 Neterian Conference. Translation by Dr. Muata Ashby

Adorations to Ra by the Scribe Hunefer

EGYPTIAN BOOK OF THE DEAD HIEROGLYPH TRANSLATIONS FOR ENLIGHTENMENT

HYMN TO RA

HYMN TO RA BY HUNEFER.
British Museum papyrus No.
9901.] XIXth dynasty.]
Translation ©2015 Dr. Muata
Ashby for Sema Institute and
Kemet University

Verse 1.

1.1. Dua   Ra   cheft   uben   f   m   akhet   abtet

1.2. *Adorations Ra   when   rising   he   in   horizon   eastern*

1.3. Adorations to the God Ra when he rises as the sun in the eastern horizon…

Verse 2.

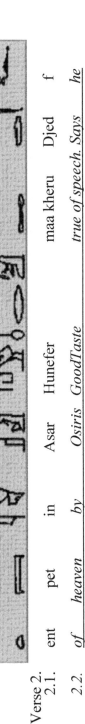

2.1. ent   pet   in   Asar   Hunefer   maa kheru   Djed   f

2.2. *of   heaven   by   Osiris   GoodTaste   true of speech. Says   he*

2.3. of heaven, emerging from the heaven/netherworld to shine on the physical plane. These are words spoken by the initiate whose name is "Osiris, One of good sense of taste," or one who is sensitive to the flavor of spiritual life, who is righteous.

Verse 3.

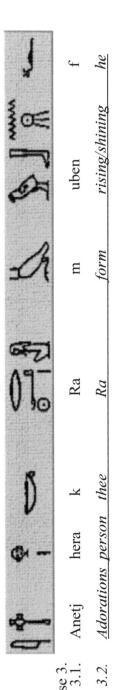

3.1. Anetj   hera   k   Ra   m   uben   f

3.2. *Adorations person thee   Ra   form   rising/shining   he*

3.3. Adorations to you who are the entity manifesting as Ra, the Creator, when shining in the sky, is he…

Verse 4.

4.1.

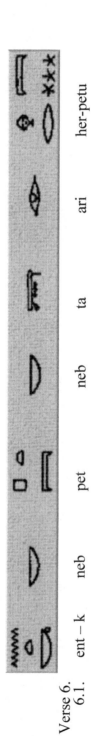

Temu	m		uben		k	sep	sen
Temu	*as*	*peace –he*	*rising/shining*	*thee*	*times*	*two*

4.2.

4.3. and also when he is in the form of Temu when he is setting at sunset. You rise twice

Verse 5.

5.1.

pezed		k	sep sen	kha	tj	m	suten	neteru
illumining	*thee*	*times two*	*crown*	*tie*	*in*	*king*	*divinities*

5.2.

5.3. lighting up the world are you, and you do this twice. Your rising is your crown as we recognize you as the king of all the gods and goddesses.

Verse 6.

6.1.

ent – k	neb	pet		neb	ta		ari	her-petu
of - thee	*lord*	*heaven*	*lord*	*earth*	*Creator*	*heavenly*

6.2.

6.3. You are the lord of heaven, the astral plane and the lord of the earth and physical Creation. You are also the maker of heavenly beings and

EGYPTIAN BOOK OF THE DEAD HIEROGLYPH TRANSLATIONS FOR ENLIGHTENMENT

Verse 7.

7.1. kheru — Neter — Uau — kheper — m — zep

7.2. *earthly beings* — **Divinity** — **One** — **creation** — **in** — **time**

7.3. earthly beings. You are the Supreme Being, only one, who self-created itself at the time of

Verse 8.

8.1. tepy — ari — tau — qemam — rekhytu

8.2. *first* — **maker** — **worlds/universe** — **creator** — **people**

8.3. the beginning of time and Creation itself. You are the maker of the physical universe and creator of human beings.

Verse 9.

9.1. Ari — nunu — qemam — hapy — ari — net

9.2. **Maker** — **primeval ocean** — **creator** — **Nile river** — **maker** — **of**

9.3. Maker of the primeval ocean, the substratum from which Creation is made. Creator of the Nile river which sustains life in our land; and maker of

Verse 10.

10.1. mu — s-ankh — im — z — it — tjezu — duu

10.2. *water* — **causing life in** — — **it** — — **knitting** — **mountains**

10.3. water and the source that causes that water to have life sustaining properties and you are also responsible for the interweaving (construction of the constituent parts) together of the mountains and all physical creation.

111

EGYPTIAN BOOK OF THE DEAD HIEROGLYPH TRANSLATIONS FOR ENLIGHTENMENT

Verse 11.
11.1. S – kheper   remteju   menmenu   ari   pet
11.2. *Cause coming into being men women cattle   maker   heaven*
11.3. You are the one who caused human beings to come into existence and likewise cattle and other animals. You are the maker of heaven

Verse 12.

12.1. ta   nyny   n   her   k   hept   tj   Maat
12.2. *earth.   Praises   to   personality thine embraced tied   truth and righteousness*
12.3. and earth. Praises be to you, the personality which is embraced, even more, tied with the justice, order and truth of existence.

Verse 13.
13.1. er   trauy   nem - k   hert   m   awet ab
13.2. *about   double period   stepping - thee   contentedly heaven in expanded heart*
13.3. Ra strides along twice daily, at morning and evening, over the heavens with contented heart full of joy.

Verse 14.

14.1. Mer-n-desdes   kheper   m   hetepu   Neka   cher
14.2. *sacred lake in the Duat becomes in peace   serpent Neka   fall*
14.3. and the sacred lake in the Nether-world has become peaceful; also, the serpent Neka, a negative spirit who is opposed to Ra and his daily course through the sky, he has been defeated and has fallen so the obstacle to Ra's shining forwards has been removed.

112

Verse 15.

15.1. Aauy   hzq   seshep   n   zektet   maau

15.2. *Arms*   *cut*   *receives*   *the*   *boat of morning*   *breezes*

15.3. The arms of that enemy of Ra have been cut off. The boat of the rising sun received breezes to make its journey effective and

Verse 16.

16.1. nefer   im   kara   -   f   ab-f   nedjm   khau

16.2. *pleased*   *in*   *sanctuary*   -   *he*   *heart –his*   *gleeful*   *rising*

16.3. the one who resides in the shrine, his heart is delighted at seeing the rising of

Verse 17.

17.1. m   sekhem   n   pet   ua   sepd   pert

17.2. *in*   *power*   *to heaven*   *one*   *provisioned*   *going forth*

17.3. Ra in his full power and glory up to the heavens going forth with all provisions needed, as all properly prepared boat voyages do.

Verse 18.

18.1. m   numu   Ra   m   maa kheru   hun   netery

18.2. *from*   *primeval waters*   *Ra*   *as*   *true of speech*   *child*   *divine*

18.3. Ra emerges from the primeval ocean of Creation, the undifferentiated primordial consciousness that is the body of Ra. Ra does this with all righteousness and truth and order, he does this as that same divine child, Nefertem,

Verse 19.

19.1. ua   heh   utet – z   mes   su   djesef   ua

19.2. **_heir   eternity   begetter (of) it   child   he   himself   one_**

19.3. who is the inheritor of timelessness, and the one who gave birth to himself by himself; Ra is one

Verse 20.

20.1. ur   tenu   aru   suten   tawiu   heqa

20.2. **_great   manifold   forms   king   Creation   prince[46]_**

20.3. great and his forms are multifarious;   he is monarch of Creation and prince of

Verse 21.

21.1. Anu   zesh   m   djeta   paut   neteru   m   henu

21.2. **_Anu   pass through   end of time, company gods goddesses form praisers_**

21.3. Heliopolis (Anu), the site of the first creation, Ra's royal city. You move through time until forever, the end of time, as the company of

gods and goddesses praises you

---

[46] In this context the term "zer" relates to nobility, royalty and specifically to a spiritual royalty. One of the 75 names of Ra is zer aah "Great noble one". The god Asar (Osiris) is similarly referred to. Nevertheless the construction of the sentence means that Ra is not The Ultimate God but a descendant of that Supreme Being.

114

Verse 22.

22.1.   n   uben – k   khenen   im   akhet   saq   m

22.2.   *the*   *rising –thine*   *rowing*   *in*   *horizon*   *exaltation*   *in*

22.3.   there as you rise and row towards the evening horizon. Shouts of exaltation are heard in

Verse 23.

23.1.   zektet   anetj hra – k   Amun-Ra   hetep   her   Maat

23.2.   *evening boat.*   *Adorations – thee*   *Hidden-Light*   *peace*   *person*   *righteousness, truth and justice*

23.3.   Your boat of the evening. We adore you in your form of Amun-Ra ["Hidden Radiance"] as you move in peace and balance and your person is the very embodiment of righteousness, order, truth and justice

Verse 24.

24.1.   udja   -   k   hert   iu   her   neb   maa   n –k

24.2.   *voyaging*   *-*   *thee*   *over the heavens. It is person all*   *seeing to thee*

24.3.   as you voyage over the heavens in your boat, the sundisk in the sky. All people look at you

Verse 25.

25.1.   red – k   seqeded   hem -   k   satu   - k

25.2.   *grow - thee*   *traversing*   *majesty -*   *thee*   *piercing rays – thine*

25.3.   as you expand while moving through the heavens in your majestic image with rays that penetrate

Verse 26.

26.1.   m   heru.

26.2.   **_in_   _persons._**

26.3.   inside all people on earth.

Chapter 4/17 Sections: Heru with Two heads and Two paths; A Follower of Neberdjer from the Pert-m-Heru - Translation by Dr. Muata Ashby

From Papyrus Nebseny

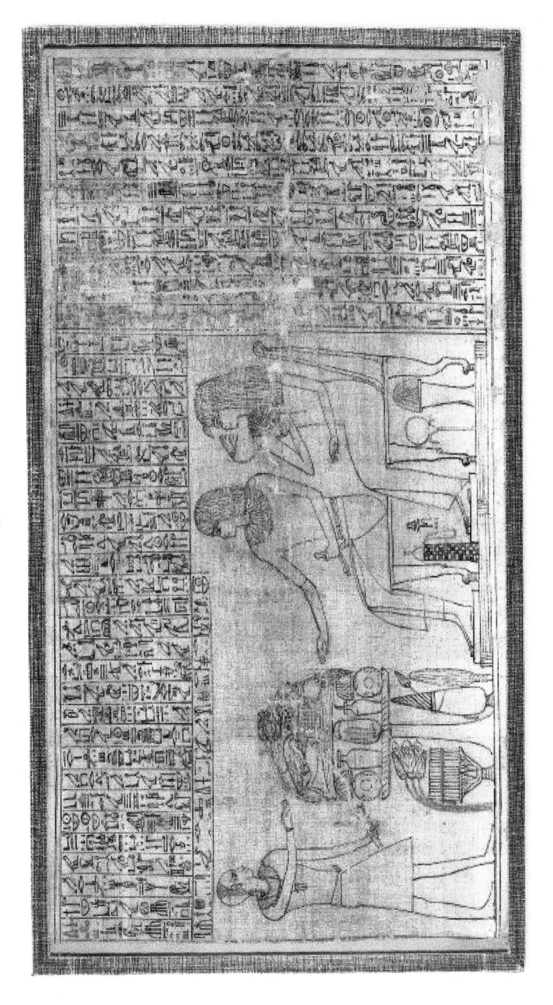

Heru with Two Heads and Two Paths

Heru with two Heads and the Two Paths

From: Pert m Heru Chap. 4/17 Papyrus Nebseni

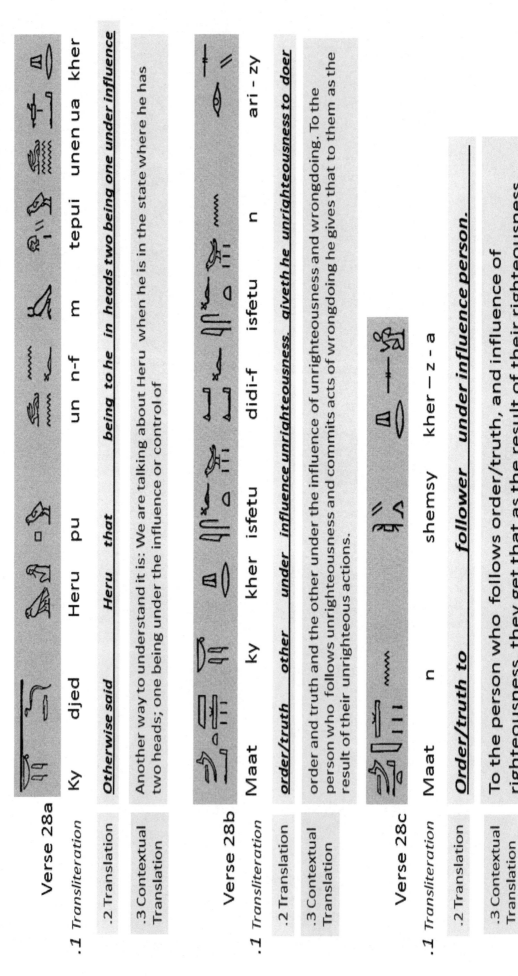

Verse 28a

.1 Transliteration	Ky	djed	Heru	pu	Heru	that	un	n-f	m	tepui	unen ua	kher
.2 Translation	*Otherwise said*				*Heru*	*that*				*being to he in heads two being one under influence*		

.3 Contextual Translation: Another way to understand it is: We are talking about Heru when he is in the state where he has two heads.; one being under the influence or control of

Verse 28b

.1 Transliteration	Maat	ky	kher	isfetu	didi-f	isfetu	n	ari - zy
.2 Translation	*order/truth*	*other*	*under*	*influence unrighteousness.*	*giveth he*	*unrighteousness to doer*		

.3 Contextual Translation: order and truth and the other under the influence of unrighteousness and wrongdoing. To the person who follows unrighteousness and commits acts of wrongdoing he gives that to them as the result of their unrighteous actions.

Verse 28c

.1 Transliteration	Maat	n	shemsy	kher – z - a
.2 Translation	*Order/truth to*		*follower*	*under influence person.*

.3 Contextual Translation: To the person who follows order/truth, and influence of righteousness, they get that as the result of their righteousness.

Translated by Sebai Dr. Muata Ashby Sema Institute ©1997-2012

A Follower of Neberdjer

Papyrus Nebseni

Verse 35b

.1 Transliteration: Nuk udja tep ta cher

.2 Translation: *I am vital upon earth before*

.3 Contextual Translation: I have vitality while I exist on earth even as I come into the presence of

Verse 35c-36a

.1 Transliteration: Ra mena a nefer cher Asar nen abu ten im a

.2 Translation: *Ra death/ending/arriving I good before Osiris not offerings yours† in me*

.3 Contextual Translation: Ra, and as a departed soul, as my death was a good death and I come into the presence of Osiris, I will not receive the offerings of that hidden god† that metes out pain to the unrighteous; that will not come into me.

Verse 36b

.1 Transliteration: Nen m heru achu zen her ntet tu a m shemsu n

.2 Translation: *Not in heavenly person altar theirs person this I in following of*

.3 Contextual Translation: The heavenly person will not be in their burning altars; so that fate does not apply, not to me, because I am in the following of

Verse 36c-37a

.1 Transliteration: Neberdjer er sheshu n kheperu

.2 Translation: *All encompassing Divinity according [to the] writings of Kheperu*

.3 Contextual: the Transcendental All-Encompassing Divinity, in accordance with the writings of the God Creator!

Translated by Sebai Dr. Muata Ashby Sema Institute ©1997-2012

Translation of the word- Neberdjer

Original Hieroglyphic- V-1   Neb - er - djer - Neter

.1- TRANSLITERATION:

Neb	er	djer	Neter

.2- TRANSLATION:

Neb	= Lord/all
er	= of
djer	= ultimate limits (as in extending to the utmost)
Neter	= divinity (spirit)

.3- CONTEXTUAL TRANSLATION:

Lord of all-encompassing divinity which enfolds all things within it to the maximum extent of existence.

Chapter 19 of Pert-m-Heru From the 2013 Neterian Conference - Presented by Dr. Muata Ashby

From Papyrus Auf Ankh

Chapter 19 of Pert-m-Heru
From the 2013 Neterian Conference – Presented by
Dr. Muata Ashby

From Papyrus Auf Ankh

PMH Chapter 19 Title

*Read
Right to
left

V-0

Netergertet m mu medma nafu sesent Ra* -0.1

(cemetery) lower heaven in water words/declaration breath nostrils Chapter -0.2*

0.3- This is the chapter of breathing air and words to have power over water in the
Cemetery, which is the lower part of heaven and its entranceway.

Nut-Goddess of heaven

Chet-Tree of Life

Hetep —Offering of Supreme
Peace

Mu-Waters of life and
Creation

PMH Chapter 19
Verse 1

Hapi

1.3 Words spoken by aspirant Osiris Living in the Flesh [Living Flesh of Osiris].. Hail God Hapi (unified), who unite the waters of Creation with life-giving essence, you in your name of weaver of the heavens. Give thee to me power. Give to me, I who am called Osiris Living in the flesh. Let me have spiritual victory and enlightenment just like Sekhemit when she was lost in the world as a deluded soul but was brought back to discover her enlightenment through the grace of her preceptor Lord Djehuty!...

Hapi of north and south

Hapi (unified)

1.2	1.1	V1
By Spoken Words	in dje Medu	
Osiris	Asar	
Flesh	Auf	
Living	Ankh	
(enlightenment / spiritual victory) Speech of True	Kheru Maa	
hail	A	
God Hapi	Hapi	
to as	ar	
of form heavens (sky)	m pet	
of thine name	n k ren	
Heavens of Weaver	pet neted	
thee give	K di	
power	sekhem	
Osiris (to)	Asar	
Flesh	Auf	
Living	Ankh	
Speech of True	Maa Kheru	
damaged	damaged	
like	mi	
Sekhemit	Sekhemit	
Sekhemit		

124

PMH Chapter 19
Verse 2

V2

2.2	2.1
Break/steal/plunder/injure	aoay
Osiris	Asar
Flesh	Auf
Living	Ankh
he	a
speech of true	Kheru Maa
Nighttime	gereh
that	puy
to of	n-n
Sick/depressed/helpless	sheny
Great	Aah
ye grant	mak
forth Going/send/	zebi
of	n
Osiris	Asar
Flesh	Auf
Living	Ankh
he	a
Speech of true	Maa kheru
(enlightenment /spiritual victory)	

zebi

2.3

at the...time of adversity of Osiris Living in the Flesh. Let him attain Enlightenment, even in the time of darkness, of great illness, helplessness and depression or death of the body. Allow this Osiris Living in the Flesh to go forward, to attain Enlightenment!

Osiris

PMH Chapter 19
Verse 3

3.2	3.1	V3
Joyful breathing	reshet	
abode	aset	
Inundation	abhu	
like	mi	
(those who) go forth	sebi	
they	zen	
that	pefy	
ancestors Honored	sheps	
Ignorant	chemen	
they	zen	
he to As	f- n - ar	
forth Going may	sebi	
those	zenu	
Osiris	Asar	
Flesh	Auf	
Living	Ankh	
he	a	
(spiritual victory) Speech of true	Kheru Maa	
is it	iu	
boat loaded	uha	

Shepsu

3.3-

Allow this initiate, Osiris Living in the Flesh, to go forward, to attain Enlightenment …to be able to breathe joyfully in the abode of inundation, where the soul is immersed in the fullness of spirit, like those honored ancestors/elders, who were originally ignorant, and yet went forth, onward to attaining Enlightenment; let me be like them, on the spiritual journey, provided with full provisions and wherewithal to succeed on the spiritual quest.

akhu   shepsu
venerable/holy ones,

PMH Chapter 19
Verse 4

4.3

The way opens to Djeddu, the abode of the backbone of the God Asar, the higher psycho-spiritual consciousness centers and the abode of the God Osiris, the center of existence, upon discovering which the soul becomes rooted in its divine source and discovers higher consciousness. So too it is homage to initiate Osiris Living in the Flesh, who is victorious in Enlightenment. *His nostrils open up in Djeddu, so he breathes after death, and lives on spirit sustenance. He has discovered Supreme Peace, the union of opposites that leads to non-duality, in the house that was built for him in the city of Anu (Heliopolis), that city of Ra and first place of Creation...*

4.1	4.2
un	open
tu	to
m	in
Djeddu	City Djeddu
kz	Homage
iu	is it
er	about
Asar	Asar
Auf	Flesh
Ankh	Living
a	he
kheru maa	speech of true (who is)
n - f	he to
Sherety	nostrils
f	His
untu	opens
m	in
Didiu	Mendes/Djeddu
htp	peace
f	he
m	in
Anu	Heliopolis
pert	house
f	his
pu	that
qed	built
iu	it

V4

Djed

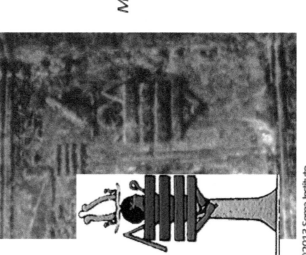

PMH Chapter 19 Verse 5

5.3

The house...built in the city of Anu by Goddess Sesheta(see next page). It was caused to be raised for Osiris Living in the Flesh by the God Khnum who is its foundation and guide for the movements of the image of the personality that is to reside there thusly: the aspirant/resident is to assume these postures when deemed appropriate: If the air is blowing to him from the north part of the heavens then move and face north from the south and breathe. And rest in the south facing north. Likewise, if the air is coming from the west...

5.2	5.1	V5
he - to	f – n	
Sesheta	Sesheta	
Raise up/support cause	aha - z	
he to	f – n	
Khnum/Djehuty	Khnum	
Person	her	
guide to	pert sebit	
he	f	
Moving image	arut	
heaven	Pet	
north	meht-n	
Air/breath/blow	Nafu	
Rest then indeed/certainly	hefd/hemz	
he to	f – n	
South	resu	
Moving image	arut	
Heaven	pet	
through of	m – n	
south	resu	
Air/breath/blow	nafu	
Rest then indeed/certainly	hefd/hemz	
to - he	f – n	
north	meht	
Moving image	arut	
heaven	pet	
in - to	m – n	
West Beautiful	Amenta	

Sesheta

Khnum

128

More about Goddess Sesheta

From
Egyptian Mysteries Vol. 2
Dictionary of Gods and Goddesses of
Shetaut Neter © 2004

time." The Persea Tree was associated with the goddess in the feline form who resided in the city of Anu (Heliopolis of the Greeks) and slew the demon serpent *Apepi*, who was the enemy of Ra and also of all souls. The terms *"Shetat"* or *"Seshetar"* are the secret rituals in the cults of the Egyptian Gods. Sesheta's writing of the mysteries creates a dwelling place for the initiate, a place wherein the opening of eternity is possible. In this house, constructed by the words of wisdom and the transformative power they have the Pillar (Seven psycho-spiritual centers of the subtle spine) of Asar is opened and the Creative force, Khnum (the god of the base of geographical Ancient Egypt), opens the floodgates of the subtle Nile, i.e. the flow of the Serpent Power out of the "house" (the energy center at the base of the spine) is opened. She is depicted as a woman with a headdress that is also the hieroglyph of her name, which is a stylized seven (or nine) pointed lotus flower on a standard that is held by a headband, all of which is beneath a set of horns that are down-turned. As her name is phonetically related to Sushen, "lotus," she is the scribe of the spirit. She also wears the leopard skin garment characteristic of *sem* priests and priestesses.

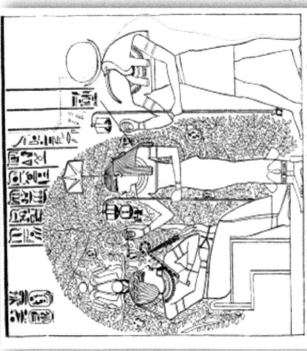

Djehuti and Sesheta write the history and name of Rameses 2 on the tree of life.

Sesheta is the goddess of writing and counterpart of Djehuti. She is a divinity of priests and priestesses and scribes. She is also the presiding deity over the seven psycho-spiritual consciousness centers of spiritual enlightenment of the Serpent Power. She is also associated with the sacred *Persea Tree* on which the names of the kings were written at the time of coronation. She was the *"Recorder of Deeds," "Mistress of Books,"* and *"Reckoner of*

PMH
Chapter 19
Verse 6

V6	6.1	6.2
	nafu	Air/breath/blow
	hefd/hemz	Rest then indeed/certainly
	n - f	to - he
	abtet	east
	ar	to as
	pet	heaven
	m – n	through of
	abtet	eastern
	nafu	Air/breath/blow
	hefd/hemz	Rest then indeed/certainly
	m - f	in – he
	amenta	West (netherworld of abode of deceased)
	athu	draw in/harness
	tu	to
	anhuu	eyebrows
	her	person
	sherety	nostrils
	f	his
	Asar	Asar
	Auf	Flesh
	Ankh	Living
	a	he
	kheru maa	speech of true (who is)
	uba	Enter/way a open /invade foreign land
	f	He
	neb bu	every place
	f – mery	he – desires
	f-pez	his backbone

6.3-

Likewise, if the air is coming from the west...then rest in the east, face from the east part of heaven to the west and relax. Finally, if it blows from the east then rest to/in the west, drawing in the breathe..etc.

Now, with the personality situated properly, focus on the part of the head of the eyebrows, you Osiris Living in the Flesh, you Enlightened being. Breathe in and restrain the breath. The way is open to enter whichever part of the spirit realm he may want to go, and his backbone is there.

PMH Chapter 19
Verse 6 Extended Definitions Study

Hefd-Rest/faint/swoon

Hefd-

Swoon/faint/during
religious ecstasy

Pezdy

Backs of men and women

Pezd-back

illumined/shining

> The illumined
> backbone
> hearkens to Verse
> 4 [psycho-spiritual
> consciousness
> centers]

V6

	6.1	6.2
	nafu	Air/breath/blow
	hefd/hemz	Rest then indeed/certainly
	n - f	to - he
	abtet	east
	ar	to
	pet	heaven
	m – n	through of
	abtet	eastern
	nafu	Air/breath/blow
	hefd/hemz	Rest then indeed/certainly
	m - f	in – he
	amenta	West
	athu	Draw in/restrain/harness
	tu	to
	anhuu	eyebrows
	her	person
	sherety	nostrils
	f	his
	Asar	Asar
	Auf	Flesh
	Ankh	Living
	a	he
	Kheru maa	speech of true (who is)
	uba	Enter/way a open /invade foreign land
	f	He
	neb bu	every place
	f – mery	he – desires
	f-pez	sun like shining his backbone

(handwritten)
Shentry untu
m Did u Hp
m Am pet
Pu qed iu

nostrils det.

Athu
Restrain

Athu
Restrain
Prison

(Highlighted sections by Dr. Ashby)

Chapter 18/110 of Pert-m-Heru From the 2012 Neterian Conference Presented by Dr. Muata Ashby

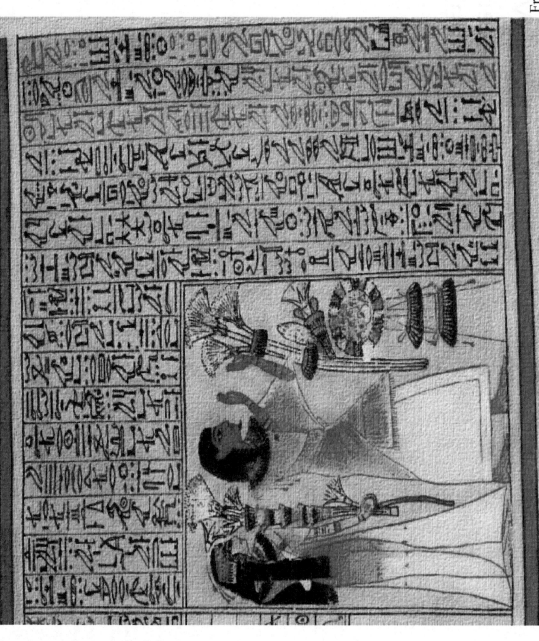

From Papyrus Ani

EGYPTIAN BOOK OF THE DEAD HIEROGLYPH TRANSLATIONS FOR ENLIGHTENMENT

Chapter 18/110: The Field of Peace and Enlightenment section 1-part1

Verse 1.

Ha	m	rau	nu Sechit htpu	Rau	nu pert	m hru	aqet	pert	m	neterchert knem	m

1.1.

1.2. *Front in words of Jurisdiction of Peace words of come out as enlightened go in come out through cemetery joining in*

1.3. Beginning of the Chapter of the realm/precinct/field/jurisdiction of peace in the Netherworld where an aspirant goes to make peace between the lower self (Set/Seth) and the Higher Self (Heru/Horus) in the Book of Enlightenment for transcending duality and becoming enlightened; to go in and out of the cemetery, the lower part of heaven, after the physical death, so as to find the passage to the higher Netherworld regions; and from the field of peace then join in

Verse 2.

Sechit yanru	un	m htp m niut	ur	nebt	nafu sekhem a	im	akht a	er skau	shine I	in	the plough	I in	a im

2.1.

2.2. *Juris. blessed souls being in peace in city/dist. great mistress freedom power I in shine I in the plough I in*

2.3. the region/field/jurisdiction of the blessed/perfected souls who are now experiencing peace, in the district of the great mistress of freedom. May I have power through perfect shining spirit being and in the ability to use the plough in that region

Verse 3.

asech	–	a im	qaqa - a	im	sura -	a	im	m	arit aritu neb dept	ta
reap	-	I in	eat - I	in	drink -	I	in	as	actions deeds all upon earth	

3.1.

3.2.

3.3. and may I reap in there, eat and drink in there, in that region of the Netherworld, which is a heavenly region where after death the personality can exist in a similar form to that on earth and carry on activities and enjoyments just as is done by those living on earth.

133

Verse 4.

Djed in Asar Any	**Any**	**maa-kheru**	**nt-k tjat**	**Heru**	**in**	**Set**	**maa**	**m**	**senb**	**er**	**Sechit htpu**	**pzshet**

4.1.

4.2. *Words spoken by Asar Any, Any True of Speech which thee carry Heru by Set see   in   wall   surrounding juris. of peace*

apportionment

4.3.   Asar Any speaks, Any the Enlightened: [recalling the Asarian resurrection teaching] this is a struggle, between Horus mind and Seth mind, within the personality of Any. It is to be settled in the Field of Peace region of the Netherworld; In the Asarian Resurrection saga, Horus and Seth were battling over control of the personality, and Horus was temporarily beaten, and Seth might have wrested control over Horus's testicles, his generative vital life force. But despite that temporary victory by Seth, for Horus there was sight through the walls surrounding the Field of Peace region of the Netherworld, so there is a path to resolve the issue there. Horus mind being lucid unlike others whose consciousness is opaque so they cannot see into the Field of Peace region was able to discover the path to inner peace or the harmony, balance and union of opposites (Heru and Set)/(hetep).

Common Events and Sections The Field of Peace

- Entrance assisted by Lord Djehuty
- Meeting the Three divinities who allow entry
- Making the HTP Offering
- Sechit Yaru
- Birthplace of gods
- Anrutef
- Boat of Asar

Architecture of the Universe

Orientation of Earth, The Heavens and the Netherworld

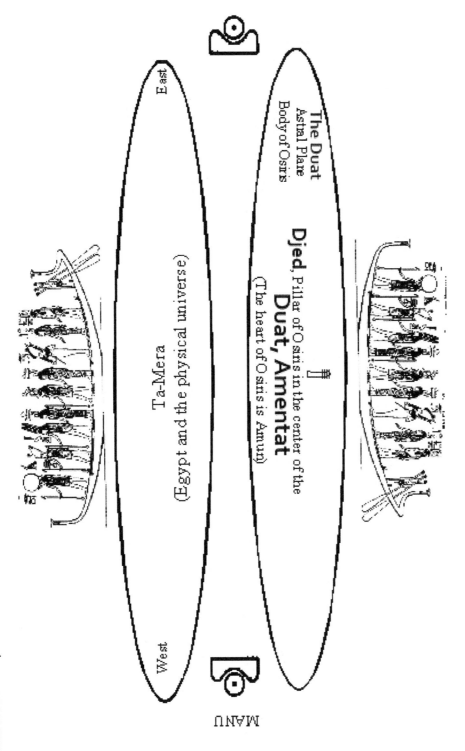

East

Ta-Mera
(Egypt and the physical universe)

West

The Duat
Astral Plane
Body of Osiris

Djed, Pillar of Osiris in the center of the
Duat, Amentat
(The heart of Osiris is Amun)

MANU

EGYPTIAN BOOK OF THE DEAD HIEROGLYPH TRANSLATIONS FOR ENLIGHTENMENT

Figure 18: Architecture of the Netherworld (Duat)

Architecture of the Duat

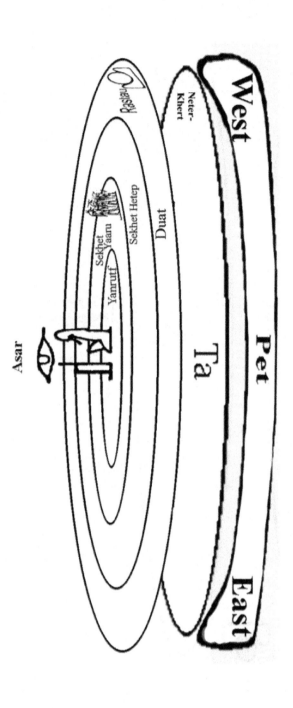

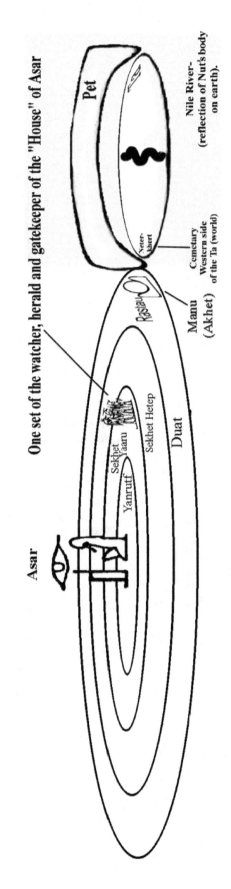

One set of the watcher, herald and gatekeeper of the "House" of Asar

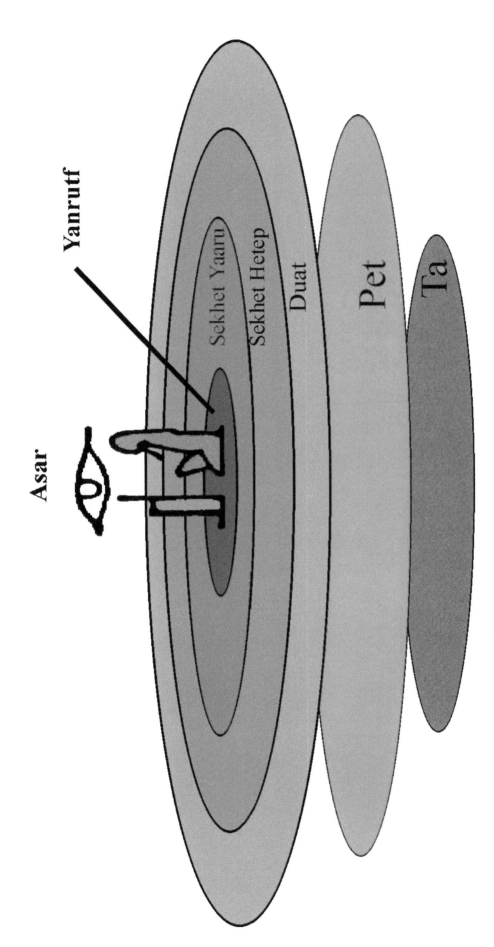

Figure 19: Main Ancient Egyptian Realms/Fields of existence

Figure 20: Plowing and sowing in the Netherworld

Plowing and sowing in the *Sechit Yanru* from the Tomb of Sennedjem

Sowing and Plowing in the Fields – Tomb of Sennedjem, Thebes (19th Dynasty: 1200s BC)
Gallup, Guitrooy and Weisberg, *Great Paintings of the Western World*, p. 38

The Ka's of Ani and his wife drinking water in the Netherworld

The "Doubles"[3] of Ani and his wife drinking water in the Netherworld

---

[3] The term "doubles" used by establishment Egyptologists is actually the Ka or astral body, which is actually the emotional body or location of the personality where thoughts and feelings manifest in the mind.

EGYPTIAN BOOK OF THE DEAD HIEROGLYPH TRANSLATIONS FOR ENLIGHTENMENT

Figure 22: Pitfalls in the Netherworld

Lake/Pool of Fire

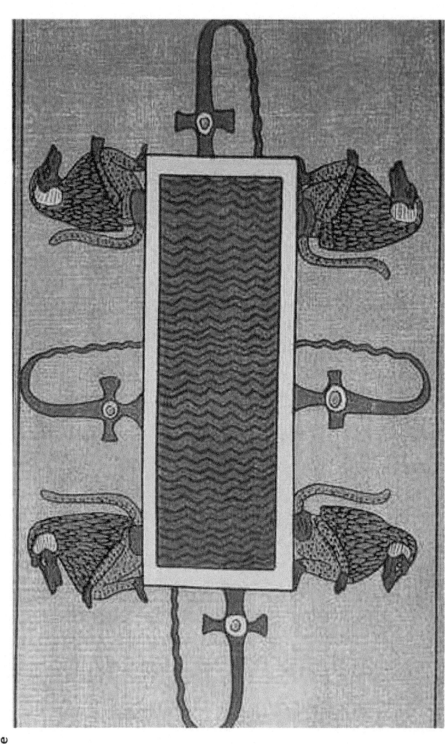

The Pool or Lake of Fiery Water, painted red, with burning braziers and baboons, from the *PertmHeru.* (plate 32)*, The Book of Enlightenment* [The Papyrus of Ani].

EGYPTIAN BOOK OF THE DEAD HIEROGLYPH TRANSLATIONS FOR ENLIGHTENMENT

Figure 23: Lake/Pool of Fire of Papyrus Nebseny

Lake/Pool of Fire of Papyrus Nebseny[4]

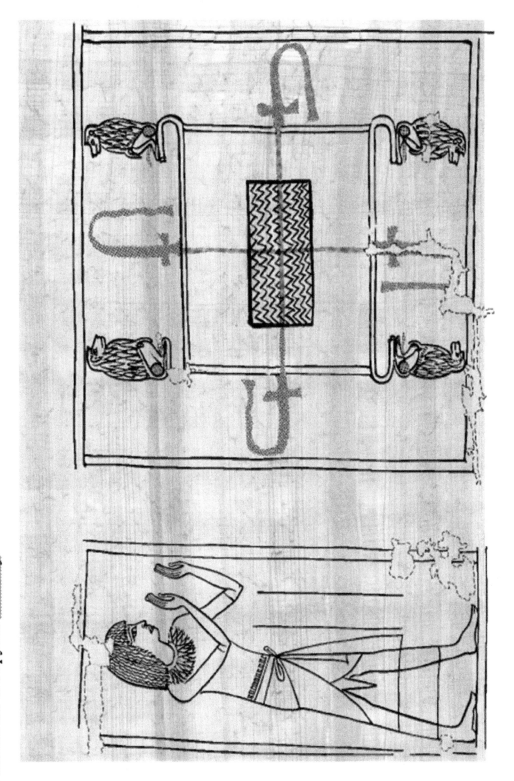

[4] Papyrus of Nebseny: sheet 31. Spell 125; spell 126 vignette.
Culture/period 18th Dynasty
Date 15thC BC (reign of Thutmose IV, by style)

Figure 24: Papyrus Bakenmut

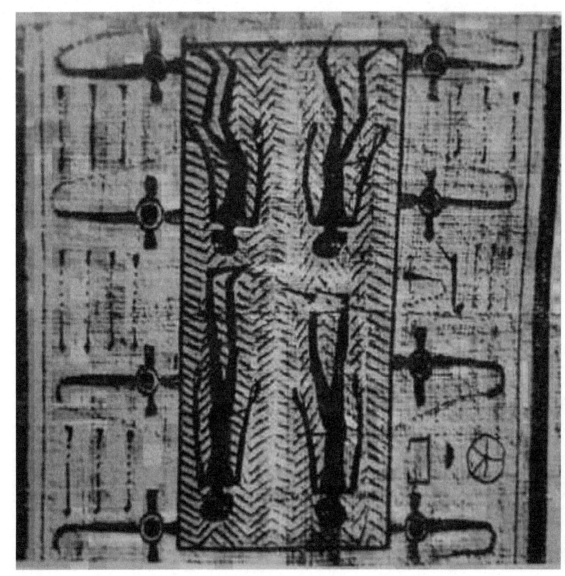

- A photo of a Papyrus of Bakenmut, 21st Dynasty (ca. 1069-945 B.C.), showing the darkened bodies of the damned floating in the Lake of Fire in the Netherworld, which is fed by flames from braziers along the lake's edges

Figure 25: Papyrus of Lady Anhai

Sechit Hetep of Lady Anhai XXII Dynasty

THE BOOK OF THE

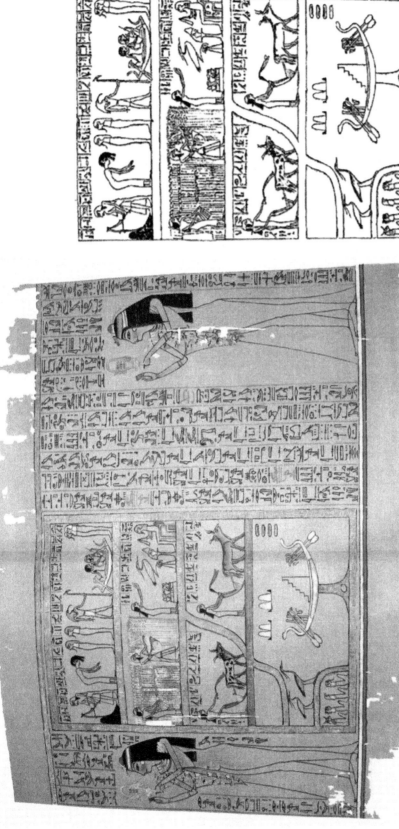

Plate 42: The Duat - Sekhet-Hetepet of Anhai from
the *Prt m Hru of Initiate Anhai*.

1- Lady Anhai pays homage to her parents and divine
beings (uppermost).
2- Anhai binds wheat into bundles, then praises exalted
souls.
3- Anhai is seen ploughing.
4- The Celestial Boat in the form of a headrest containing
a shrine with seven steps.

143

Figure 26: The Ka of Ani and His wife

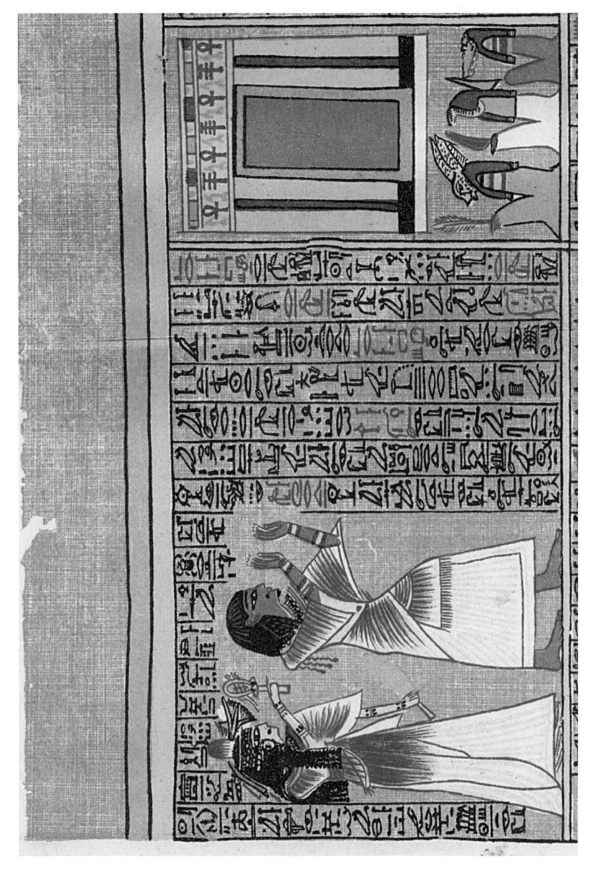

The Ka of Ani and his with Thuthu, a priestess, address the three divinities at the entrance to the *Sechit Yanru*

Chapter 18: Cont.

Verse 5.

5.1. Nafu her ba n Heru - f im suhyt nehem – f chanu khat n Heru nuk a seshed –a su im at

5.2. *Freedom person soul of Horus – he in. testicles godly rescue – he interior body of Heru I am crowned I he in temple*

5.3. The soul of Heru has been freed within his own being, from the grasp of Seth (egoism). The divine testicles, the generative power of spiritual aspiration, have been rescued and are now in service of spiritual enlightenment as opposed to worldly illusions and desires. In the inner chamber of the body of Horus, the abode of spiritual awakening. Horus (the spiritual aspirant) is freed. I crowned him in the temple

Verse 6.

6.1. Shu iu at chabasu–f nuk-a as hetep m zpu - f zeshem -f mehtu n paut neteru semzu – f

6.2. *Shu it is temple stars – his I am indeed peace in district his directed he fullness of company of gods and goddesses elders his*

6.3. of Shu, in the stars, he who is the lord of air and space, the nexus between heaven and earth, the conduit between the physical realm and the astral and a luminous manifestation of Ra himself, who expresses through the gods and goddesses on earth. I indeed have achieved peace in the realm guided by him, a dominion of fullness of the Group of his Elder Gods and Goddesses under his guidance and management.

Verse 7.

7.1. Z-htp – f   ahaui   derp   Z-htp – f   ahaui

Z-htp – f   ahaui   ankh   qemam-f nefer   anu

n   aru

7.2. *Made peace he fighting gods [Heru and Set] of overseers life created he good   Bringing   offering   made peace –he combatants*

7.3. He made peace between the gods Horus and Seth, the overseers of life. He created what is good by bringing an offering of peace which is the union of opposites that brings duality to an end; thereby he made peace between the combatants, one who represents the quality of righteousness versus the other who represents the quality of egoism in the personality,

Verse 8.

8.1. zenu behen - f iakebu   er   ahaui   zenu der – f   khennu   er   sheriu   ah   nkk-f

n aryu

8.2. *of duty   theirs. Cut - he   crops[hair]   the fighters   they. Forced away –he, trouble   about   children   smite thou–he*

8.3. which is their duty, to combat and also make peace. He cut the crops, in other words, the hair of the fighters, which was obstructing their vision of non-duality, by falling over their foreheads and blocking their third eye, the spiritual vision beyond the other two eyes that perceive the worldly existence.   He forced away, drove out, the trouble their children, the personalities that they would have given rise to in the future, the incarnations in human existence and the giving birth to deluded thoughts and worldly desires born of ignorance and egoism that would have occurred while under the unenlightened state of mind affected by the ongoing conflict. Also removed is what might have suffered otherwise and he struck it down and destroyed that trouble utterly.

The Field of Purified Souls the Ancient Egyptians according to the Papyrus of Ani

SUMMARY: 1. Ani adoring the gods of Sekhet-Aaru. **2.** Ani ploughing in the Other World. **2.** Ani reaping in the Other World. **4.** The abode of the perfect spirits, and the magical boats.

DETAIL: 1. Ani making an offering before a hare-headed god, a snake-headed god, and a bull-headed god; Djehuty confirms the reading of the Maat scales as Ani makes the offering to the divinities collectively referred to as "Pauti" or "company". Ani traverses over water with a Hetep, arrives and makes the "Offering of peace in the Field of Peace."

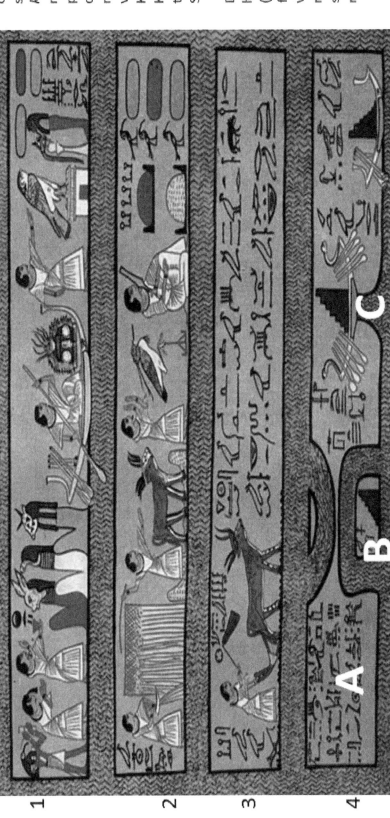

1

2

3

4

A

B

C

DETAIL: 2. Ani reaping corn, Ani driving the oxen which tread out the corn; Ani adoring a Bennu bird perched on a stand; Ani seated holding the *kherp* sceptre-mastery and power-sekhem-dominion; a heap of red and a heap of white corn; three KAU and three KHU,, "the food of the Kas of the Shining spirits.

DETAIL: 3. Ani holding the nekaku (flail) ploughing a field near a stream which contains neither fish, nor serpents, in the region Sechit yanru.

147

4. DETAIL: A abode of the AKHU-Shining spirits, the enlightened. a region called the "place of the spirits" who are seven cubits high, where the wheat is three cubits high, and where the SÃHU, or Glorious spiritual bodies, reap it B-The birthplace of the "gods and goddesses" an island on which is a flight of steps; C-The place where the god therein is Un-nefer (Asar) in a boat with seven steps, lying at the end of a canal and having two serpents at the bow and stern (Aset and Nebethet); and a boat floating on a canal. The name of the first boat is Behutu-tcheser, the sacred steps and throne and that of the second Djefau the boat of the God who is movement and divine food sustaining all life.

Chapter 18: Cont.

Verse 9.

9.1. Nekent bau sekhem- a ams nuk rech nes kheny m shem muz er seper er niutu– z user - a

9.2. *Injury souls power - I control I am know it sailing in waters those and arriving at towns dominion -I*

9.3. The injury of the souls has been struck down. I have power to control the conflict between Horus and Seth, because I know the teaching, I know Horus and Seth, I know myself; even as I sail over the waters of the netherworld, and I arrive at the towns/districts of the netherworld, unobstructed and I have dominion over

Verse 10.

10.1. Ra – a zepd akhu an sekhem zenu im deb im m

10.2. *Mouth mine may given glorious spirit not power they in outfitted inside in*

10.3. my mouth, which is the emancipation of spirit and freedom to express my consciousness without the obstructions of Seth, the ego, due to spiritual ignorance. May I be given enlightenment; the gods and goddesses do not have power over the Enlightened beings, no power within. I am equipped/outfitted/qualified and ready to be in

Verse 11.

11.1. Sechitu–k hetep merert – a -k arit- k nt

11.2. *Field –thine peace desire – I - thine actions-thine it*

11.3. your Field/Realm of Peace. My desires are yours and my actions yours, they are. Oh Shu, Lord of the Field of Peace, you who are the luminous manifestation of Ra in this realm, I have realized that you and I are one. So my desires and actions are as yours and I can do as I please, as you do, because I am you and you are me…

148

Chapter 11/23 of Pert-m-Heru Presented at the 2011 Neterian Conference – Translation by Dr. Muata Ashby

From Papyrus Ani

Figure 27: Opening the mouth in Papyrus Ani

EGYPTIAN BOOK OF THE DEAD HIEROGLYPH TRANSLATIONS FOR ENLIGHTENMENT

Verse 1.

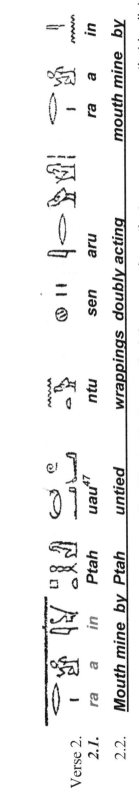

ra	un	ra	n	Asar	sesh	Any	Djemediu	Un
chapter	*opening*	*mouth*	*of*	*Osiris*	*scribe*	*Any*	*Speech*	*Open*

1.1. ra un ra n Asar sesh Any Djemediu Un

1.2. *chapter opening mouth of Osiris scribe Any Speech Open*

1.3. This is the chapter of the Ancient Egyptian Book of Enlightenment is for opening the mouth of the Osiris, who is, in this case, the scribe by the name, Any. Opening the mouth means opening the mind to unobstructed higher consciousness. These are the words to be said that accomplish the desired opening process of higher consciousness.

Verse 2.

2.1. ra a in Ptah uau⁴⁷ untied ntu sen aru wrappings doubly acting ra a in

Mouth mine by Ptah untied   *wrappings doubly acting*   *mouth mine by*

2.2. *Mouth mine by Ptah*

2.3. My mouth is opened by the God Ptah. He has untied the wrappings that were over my mouth (dually) as I was wrapped as a mummy, to free my lower conscience and my higher consciousness, from the wrappings that were blocking my mouth, shutting me in to the miserable, limited and mortal existence. Those wrappings were placed over my mouth by

THE GOD PTAH

151

⁴⁷ Alternative spelling

What does Ptah provide?

1- Transliteration
Ptah resu anab f

Translation
Ptah south of his wall

2- Transliteration
Di f ankh was

Translation
He gives life and power

3- Transliteration
Di n ankh, djed, was neb
Senab neb awet ab neb
N nesu biti Kheper Ka Ra

Translation

I give life, spiritual stability, and all power
All health and expansion of heart (for)
To the king "Kheper Ka Ra" (a title of Senusert I: The coming into being of the essence of Ra)

Translate

4. He gives life, stability and power like Ra

5. the good god (the Pharaoh)

6. Senusert (brother of goddess Usert

7. gives life and power

8 divine embrace

9. beloved, gives life stability, power and health all the days, [like] Ra

---

Translation for Lesson 17

Transliterate

4. *Di ankh djed was mi Ra*   ankh, djed, was

5. *neter nefer*

6. *Senusert*   ankh, djed, was

7. *di ankh was*

8. *hept*   ankh, djed, was

9. *mer di ankh djed was senab neb ra* [mi]

Verse 3.

3.1. **Neter nut a ai ar - f Djehuty meh aper m hekau**

3.2. *the God town mine. Comes that he Lord Djehuty full, equipped Means of words of power*

3.3. the God of my town, of my local time and space residence, who refers me to time and space and physical human existence. But now comes in Lord Djehuty, filled and equipped with words of power that have the capacity to remove obstacles and transform the mind, and he is

THE GOD DJEHUTY

Verse 4.

4.1. **uhau ntu sen n Setesh saiu Ra - a chesef - tu**

4.2. *loaded. that double of Set fetter mouth mine. Repulsion – that*

4.3. loaded with those powers to assist the worthy spiritual aspirant to overcome that which binds the mouth doubly, the fetters of Set. However, there is a force that repulses that blocking, that obstruction from the fetters of Set.

THE GOD SET

153

EGYPTIAN BOOK OF THE DEAD HIEROGLYPH TRANSLATIONS FOR ENLIGHTENMENT

Verse 5.

5.1.	**Tem**	**uden**	**n - f**	**zenu**	**- f**	**saiu**	**Set**
5.2.	***Tem***	***tears down/apart***	***of he***	***those***	***his***	***fetters***	***Set***

5.3.   The God Tem, the Lord of Heliopolis(Anu) the site of the first creation, Ra's royal city, and third Aspect of Ra who brings to a successful completion the spiritual journey, he is there to tear down those fetters of Set.

THE GOD TEM

Verse 6.

6.1.	**Un**	**ra - a**	**wepu**	**ra - a**	**ar**	**Shu**	**m**	**uat -f**	**tuy**
6.2.	***Open***	***mouth mine***	***open/clear/expand***	***mouth mine***	***by***	***Shu***	***through harpoon***	***his***	***that***

6.3.   Opened is my mouth with clarity and expansion; my conscious awareness is expanded, owing to Shu who used his one-pointed harpoon, the non-dual vision of spirit, that pierces and destroys the ignorance of duality in me. He did this with

THE GOD SHU

One-pointed harpoon

154

What does Shu Provide?

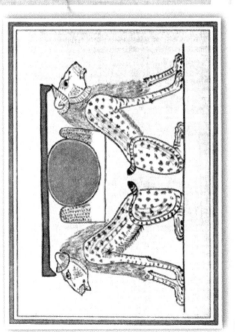

- Separates Geb and Nut -- Air and space (ether} --Heh-- millions

- So Shu is to be worshipped with beautiful fragrances, oils and incense. He is in the air. He is in the space between objects and he connects heaven to earth.

- You should practice breathing exercises. These exercises allow one to discover the subtlety of breath and that leads to the subtlety of higher energies and planes of existence. Watch your breath, allowing it to go on with its normal rhythm.

- *SHU IS A ENTRANCE WAY BETWEEN THE DUALITY OF PHYSICAL EXISTENCE [breath]*

- This teaching is also symbolized in the *Aker* wisdom, the *Aker* symbolism. *Aker is the two lions who sit back to back, and they support on their backs. The sun disk is supported on their backs. Shu and Tefnut are known* as the *Ruty. Shu and Tefnut are known* as the same *Ruty, the two lion god and goddess. The Akerui are known as Sef & Duau, and* The *Akerui [Aker is one, Akerui is two], are the two lions, the Ruty. Shu and Tefnut are known* *also Bakau & Manu, the* mountain of the morning is Bakau and the mountain of the evening is Manu. Sef is yesterday and Duau is today the present and also the future, in other words, the before and the now and what will be. So the Akerui symbolizes time and space. The sundisk between them is eternity.

What are the "Fetters of Set"?

(What is Saiu Set?)

(i.e., What obstructs your expansion in consciousness?)

saiu Set

"The fetters of Set."

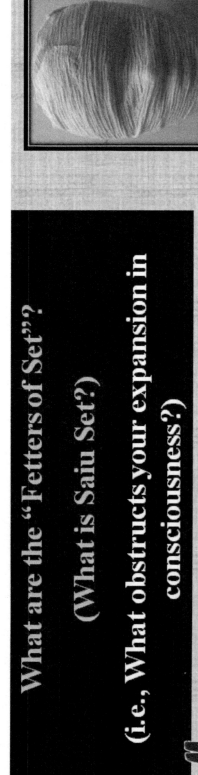

Fetters of Set:

Fear, Insecurity, Worries, Anxieties, Attachment, Lust, Jealousy, Anger, Hatred, Greed, Controlling-type of behaviors, Selfishness, Envy, lack of self control, Impotence - inability to fulfill divine purpose of life - practically and spiritually, Ignorance of the Divine, etc.

156

Verse 7.

ent	baat	n	pet	enty	wep	n - f	er	n	neteru	im se

7.1.

7.2. *the   iron instrument   of   heaven that   opens   for- he   mouth   of   gods & goddesses in cause*

7.3. made of the iron instrument of the gods & goddesses, that fell from the sky,[48] that opens the mouth/mind, in other words, opens consciousness and frees the mind from the delusions of egoism.

Verse 8.A

8.1. A- **nuk**   **Sekhemit hems**   **a**   **her**   **m**   **imt**   **- urt**

8.2. A- *I am*   *Sekhemit sit*   *I person pedestal in*   *-great*

8.3. A- I am the goddess Sekhemit who sits on the great pedestal of Maat, the source of the

Verse 8-B

8.1. B   **naf**   **aahta**   **ent**   **pet**   **nuk**

8.2. B   ***wind, the magnanimous heavens.   I am***

8.3. B   wind of life of the great heavens and allows the strength to sustain life and the spiritual strength to attain victory and enlightenment. That is who I am

Goddess
Sekhemit

157

[48] Scientifically, iron is a metal forged in stars and emitted by them into space where they can become parts of forming planets by coalescing with other elements or falling on planets as meteorites. In Ancient Egyptian Religion, iron is recognized as a heavenly/solar element, also related to the region of the sky where stars are always visible(never resting/setting stars) , meaning do not fall and rise at the horizon; so when the ritual and wisdom of this instrument touches the mouth of the initiate it opens the mind to steady and not fluctuating consciousness such as waking consciousness that fluctuates between waking and sleep. Thus, removes obstructions allowing liberty of Spirit to express freely in time and space.

What does Sekhemit Provide?

From the
Scripture:
Story
Of Hetheru &
Djehuty

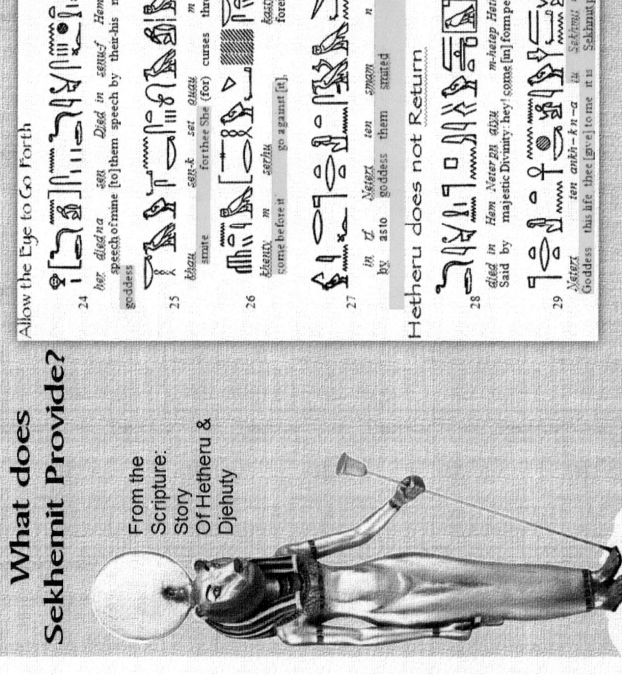

Allow the Eye to Go Forth

24 *her. died na   sen   Died in   senu-f   Hem-f   dishm   arat*
speech of mine [to] them   speech by   their-his   majesty he. Allow go forth eye
goddess

25 *than   sen-k   set   quau   m   dju   an qit*
smite   for thee She (for)   curses   through mountains death no eye

26 *khenty   m   serhu   kasty   has   m   Hetheru*
come before it   go against [it].   foreign lands   moving   form Hetheru

27 *in   it   Neteri   ten   smam   n   s-rawigiu   heri*
by   as to   goddess   them   smited   caused men and graves in desert
women

Hetheru does not Return

28 *died in   Hem   Neter pu   aiu   m-hetep Hetheru au ten.   Died   in*
Said by   majestic Divinity: hey! some [in] form peace Hetheru deeds done. Said by

29 *Neteri   ten   ankh-kn-a   iu   Sekhaut   n   remigiu   iu   ngim*
Goddess   this life   thee [give] to me   it is   Sekhaut power on men and woman [is] sweet

158

Verse 9.

9.1.

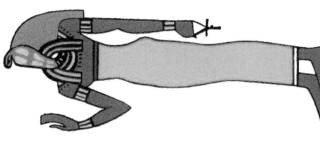

| *Sahyt* | *urt* | *her* | *ab* | *bau* | *Anu* | *ar* | *hekau* |

9.2. *Sah*   *Great,*   *the innermost person in the heart of souls in Heliopolis.*   *As (for)*   *Hekau*

9.3. The Ultimate Understanding Goddess and the innermost reality who is the heart of the souls of Heliopolis(Anu) the site of the first

creation, Ra's royal city;; As for the Words of Power

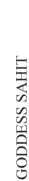

GODDESS SAHIT

What does Saahit Provide?

Saah = understanding

Sahu = Divinity of Orion (Asar)

Saahyt = Goddess of Orion (aspect of Aset)

Saah and Uadjit

Worshipping Heru at his birth

Artu = Aset & Nebthet)

Aset

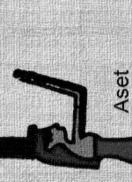

Saahyt

Sba

Uadjit

Understanding

illumination

Serpent Power

Ur   Great

Verse 10.

10.1. | neb | medtu | neb | djedu | er | a | sut | aha | neteru | er | ze - n
all | words | all | spoken | about me | those, | stand up | gods & goddesses | about that they

10.2. **all words spoken against me, the company of gods and goddesses will stand up for me against those negative words that**

10.3. seek to name me as having lived unrighteously,

Verse 11.

11.1. | pauty | neteru | demdyu
the company of gods & goddesses together!

11.2. **the company of gods & goddesses together!**

11.3. the company of gods & goddesses will stand up for me, united in force on my behalf, due to my faith, virtue and

knowing the wisdom of this chapter!

The Signature
Teaching of Chap 11

Saiu Set	Ra	Kemn
Fetters of Set	Mouth	Ignorance
Abu Neteru	Un ra	Maa kheru
Purity through Gods and Goddesses of Chap 11	Mouth opens	Truth o Speech (i.e. Enlightenment)
Djedu	Aha	Neteru
Words (witnessing about the life of the initiate)	Protection and support from the	Gods and Goddesses

Coffin Text: Invocation 714: Becoming Nun, The primeval Ocean

Original translation by Muata Ashby © 2011

Figure 28: Samples of Ancient Egyptian Coffins

Original Text	Transliteration	Translation [Word for word]	Translation [Contextual]
Verse 1	1.1	1.2	1.3
	Nu K Nun	I am Nun	I am the god Nun,
	Ua anut	One not	The Only One, without a second or
	ua Nun - F	One Nun self	another as I am Nun himself
Verse 2	2.1	2.2	2.3
	Ch p r	Chepera [Khepera] the Creator	I am Khepera the Creator who created Creation
	er n a im	As to of me in/as	As concerns Myself, I performed the creation through
Verse 3	3.1	3.2	3.3
	Z P	deed	a grand thing that was done by me. I came into being by creating Creation out of myself, from my own fullness, which is the primeval ocean [undifferentiated consciousness]. So just as I am full, the Creation I created out of myself is also full of me and as me.
	Ur n meht	great of fullness	
	A Cheper r N A	me creator as to of me	

Original Text	Transliteration	Translation [Word for word]	Translation [Contextual]
Verse 4	4.1	4.2	4.3
	Nuk	I Am	I am the Creator, himself, who places creation in place (equivalent) for the God [Creation is there as manifestation of God out of God and Created by God out of himself] {God and Creation are equivalent, one and the same; so God was in the place where time and space (the Universe) is currently but Creation is composed of God so they are equivalent: actually the same thing in different form}
	P	The	
	a		
	Cheper	Creator	
	F	He	
	Djb	Exchange	
	n	of	
	n	to	
	Tj	[determ.] encompassing/encircling]	
	Neter	[determ.] God	
Verse 5	5.1	5.2	5.3
	Im	Within	…from… within himself.
	Suht	Egg	That Creation came forth from his egg from which sprang forth Creation of the Divine self [God]
	f	He	
	Neter	God	
Verse 6	6.1	6.2	6.3
	Nuk	I Am	I am the same one; the God of the inundation, the primeval waters, which itself is me, who was in it, in the primeval waters from which all Creation was brought forth by me.
	a	Me	
	Sha	Inundation	
	Im	In	
	Nu	Nun	

Original Text	Transliteration	Translation [Word for word]	Translation [Contextual]
Verse 7	7.1	7.2	7.3
	M A K Heh u Neter P er n a	Behold The god Hehu [determ.]The divinity Going forth Of me	Behold, it is the god Hehu, the primeval winds that stirred up the primeval ocean and caused waves to take shape into the forms of Creation. He goes out from me to do the work of creation.
Verse 8	8.1	8.2	8.3
	M a k U Dj A a	Behold Vitality I	Behold! I am the vitality, the Life Giving fire, life force, strength, soundness, health, etc…of Creation.
Verse 9	9.1	9.2	9.3
	S Cheper er N A Hau A m Achu A	Caused to be created as to of I Body parts mine Through Shining spirits mine	I have been the source and reason that created Creation from my body parts, which are the elements that gave rise to the objects of Creation…by means of my spirits which enliven all things in Creation.

Original Text	Transliteration	Translation [Word for word]	Translation [Contextual]
Verse 10	10.1	10.2	10.3
	Nu	I	I am the maker of building, fashioning things and also the one who tears them down, so I am the Creator/Destroyer of Creation as I see fit to do with things, [the objects of Creation], that are mine; to do with as I please, in accordance with my heart's desire.
	K	Am	
	A		
	Aru	Actions	
	A	I	
	Chem	Build/teardown	
	n		
	u		
	A	I	
	er	As to	
	Merr	Please/heart's desire	
	A	I	
	Cht	Things	
	F	he	
	Ab	Heart	
	A	mine	

Chapter 31/64 of the Ancient Egyptian Book of the Dead translated by Dr. Muata Ashby and presented at the 2008 Neterian Conference

From Papyrus Auf Ankh

168

Highlights of Chapter 31/64

Title of Chapter 31/64

Title

T1.1 *Ra n pert m Hru   m   Ra ua*

T1.2 *Chapters of coming forth as Light in chapter one*

T1.3 The Chapter of Knowing That Is To Be Known To Attain Enlightenment:

All In One Chapter

Chapter 31/64 Verse 1-2

Verse 1A	Transliteration 1A.1	Translation 1A.2
	Medu	These words are to be said
	in	by
	Asar	Asar
	Iu-f	It is he / living flesh
	ankh	living
	uhem	Again
	nuk	I
	sef ra	yesterday / lion god
	iu A	It is me
	Rech	know
	-	-
	a	I
	nehpu	Yesterday/tomorrow
	cha	Shining

Verse 1B	Transliteration 1B.1	Translation 1B.2
	Herd	Personality
	mestu f	birth His
	m	through
	kyzpch	Again
	-	-
	Shta	Mystery
	Ba	Soul

1A-B.3 Translation Contextual

These words are to be said by
Osiris Living In The Flesh {Living Flesh Of Osiris}. It is he
who lives again, and has not died. These are his words:

I am yesterday, It is me, I also know tomorrow."

He is an enlightened personality by virtue of having been
born again, a second time, now beyond worldly life and
into spiritual consciousness.

What has been said, just now, is a great mystery of the
soul and what comes next will elaborate further.

Figure 29: The Divinities of Past and Future and Present

Yesterday and Tomorrow

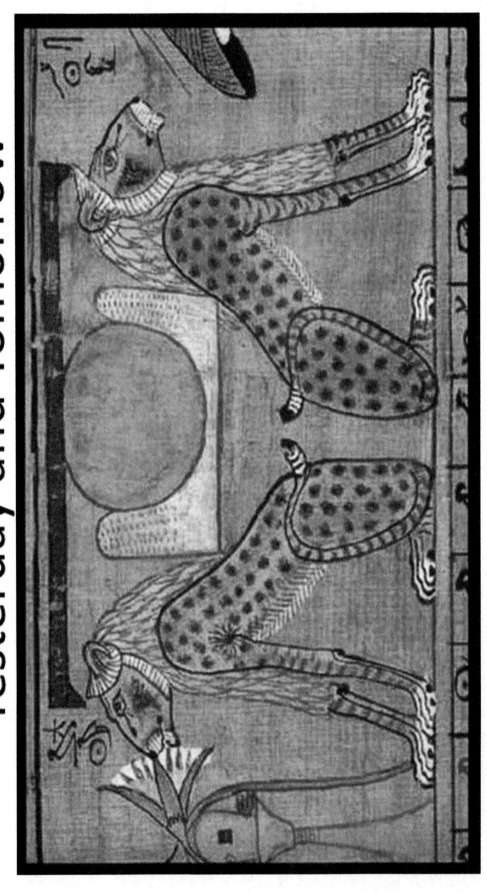

The divinities of yesterday and tomorrow and the horizon with sundisk symbolize the trinity of time (past and future) as well as the eternal present. Knowing the past and the future means transcending time. The ever-shining sun symbolizes fullness of spirit and conscious awareness, consciousness that does not fluctuate as opposed to the moon which symbolizes fluctuations in consciousness (cycle of conscious, unconscious, then conscious again, etc.) The lion divinities are related to Akher, the double leonine divinities Shu and Tefnut, the first children of Ra symbolizing air, wind, space, light, male generative power of Spirit and moisture, life force and female generative power of Creation.

THEMES: Identification–Nuk Pu

Verse 4B	Transliteration 4B.1	Translation 4B.2	Translation-Contextual 4B.3
	Her	Personality heavenly	The heavenly person in the inner shrine is the heart, the essence, the source. This is the Divine Self, the God Asar who is no longer lying horizontal in a repose of death; rather, this personality has been raised erect, strong as a wall and I identify with that: *He is I and I am he! We are one and the same, inexorably tied together.*
	Her ab	Shrine Heart of	
	kerau	shrine	
	aha	standing	
	m	in/through	
	um	raised	
	t – ta	wall	
	n – tef	The he;	
	pu nuk	That I am	
	Tjsy wedjb	tied reciprocally {formula}	

Text emphasis by Dr. Muata Ashby

tf	he	*He*
pu	is	*is*
nuk	me	*I*
tjsy	tied to	*and*
wdjb	each other	*I am he*

Tjsy-knoted together/reciprocal

EGYPTIAN BOOK OF THE DEAD HIEROGLYPH TRANSLATIONS FOR ENLIGHTENMENT

Verse 7A	Transliteration 7A.1	Translation 7A.2	Translation-Contextual 7A.3
	tek	Coming towards, entering, the Divinity	When entering to see the Divinity, the special words should enter the ears like medicine. When in the Duat (Netherworld), there should be no sin, no taint of wrongdoing against you from the mother. The mother is the heart, which accumulates the sum total of the actions of the past, {aryu} that impel and compel the fate of the future of the soul. This is for me a protection against a negative fate after death.
	n neter		
	djedtu	words	
	sedjm	heard	
	mes-tjeru	ears, - [pun with Medicine]	
	a	mine	
	m duat	In the Duat	
	an iutu	not is sin, evil, wrong	
	zer du	little things given, bad	
	neb	all	
	mut	Mother**	
	a	my	
	r – ten n	to you	
	hemu	to but, to gore with horns	
	makit-u	protections	

Themes:
•Coming Close to The Divine

•Sins of the Mother

See this Chapter 31/64 verse: 20D-21A, Verse 34 & Chapter 30A (section) Pert-m-Heru

174

** About the concept of the heart as mother of a persons destiny-

Mother

Translation-Contextual

Not is there found in me any going in the wrong direction, against righteousness; and that has allowed there to be no reason for me to cry as I face the judgment based on my actions {aryu} while alive on earth, in the past or in previous lives.

THEMES: No Crying (cause for suffering)-Purity of Feeling through participation in divine rituals and festival (Devotion to the Divine)

I see through my journeys of this life and lifetimes and I witnessed the rituals and festival of the last quarter of the month, a most important one in the city of Osiris and the appearance of the journey of the divine boat, which increased my devotion and spiritual purity. {carrying of the divine boat at the festivals}

Verse 9B	Transliteration	Translation
	an gem	Not find
	m – a	in I
	un	going wrong
	im	through
	r – remí	Crying
	–	-
	maa – a	See I
	m	through
	seqdut	sailings
	–	-
	denaut Heb	Last quarter of month festival
	Abd	City of Osiris

THEMES: Identification- Nuk Pu-with the Devourer

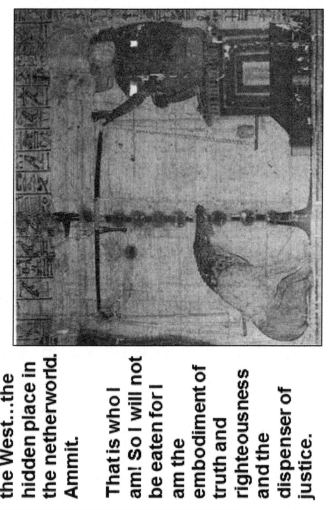

Verse 20B	20B.1 Transliteration	20B.2 Translation	20B.3 Translation-Contextual
	Nz	Devourer	The devourer who watches over the balance so as to eat the hearts of unrighteous souls in the in the region of the West…the hidden place in the netherworld. Ammit.
	pu	That	
	m	In	
	Amunt	hidden residence	
	nuk	I am	That is who I am! So I will not be eaten for I am the embodiment of truth and righteousness and the dispenser of justice.

176

Verse 20D-21A	20D-21A.1 Transliteration	20D-21A.2 Translation	20D-21A.3 Translation-Contextual
	iu	conceived	I was conceived by the woman (mother) that carried and then laid down the load and then turned away absolutely, without looking back. That is the opposite {reverse} of how people live in the world. So, the mother mind that gage birth to me now goes in a different direction from me and I am free from that path of worldly delusion.
	r – a	I	
	usekad	Lay down	
	p –fai	p-the, fai-[det. carry], [det. Force], [scroll -det. Abstract]	
	s-mes	Cause to give birthing	
	hu	Turn away [emphatic] +reverse legs [det.]	
		[Det. –woman/She [mother]]	
	sekd	Turn upside down	

THEMES: Dispassion, Detachment and Forsaking the values of the worldly minded. Turning away from the usual worldly desires engendered by the mother that gave rise to the personalities desires (the aryu in the heart).

177

EGYPTIAN BOOK OF THE DEAD HIEROGLYPH TRANSLATIONS FOR ENLIGHTENMENT

Verse 22B	22B.1 Transliteration	22B.2 Translation	22B.3 Translation-Contextual
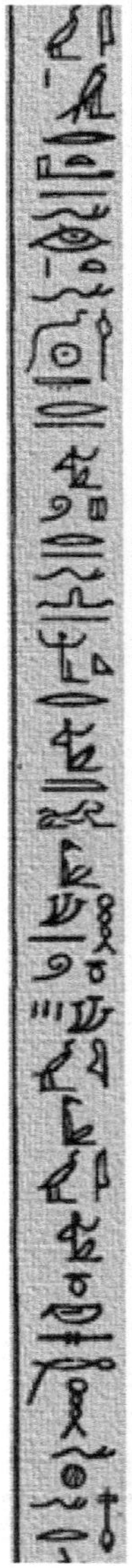	iu	It is	It is Heru, whose eye shines on the earth. That name, "Heru", is my name. {i.e. Heru, the God, and I are one and the same}
	her r-tan-f	Heru that of his	
	arit-f	eye his	
	wdj-ta	shine earth	
	ren – a	name mine	
	pu ren – f	that name his!	
	an qa	Not exalted	In comparison to me, in the form of the lion God, there is nothing more exalted. The name is *Blossoms of Shu*, i.e. "Light".
	r – a	in relation to me	
	m – ru	in form as lion god	
	henu	"Blossoms of Shu 'Light'"	
	Shu	The god Shu	That is the god Shu, who is a manifestation of Ra, and expression of air, its power, vitality and space/ether; that is actually my very self. It is I who cause the fullness of Creation and that is the highest good!
	iu – a	it is me	
	Nuk	I	
	z-meh-f	cause -fullness in –him	
	chef nefer	Completion, beautiful/good	

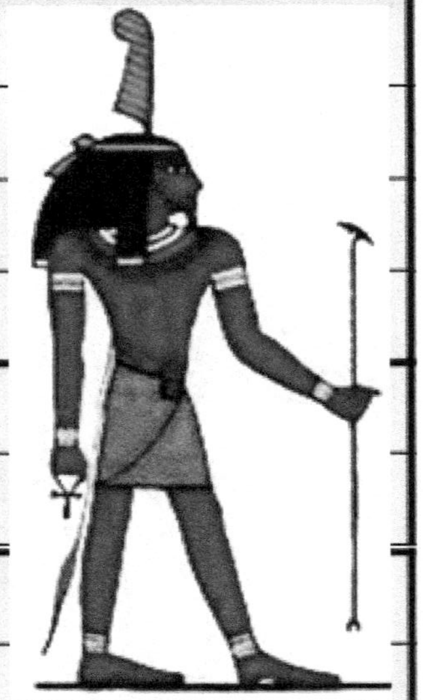

THEMES: Identification-NukPu

178

Verse 28C-29A	28C-29A.1 Transliteration	28C-29A.2 Translation	28C-29A.3 Translation-Contextual
	ru	Lion	I am the lion divinity, that sun divinity, Shu, carrying the Creation in his arms. In Kemet, the venerable land, it is you who are in me and I am in you!
	aton neter	sun divinity	
	fai – ai	carrying with arms	
	im	in	
	ta	the land [Kemet]	
	tjeser	exhaled	
	iu – k	It is thee	
	im – a	in me	
	iu – a	It is I	
	im – k	in thee	

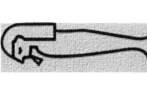

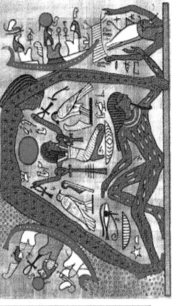

	aru	Image	Your image, your form, that is me!
	k	thine	
	nuk	me	

THEMES: Relationship with the divinity, Identification {Nuk Pu} and Realization {Iu kim-a, iu-a im k}

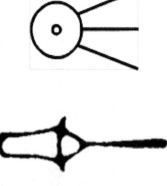

Verse 29C	29C.1 Transliteration	29C.2 Translation	29C.3 Translation-Contextual
	Aqn –a	Go in -I	I go inside, into the region of Sekhem, which is the abode of the Life Force that enlivens the personality through the solar lion power of that divinity. I stay there for a time, purifying and transforming myself with that life force, in that air, in that light, that is Shu; then I come forth now as an enlightened being. Therefore, I am Osiris.
	m	Into	
	Zechmt	Sekhem region –inner shrine, holy of holies, place of leonine power	
	pert – a	going out -I	
	m	form	
	akh	Glorious shining spirit, enlightened being	
	nuk	I am	
	Asar	Osiris	

THEME: Becoming Akh through Sekhem

There are 9 parts to the human personality. Sekhem, the vital life force, is an aspect of the human personality. [see section: "The Elements of the Human Personality"]
The Sekhem is the Life Force or Power that exists in the universe. The symbol of Sekhem is the hand held staff pictured at right. When used in worldly terms it refers to a scepter that means physical power, authority and strength. In spiritual terms, the Sekhem is the power or spiritual personification of the vital Life Force in humans, derived from God Ra through the leonine aspect of the divinity Shu. Its dwelling place is in the heavens (astral plane) with the Akhu (Shining Spirits), but all life draws upon this force in order to exist. Sekhem also denotes the potency, the erectile power or force of the quality of lion nature used in fashioning one's own glorious new body for resurrection.

180

Verse 30	30.1 Transliteration	30.2 Translation	30.3 Translation-Contextual
	iu – f	It is he	It is that Divinity that is the source of my life. Truly that is also the source sustaining the manifestations of all people.
	ankh – a	life I	
	maakheru	truthfully	
	maa	see	
	aru	forms	
	remtju	people	This mystery teaching of this chapter will make a person attain spiritual victory, i.e., enlightenment. That person will be a controller, a master while on earth. In the Netherworld it means assuming all forms; realizing oneness with all things. This realization of oneness is a protection from the Great Divinity, preventing any adverse action from any form since a form that is oneself would not hurt oneself.
	djeta	forever	
	ar	As to	
	gerr	Mastery	
	ra pen	chapter this one	
	z-maakheru –f –	Causes -truth of speech [of] –person	
	pu her tpy ta	that person controller on earth	
	m Netergert	In Netherworld	
	iu – f	It is -person	
	ari – f	Doing [that] –person	
	aru neb n	forms all the	
	ankhu	living	
	makit	protections	This chapter was found…
	pu ent	this the	
	Neter aah	Divinity Great	
	Gemtu	Found	

Theme: Being rooted in Divinity

EGYPTIAN BOOK OF THE DEAD HIEROGLYPH TRANSLATIONS FOR ENLIGHTENMENT

Verse 30D-31	30D-31.1 Transliteration	30D-31.2 Translation	30D-31. Translation-Contextual
	Gemtu	Found	This chapter was found in the city of Khemenu inscribed on the soles of the feed of the god of Khemenu, Lord Djehuty in iron, which comes from the stars as a gift of the Divine ((Iron is a meteorite metal forged in the sun).
	ra khemnu	chapter [in] Khemenu	
	her deb	personality [Djehuty] soles of feet	
	pent / bau	One who / Iron	
	Sesh m	writings in	These writings were in blue color on the soles of the feet of the Divinity, the blue color of transcendental consciousness.
	chezbed	[in] blue	
	geru	Possessor	
	n ~ Neter pen	Of Divinity this	
	Gem m	Found in	These writings were found in the time of the Pharaoh Menkaura {Old Kingdom} who is spiritually victorious.
	hu	Time	
	n ~nesu bity	Of -ruler of upper and lower Egypt [Pharaoh]	
	Menkau-Ra	One established in the Ka of Ra	
	Maakheru erta	True of speech related to	Now, the prince Hardidif, who was then functioning as a priest...
	n – Suten sa	The -royal son	
	Hardidif	Heru the giver	
	im ~ f zm	In form -he priest	

Theme: PROVENANCE of this chapter, the artefact for the ritual of enlightenment and the color of enlightenment.

182

EGYPTIAN BOOK OF THE DEAD HIEROGLYPH TRANSLATIONS FOR ENLIGHTENMENT

Verse 32	32.1 Transliteration	32.2 Translation	32.3 Translation-Contextual
	chet	Penetrating/visiting	Going into temples to inspect them in the capacity of overseer, for himself; this chapter penetrated this person and he became introspective, prayerful, awestruck and engaged in meditative trance for a period of time.
	menmen	Firm places [temples]	
	r	Purpose	
	arit	eyewitness	
	sap	inspecting	
	m -rau	In chapters	
	tu	It is	
	chet	Penetration	
	hna –f	With -he	
	her	Person	
	dbhu	Prayer / awestruck, transfixed	
	su	He and or period of time	He then brought the scripture on a sledge in a box of copper, to the King and presented this writing containing the Great Mystery to him in private.
	m	in	
	s-uash	Worship	
	ini –f	Bringing he	
	su m unsh	in sledge (copper)	
	tu n Suten	to the Pharaoh	
	cheft maa –f	Before [him] see -he	
	nty her	without anyone [else]	
	z-zsheta	causing -writings mystery	
	pu aah medjet	this [is a] Great! [mystery] [det. Scroll]	sledge

Theme: Realization of the wisdom of this chapter, Transfixion

Verse 33	33 Transliteration	33 Translation	33 Translation-Contextual
	an maa an sedm	Seeing no more, hearing no more	When the looking with eyes stops, the hearing stops; when the outgoing speech (thought process) is turned to inwards and when there is abstaining from sex relations and when no meat or fish is consumed...
	sekd	reverse speaking	
	ra hn ab	Chapter recite, clean	
	n turi	of purity	
	an tekn	Not coming to, to enter, invade	
	m	into	
	hemetu	women	
	an imyu	not meat	This chapter is to be recited and an amulet of a scarab, purified with gold, symbolizing being anchored in fullness of heart (mind), immortality and establishment in the spiritual personality. This amulet is placed over the heart and its wisdom in the unconscious mind.
	hy remu	foodstuff, fish	
	ask khepr	Thus a scarab of	
	rr Sa n	as to	
	Mehp mendnu	fullness, mooring post (placed)	
	z – ab	cause -cleansing	
	m nub	in gold	
	er – ta – m	this -thing -in	A person should do this....
	het ab n	chamber heart of	
	za ari n f	person do this for	

Theme: PREPARATION

Withdrawal of the senses and inward reflection, abstinence, vegetarianism and ritual meditation.

EGYPTIAN BOOK OF THE DEAD HIEROGLYPH TRANSLATIONS FOR ENLIGHTENMENT

Verse 34	34.1 Transliteration	34.2 Translation	34.3 Translation-Contextual
[hieroglyphs]	awet ra sshedu	opening mouth (ceremony), bound up	…for the ritual of opening the mouth, together with a jar with water from the head of the celestial waters, the speech of a person should be the words of power thusly…
	m znu m	in jar in	
	tepy nui	head of celestial waters	
	djedu her f m	Speech of person through	
	Hekau	words of power	

	Ab Ab
	a – n a – n
	Mut Mut
	a a
		Say twice: Heart Heart
		            My - the My - the
		            Mother Mother
		            Mine Mine
			My heart my mother, {say twice}, the heart in my breast, the repository of the record of my past deeds upon which the Great Judgment is based, that decides my fate, and through which I transform and manifest in varied incarnations and forms; do not stand up as a witness against me when I come before the councils of gods and goddesses who judge the soul. And do not turn away…

	Haty ab ua	Breast heart mine	
	m kheperu a	Through transformation mine	
	m aha r a	Manifest [not] standing up as to me	
	m met	as witness	
	m chesf	in form of opposing	
	er – a	Referring to -me	
	m djedja nutu	Manner of councils	
	m r	Manner speaking	
	chaa	turn away from (against)	

185

EGYPTIAN BOOK OF THE DEAD HIEROGLYPH TRANSLATIONS FOR ENLIGHTENMENT

Verse 35	35.1 Transliteration	35.2 Translation	35.3 Translation-Contextual
	Ar –a	Referring to -me	from me when I come into the presence of the "Master of the scales", Lord Anubis.
	m mbah	In presence of	
	ari-makhat	Master -of the Scale (Lord Anpu)	
	tek- ka	Thine -personality	O Lord Anubis, your very being is in my body.
	m khat a	in body mine	The cosmic force of the god Khnum, the virile Creator, is in me is my vitality.
	Khnum	The god Khnum	
	z-udja	causes -vitality	
	hau-a	body -mine	
	Per k	Going forth thee	As you go forth to the "Good House"; as to the coffin's dwelling place, may there be no indignations against me; may no disgrace come to my name from them {the council}, and the lord of eternity.
	r bhet	to the house	
	nefer	goodness/beneficent	
	Han-nu	coffin	
	kenu im	Indignations, in	
	Zet	they, them	
	sheptu	disgrace	
	ren – a	name -mine	
	shenynu	Ra/Asar lord of eternity	

Theme: DECLARATION

186

Verse 36	36.1 Transliteration	36.2 Translation	36.3 Translation-Contextual
	rr – au	About -me	As pertaining to me, this means standing as a positive witness in the house of goodness, experiencing happiness there and as I have been judged righteous through the words of power that I possess and am a master of, that provide purity of heart that affords knowledge and immortality.
	m aha ua	by means of standing	
	m met	as witness	
	aha – f –m	Stand -he -in	
	Bhet neferu	the house of goodness	
	m	Manifest as	
	awet	happiness	
	n tu dja	to the judge	
	m	through	As pertaining to me, this means I am a Divinity and a protected being; I am your child, you who exist within there (House of Goodness, i.e. Osiris).
	djed	words	
	ger	Possessor or master	
	r – a	as to- me	
	r – m Neter aah	as to -being Divine, a god/goddess great	Therefore, I am pure being, a divinity knowing myself as your offspring and your very existence, one with you, I here and you there, I am you and you are me.
	makit	protections	
	sa – k	child -thine	
	un – tj	existing -there	

Theme: **CULMINATION of the mystic quest**

Chapter 30A (section) Pert-m-Heru: The Heart as Cause of Incarnation, Ma'at as the path of Enlightenment

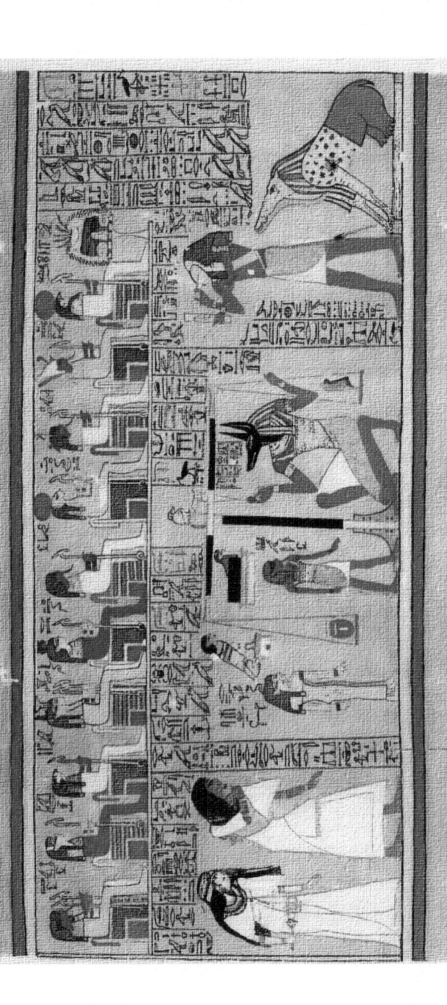

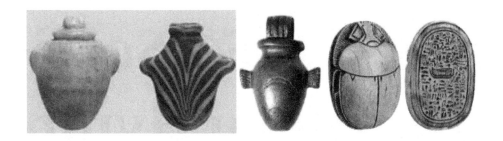

Verse 1.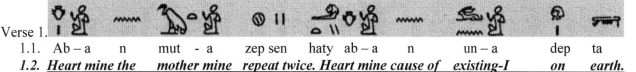

1.1. Ab – a   n   mut - a   zep sen   haty ab – a   n   un – a   dep ta

*1.2. **Heart mine the**   **mother mine**   **repeat twice. Heart mine cause of**   **existing-I**   **on**   **earth.***

1.3. My heart, my mother, my heart, my mother. My heart which is the mother which gives birth to my desires that cause my soul's coming into human incarnation.

Verse 2.

2.1. m   aha   er   a   m   **meteru**   rem   neb   chetu

*2.2. **Manner rising**   **not**   **me**   **by**   **obstructing**   **as witness**   **in presence**   **lord judgment balance***

2.3. At the time of my judgment in the Hall of Maati, in the presence of the lord of the judgment, Lord Anubis (Anpu), when you step up to bear witness about me, oh my heart, the place in my unconscious mind, wherein are stored impressions of my past, the sum total of my thoughts, feelings and actions over many lifetimes, do not obstruct my spiritual journey by bearing witness about negative things I may have done while alive in the land of the living, since I strived to follow Maat and a life or righteousness, order and truth; so there should be no negative things to bear witness about.

Verse 3.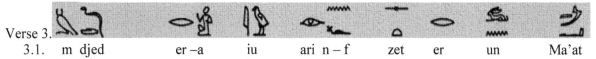

3.1. m   djed   er –a   iu   ari n – f   zet   er   un   Ma'at

*3.2. **Manner speaking about me**   **it is**   **worked he against the**   **about**   **absolute**   **right & truth, order, justice.***

3.3. When you speak about me, report about me as one who lived in a manner not against what is real, what really exists, the ever-presence, abiding reality, God, as what is real and not the illusory world of time and space as if it were an abiding reality. So do not speak about me as being an advocate of that which is egoistic, self-serving, against truth, such as the ideal of greed, callousness and the idea of physical vanity ignoring the ephemeral nature of life and dismissing the infinite and immortal spirit, Neter, beyond the ephemeral time and space relative reality of life. Bear witness about me as one who lived in a manner not against what is right & truth, order, and justice.

Chapter 7/151 Section 3 Pert-m-Heru Hymn by Aset from PertemHeru-Translation by Dr. Muata Ashby (C)2000-2013 Sema Institute

From Papyrus Ani

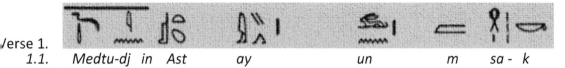

Verse 1.
1.1. Medtu-dj in Ast   ay   un   m   sa - k

1.2. _Words spoken by Aset   coming   being   in form   protection -thine_

1.3. These words are spoken by Goddess Isis: "I come to you in a role as your protector

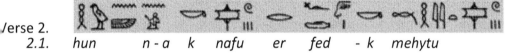

Verse 2.
2.1. hun   n - a   k   nafu   er   fed   - k   mehytu

2.2. _rejuvenation blow of I thee   liberating air for cleansing nose yours, fullness_

2.3. I blow, from me to you, the liberating and rejuvenating air from the north, with fullness of

consciousness, which cleanses your nose,

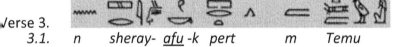

Verse 3.
3.1. n   sheray- _afu_ -k pert   m   Temu

3.2. _the   nostrils [for] body part yours comes in form of Temu_

3.3. to the nostrils for your body. This air comes in the form of the god Temu, who is in the north,

which is the spirit essence of Ra, the source and sustenance of all life and the successful

completion of the spiritual journey.

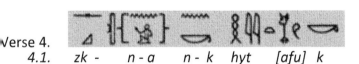

Verse 4.
4.1. zk -   n - a   n - k   hyt   [afu] k

4.2. _Gathered   to/by me to/for - thee throat body part thine_

4.3. I have collected the pieces of your throat for you so you can breathe and live. I pieced your throat

back together and cleared obstructions to the air from Temu that conveys the vital life force. So

now you have the capacity to experience unobstructed vitality; now you do not have internal

obstructions to existing as a conscious living being.

Verse 5.

5.1.   erdy   n - a   un   n - k   m   Neter

5.2.   <u>*given from I*</u>   <u>*being   to thee*</u>   <u>*form of Divine*</u>

5.3.   I have given to you the capacity to exist in the form of a God and

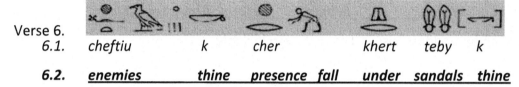

Verse 6.

6.1.   cheftiu   k   cher   khert   teby   k

6.2.   <u>*enemies   thine   presence fall   under sandals thine*</u>

6.3.   in your presence, I present to you your enemies which have fallen under your feet. So now you do not have external obstructions to existing in your divine form.

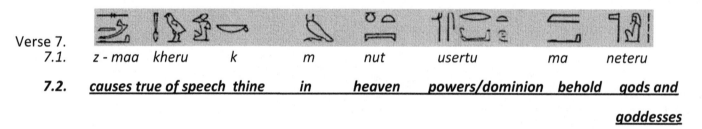

Verse 7.

7.1.   z - maa kheru   k   m   nut   usertu   ma   neteru

7.2.   <u>*causes true of speech thine   in   heaven   powers/dominion behold gods and*</u>

                                                                           <u>*goddesses*</u>

7.3.   By doing these things, I, the goddess of intuitional wisdom, the embodiment of wisdom, have caused for you to have divine state in heaven, over which you have power and dominion and all the gods and goddesses behold you!"

Chapter 12/25 of the Pert-m-Heru: Remembering one's name after death. Translation by Dr. Muata Ashby ©2000-2015

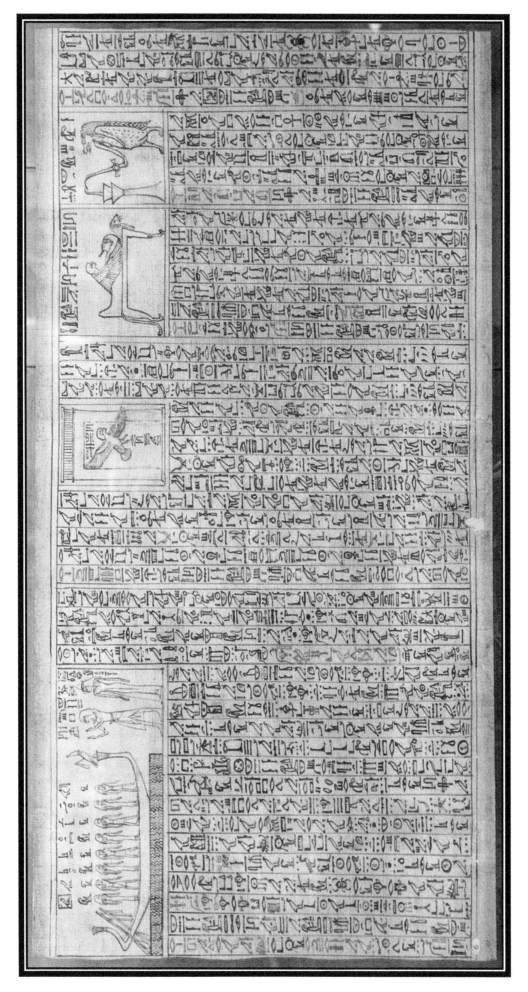

From Papyrus Nebseny

Verse 1.

1.1.	Ra	n	r - dit	s- khau	- a	ren	f	m	Neterkhert
1.2.	*words of*	*giving*	*causing remembrance*			*name*	*(his)*	*in*	*cemetery*

1.3. This is the chapter that provides the activation of remembering one's name while in the cemetery, which is the region of the lower part of heaven, that place that is entered after leaving the land of the living and where the movement towards the inner Netherworld begins.

Verse 2.

2.1.	r -di	n- a	ren	a	m		per	ur
2.2.	*May be given to me name*		*mine*	*in*			*great*	*house.*

2.3. May my name be given to me even while I may still be in my burial chamber as I prepare for the journey into the Duat (Netherworld).

Verse 3.

3.1.	s-kha	a	ren	a	m		per	nezer
3.2.	*May remember*	*I*	*name*	*mine*	*in*		*house*	*fire.*

3.3. May I remember my name, the essence of who I am, when my ethical conscience is tested in the house of fire region of the Netherworld

Verse 4.

4.1.	gereh	puy	n	ap	renptu	n	tenutu	abed
4.2.	*night*	*that*	*of*	*computing*	*years*	*and*	*reckoning*	*months.*

4.3. on the night where takes place the computation and accounting for the deeds done in my time while on earth.

Verse 5.

5.1.	nuk	*amy*	puy	hem	a	her	m	abtet	n
5.2.	*I am*	*within*	*that Divinity.*	*Rest*	*I*	*person*	*in*	*eastern*	*of*

5.3. I am within the Divine Being. I rest myself in the eastern part of

Verse 6.

6.1.	pet	neter	neb	temu	fy	m	saa	djed	ren - f	m	chet
6.2.	*heaven.*	*Deity*	*all*	*obstruct*	*they*	*in;*	*know I*	*speech*	*name -his*		*form advancing.*

6.3. heaven which is where I enter the Netherworld, after exiting the land of the living, in the beautiful west of the land of the living on earth. From the land of the living I go to the Neterkhert and from there I am born into the Netherworld and to discover higher consciousness. So about any god or goddess who may come forward to obstruct my progress in the Netherworld, as I move towards the center where the Supreme Being is, since I know my name, and I also know their names, the essential nature of all of them, which affords power over that which is known, I can speak their names and thereby control and neutralize their powers over me, thus I have the freedom to go forward to my destination, the ultimate abode of the Divine, unobstructed.

INDEX

Other Books From C M Books

P.O.Box 570459
Miami, Florida, 33257
(305) 378-6253 Fax: (305) 378-6253

Prices subject to change.

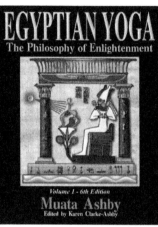

1. *EGYPTIAN YOGA: THE PHILOSOPHY OF ENLIGHTENMENT* An original, fully illustrated work, including hieroglyphs, detailing the meaning of the Egyptian mysteries, tantric yoga, psycho-spiritual and physical exercises. Egyptian Yoga is a guide to the practice of the highest spiritual philosophy which leads to absolute freedom from human misery and to immortality. It is well known by scholars that Egyptian philosophy is the basis of Western and Middle Eastern religious philosophies such as *Christianity, Islam, Judaism,* the *Kabala,* and Greek philosophy, but what about Indian philosophy, Yoga and Taoism? What were the original teachings? How can they be practiced today? What is the source of pain and suffering in the world and what is the solution? Discover the deepest mysteries of the mind and universe within and outside of your self. 8.5" X 11" ISBN: 1-884564-01-1 Soft $19.95

2. *EGYPTIAN YOGA: African Religion Volume 2*- Theban Theology U.S. In this long awaited sequel to *Egyptian Yoga: The Philosophy of Enlightenment* you will take a fascinating and enlightening journey back in time and discover the teachings which constituted the epitome of Ancient Egyptian spiritual wisdom. What are the disciplines which lead to the fulfillment of all desires? Delve into the three states of consciousness (waking, dream and deep sleep) and the fourth state which transcends them all, Neberdjer, "The Absolute." These teachings of the city of Waset (Thebes) were the crowning achievement of the Sages of Ancient Egypt. They establish the standard mystical keys for understanding the profound mystical symbolism of the Triad of human consciousness. ISBN 1-884564-39-9 $23.95

3.   *THE KEMETIC DIET: GUIDE TO HEALTH, DIET AND FASTING* Health issues have always been important to human beings since the beginning of time. The earliest records of history show that the art of healing was held in high esteem since the time of Ancient Egypt. In the early 20th century, medical doctors had almost attained the status of sainthood by the promotion of the idea that they alone were "scientists" while other healing modalities and traditional healers who did not follow the "scientific method' were nothing but superstitious, ignorant charlatans who at best would take the money of their clients and at worst kill them with the unscientific "snake oils" and "irrational theories". In the late 20th century, the failure of the modern medical establishment's ability to lead the general public to good health, promoted the move by many in society towards "alternative medicine". Alternative medicine disciplines are those healing modalities which do not adhere to the philosophy of allopathic medicine. Allopathic medicine is what medical doctors practice by an large. It is the theory that disease is caused by agencies outside the body such as bacteria, viruses or physical means which affect the body. These can therefore be treated by medicines and therapies   The natural healing method began in the absence of extensive technologies with the idea that all the answers for health may be found in nature or rather, the deviation from nature. Therefore, the health of the body can be restored by correcting the aberration and thereby restoring balance. This is the area that will be covered in this volume. Allopathic techniques have their place in the art of healing. However, we should not forget that the body is a grand achievement of the spirit and built into it is the capacity to maintain itself and heal itself. Ashby, Muata ISBN: 1-884564-49-6 $28.95

4.   INITIATION INTO EGYPTIAN YOGA Shedy: Spiritual discipline or program, to go deeply into the mysteries, to study the mystery teachings and literature profoundly, to penetrate the mysteries. You will learn about the mysteries of initiation into the teachings and practice of Yoga and how to become an Initiate of the mystical sciences. This insightful manual is the first in a series which introduces you to the goals of daily spiritual and yoga practices: Meditation, Diet, Words of Power and the ancient wisdom teachings. 8.5" X 11" ISBN 1-884564-02-X Soft Cover $24.95 U.S.

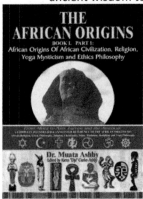

5.   *THE AFRICAN ORIGINS OF CIVILIZATION, RELIGION AND YOGA SPIRITUALITY AND ETHICS PHILOSOPHY* HARD COVER EDITION Part 1, Part 2, Part 3 in one volume 683 Pages Hard Cover First Edition Three volumes in one. Over the past several years I

have been asked to put together in one volume the most important evidences showing the correlations and common teachings between Kamitan (Ancient Egyptian) culture and religion and that of India. The questions of the history of Ancient Egypt, and the latest archeological evidences showing civilization and culture in Ancient Egypt and its spread to other countries, has intrigued many scholars as well as mystics over the years. Also, the possibility that Ancient Egyptian Priests and Priestesses migrated to Greece, India and other countries to carry on the traditions of the Ancient Egyptian Mysteries, has been speculated over the years as well. In chapter 1 of the book *Egyptian Yoga The Philosophy of Enlightenment,* 1995, I first introduced the deepest comparison between Ancient Egypt and India that had been brought forth up to that time. Now, in the year 2001 this new book, *THE AFRICAN ORIGINS OF CIVILIZATION, MYSTICAL RELIGION AND YOGA PHILOSOPHY,* more fully explores the motifs, symbols and philosophical correlations between Ancient Egyptian and Indian mysticism and clearly shows not only that Ancient Egypt and India were connected culturally but also spiritually. How does this knowledge help the spiritual aspirant? This discovery has great importance for the Yogis and mystics who follow the philosophy of Ancient Egypt and the mysticism of India. It means that India has a longer history and heritage than was previously understood. It shows that the mysteries of Ancient Egypt were essentially a yoga tradition which did not die but rather developed into the modern day systems of Yoga technology of India. It further shows that African culture developed Yoga Mysticism earlier than any other civilization in history. All of this expands our understanding of the unity of culture and the deep legacy of Yoga, which stretches into the distant past, beyond the Indus Valley civilization, the earliest known high culture in India as well as the Vedic tradition of Aryan culture. Therefore, Yoga culture and mysticism is the oldest known tradition of spiritual development and Indian mysticism is an extension of the Ancient Egyptian mysticism. By understanding the legacy which Ancient Egypt gave to India the mysticism of India is better understood and by comprehending the heritage of Indian Yoga, which is rooted in Ancient Egypt the Mysticism of Ancient Egypt is also better understood. This expanded understanding allows us to prove the underlying kinship of humanity, through the common symbols, motifs and philosophies which are not disparate and confusing teachings but in reality expressions of the same study of truth through metaphysics and mystical realization of Self. (HARD COVER) ISBN: 1-884564-50-X $45.00 U.S. 81/2" X 11"

6.   *AFRICAN ORIGINS BOOK 1 PART 1* African Origins of African Civilization, Religion, Yoga Mysticism and Ethics Philosophy-Soft Cover $24.95 ISBN: 1-884564-55-0

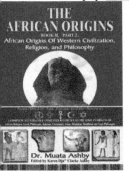

7.   *AFRICAN ORIGINS BOOK 2 PART 2* African Origins of Western Civilization, Religion and Philosophy (Soft) -Soft Cover $24.95 ISBN: 1-884564-56-9

8.   *EGYPT AND INDIA AFRICAN ORIGINS OF Eastern Civilization, Religion, Yoga Mysticism and Philosophy*-Soft Cover $29.95 (Soft) ISBN: 1-884564-57-7

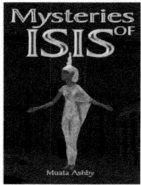

9.   *THE MYSTERIES OF ISIS: **The Ancient Egyptian Philosophy of Self-Realization*** - There are several paths to discover the Divine and the mysteries of the higher Self. This volume details the mystery teachings of the goddess Aset (Isis) from Ancient Egypt- the path of wisdom. It includes the teachings of her temple and the disciplines that are enjoined for the initiates of the temple of Aset as they were given in ancient times. Also, this book includes the teachings of the main myth of Aset that lead a human being to spiritual enlightenment and immortality.   Through the study of ancient myth and the illumination of initiatic understanding the idea of God is expanded from the mythological comprehension to the metaphysical. Then this metaphysical understanding is related to you, the student, so as to begin understanding your true divine nature. ISBN 1-884564-24-0 $22.99

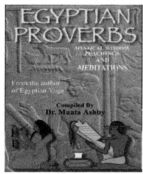

10.   *EGYPTIAN PROVERBS:* collection of —Ancient Egyptian Proverbs and Wisdom Teachings -How to live according to MAAT Philosophy. Beginning Meditation. All proverbs are indexed for easy searches. For the first time in one volume, ——Ancient Egyptian Proverbs, wisdom teachings and meditations, fully illustrated with hieroglyphic text and symbols. EGYPTIAN PROVERBS is a unique collection of knowledge and wisdom which you can put into practice today and transform your life. $14.95 U.S   ISBN: 1-884564-00-3

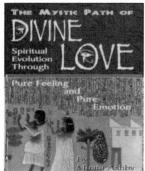

11.   *GOD OF LOVE: THE PATH OF DIVINE LOVE The Process of Mystical Transformation and The Path of Divine Love*   This Volume focuses on the ancient wisdom teachings of "Neter Merri" –the Ancient Egyptian philosophy of Divine Love and how to use them in a scientific process for self-transformation. Love is one of the most powerful human emotions. It is also the source of Divine feeling that unifies God and the individual human being. When love is fragmented and diminished by egoism the Divine connection is lost. The Ancient tradition of Neter Merri leads human beings back to their Divine connection, allowing them to discover their innate glorious self that is actually Divine and immortal. This volume will detail the process of transformation from ordinary consciousness to cosmic consciousness through the integrated practice of the teachings and the path of Devotional Love toward the Divine. 5.5"x 8.5" ISBN 1-884564-11-9 $22.95

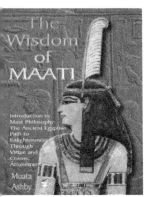

12.   *INTRODUCTION TO MAAT PHILOSOPHY: Spiritual Enlightenment Through the Path of Virtue*   Known commonly as Karma in India, the teachings of MAAT contain an extensive philosophy based on ariu (deeds) and their fructification in the form of shai and renenet (fortune and destiny, leading to Meskhenet (fate in a future birth) for living virtuously and with orderly wisdom are explained and the student is to begin practicing the precepts of Maat in daily life so as to promote the process of purification of the heart in preparation for the judgment of the soul. This judgment will be understood not as an event that will occur at the time of death but as an event that occurs continuously, at every moment in the life of the individual. The student will learn how to become allied with the forces of the Higher Self and to thereby begin cleansing the mind (heart) of impurities so as to attain a higher vision of reality. ISBN 1-884564-20-8 $22.99

13.   *MEDITATION The Ancient Egyptian Path to Enlightenment*   Many people do not know about the rich history of meditation practice in Ancient Egypt. This volume outlines the theory of meditation and presents the Ancient Egyptian Hieroglyphic text which give instruction as to the nature of the mind and its three modes of expression. It also presents the texts which give instruction on the practice of meditation for spiritual Enlightenment and unity with the Divine. This volume allows the reader to begin practicing meditation by explaining, in easy to understand terms, the simplest form of meditation and working up to the most advanced form which was practiced in ancient times and which is still practiced by yogis around the world in modern times. ISBN 1-884564-27-7 $22.99

14.   *THE GLORIOUS LIGHT MEDITATION* TECHNIQUE OF ANCIENT EGYPT New for the year 2000. This volume is based on the earliest known instruction in history given for the practice of formal meditation. Discovered by Dr. Muata Ashby, it is inscribed on the walls of the Tomb of Seti I in Thebes Egypt. This volume details the philosophy and practice of this unique system of meditation originated in Ancient Egypt and the earliest practice of meditation known in the world which occurred in the most advanced African Culture. ISBN: 1-884564-15-1 $16.95 (PB)

15.   *THE SERPENT POWER: The Ancient Egyptian Mystical Wisdom of the Inner Life Force.*   This Volume specifically deals with the latent life Force energy of the universe and in the human body, its control and sublimation. How to develop the Life Force energy of the subtle body. This Volume will introduce the esoteric wisdom of the science of how virtuous living acts in a subtle and mysterious way to cleanse the latent psychic energy conduits and vortices of the spiritual body. ISBN 1-884564-19-4 $22.95

16.   *EGYPTIAN YOGA The Postures of The Gods and Goddesses* Discover the physical postures and exercises practiced thousands of years ago in Ancient Egypt which are today known as Yoga exercises. Discover the history of the postures and how they were transferred from Ancient Egypt in Africa to India through Buddhist Tantrism. Then practice the postures as you discover the mythic teaching that originally gave birth to the postures and was practiced by the Ancient Egyptian priests and priestesses. This work is based on the pictures and teachings from the Creation story of Ra, The Asarian Resurrection Myth and the carvings and reliefs from various Temples in Ancient Egypt 8.5" X 11" ISBN 1-884564-10-0 Soft Cover $21.95 Exercise video $20

17.   *SACRED SEXUALITY: ANCIENT EGYPTIAN TANTRA YOGA: The Art of Sex* Sublimation and Universal Consciousness This Volume will expand on the male and female principles within the human body and in the universe and further detail the sublimation of sexual energy into spiritual energy. The student will study the deities Min and Hathor, Asar and Aset, Geb and Nut and discover the mystical implications for a practical spiritual discipline. This Volume will also focus on the Tantric aspects of Ancient Egyptian and Indian mysticism, the purpose of sex and the mystical teachings of sexual sublimation which lead to self-knowledge and Enlightenment. ISBN 1-884564-03-8 $24.95

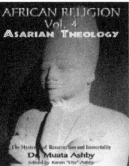

8. *AFRICAN RELIGION Volume 4: ASARIAN THEOLOGY: RESURRECTING OSIRIS* The path of Mystical Awakening and the Keys to Immortality NEW REVISED AND EXPANDED EDITION! The Ancient Sages created stories based on human and superhuman beings whose struggles, aspirations, needs and desires ultimately lead them to discover their true Self. The myth of Aset, Asar and Heru is no exception in this area. While there is no one source where the entire story may be found, pieces of it are inscribed in various ancient Temples walls, tombs, steles and papyri. For the first time available, the complete myth of Asar, Aset and Heru has been compiled from original Ancient Egyptian, Greek and Coptic Texts. This epic myth has been richly illustrated with reliefs from the Temple of Heru at Edfu, the Temple of Aset at Philae, the Temple of Asar at Abydos, the Temple of Hathor at Denderah and various papyri, inscriptions and reliefs.   Discover the myth which inspired the teachings of the *Shetaut Neter* (Egyptian Mystery System - Egyptian Yoga) and the Egyptian Book of Coming Forth By Day. Also, discover the three levels of Ancient Egyptian Religion, how to understand the mysteries of the Duat or Astral World and how to discover the abode of the Supreme in the Amenta, *The Other World*   The ancient religion of Asar, Aset and Heru, if properly understood, contains all of the elements necessary to lead the sincere aspirant to attain immortality through inner self-discovery. This volume presents the entire myth and explores the main mystical themes and rituals associated with the myth for understating human existence, creation and the way to achieve spiritual emancipation - *Resurrection*. The Asarian myth is so powerful that it influenced and is still having an effect on the major world religions. Discover the origins and mystical meaning of the Christian Trinity, the Eucharist ritual and the ancient origin of the birthday of Jesus Christ. Soft Cover ISBN: 1-884564-27-5 $24.95

19. *THE EGYPTIAN BOOK OF THE DEAD MYSTICISM OF THE PERT EM HERU* " I Know myself, I know myself, I am One With God!–From the Pert Em Heru "The Ru Pert em Heru" or "Ancient Egyptian Book of The Dead," or "Book of Coming Forth By Day" as it is more popularly known, has fascinated the world since the successful translation of Ancient Egyptian hieroglyphic scripture over 150 years ago. The astonishing writings in it reveal that the Ancient Egyptians believed in life after death and in an ultimate destiny to discover the Divine. The elegance and aesthetic beauty of the hieroglyphic text itself has inspired many see it as an art form in and of itself. But is there more to it than that? Did the Ancient Egyptian wisdom contain more than just aphorisms and hopes of eternal life beyond death? In this volume Dr. Muata Ashby, the author of over 25 books on Ancient Egyptian Yoga Philosophy has produced a new translation of the original texts which uncovers a mystical teaching underlying the sayings and rituals instituted by the Ancient Egyptian Sages and Saints. "Once the philosophy of Ancient Egypt is understood as a mystical tradition instead of as a religion or primitive mythology, it reveals its secrets which if practiced today will lead anyone to discover the glory of spiritual self-discovery. The Pert em Heru is in every way comparable to the Indian Upanishads or the Tibetan Book of the Dead." ⬜ $28.95   ISBN# 1-884564-28-3 Size: 8½" X 11

20.   *African Religion VOL. 1- ANUNIAN THEOLOGY THE MYSTERIES OF RA* The Philosophy of Anu and The Mystical Teachings c The Ancient Egyptian Creation Myth Discover the mystical teachings contained in the Creation Myth and the gods an goddesses who brought creation and human beings into existence. The Creation myth of Anu is the source of Anunia Theology but also of the other main theological systems of Ancient Egypt that also influenced other world religion including Christianity, Hinduism and Buddhism. The Creation Myth holds the key to understanding the universe and fo attaining spiritual Enlightenment. ISBN: 1-884564-38-0 $19.95

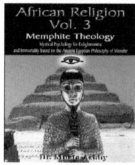

21.   *African Religion VOL 3: Memphite Theology: MYSTERIES OF MIND* Mystical Psychology & Mental Health for Enlightenmen and Immortality based on the Ancient Egyptian Philosophy of Menefer -Mysticism of Ptah, Egyptian Physics and Yog Metaphysics and the Hidden properties of Matter.   This volume uncovers the mystical psychology of the Ancient Egyptia wisdom teachings centering on the philosophy of the Ancient Egyptian city of Menefer (Memphite Theology). How t understand the mind and how to control the senses and lead the mind to health, clarity and mystical self-discovery. Thi Volume will also go deeper into the philosophy of God as creation and will explore the concepts of modern science and hov they correlate with ancient teachings. This Volume will lay the ground work for the understanding of the philosophy o universal consciousness and the initiatic/yogic insight into who or what is God? ISBN 1-884564-07-0 $22.95

22.   *AFRICAN RELIGION VOLUME 5: THE GODDESS AND THE EGYPTIAN MYSTERIESTHE PATH OF THE GODDESS THE GODDES PATH* The Secret Forms of the Goddess and the Rituals of Resurrection The Supreme Being may be worshipped as father o as mother. *Ushet Rekhat* or *Mother Worship*, is the spiritual process of worshipping the Divine in the form of the Divine Goddess. It celebrates the most important forms of the Goddess including *Nathor, Maat, Aset, Arat, Amentet and Hatho* and explores their mystical meaning as well as the rising of *Sirius,* the star of Aset (Aset) and the new birth of Hor (Heru) The end of the year is a time of reckoning, reflection and engendering a new or renewed positive movement towarc attaining spiritual Enlightenment. The Mother Worship devotional meditation ritual, performed on five days during the month of December and on New Year's Eve, is based on the Ushet Rekhit. During the ceremony, the cosmic forces symbolized by Sirius - and the constellation of Orion ---, are harnessed through the understanding and devotional attitude

of the participant. This propitiation draws the light of wisdom and health to all those who share in the ritual, leading to prosperity and wisdom. $14.95 ISBN 1-884564-18-6

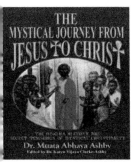

23.   *THE MYSTICAL JOURNEY FROM JESUS TO CHRIST* Discover the ancient Egyptian origins of Christianity before the Catholic Church and learn the mystical teachings given by Jesus to assist all humanity in becoming Christlike. Discover the secret meaning of the Gospels that were discovered in Egypt. Also discover how and why so many Christian churches came into being. Discover that the Bible still holds the keys to mystical realization even though its original writings were changed by the church. Discover how to practice the original teachings of Christianity which leads to the Kingdom of Heaven. $24.95 ISBN# 1-884564-05-4 size: 8½" X 11"

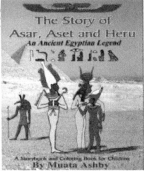

24.   *THE STORY OF ASAR, ASET AND HERU:* An Ancient Egyptian Legend (For Children)   Now for the first time, the most ancient myth of Ancient Egypt comes alive for children. Inspired by the books *The Asarian Resurrection: The Ancient Egyptian Bible* and *The Mystical Teachings of The Asarian Resurrection, The Story of Asar, Aset and Heru* is an easy to understand and thrilling tale which inspired the children of Ancient Egypt to aspire to greatness and righteousness.   If you and your child have enjoyed stories like *The Lion King* and *Star Wars you will love The Story of Asar, Aset and Heru.* Also, if you know the story of Jesus and Krishna you will discover than Ancient Egypt had a similar myth and that this myth carries important spiritual teachings for living a fruitful and fulfilling life. This book may be used along with *The Parents Guide To The Asarian Resurrection Myth: How to Teach Yourself and Your Child the Principles of Universal Mystical Religion.* The guide provides some background to the Asarian Resurrection myth and it also gives insight into the mystical teachings contained in it which you may introduce to your child. It is designed for parents who wish to grow spiritually with their children and it serves as an introduction for those who would like to study the Asarian Resurrection Myth in depth and to practice its teachings. 8.5" X 11"   ISBN: 1-884564-31-3 $12.95

25.   *THE PARENTS GUIDE TO THE AUSARIAN RESURRECTION MYTH:* How to Teach Yourself and Your Child the Principles of Universal Mystical Religion.   This insightful manual brings for the timeless wisdom of the ancient through the Ancient Egyptian myth of Asar, Aset and Heru and the mystical teachings contained in it for parents who want to guide their children to understand and practice the teachings of mystical spirituality. This manual may be used with the children's storybook *The Story of Asar, Aset and Heru* by Dr. Muata Abhaya Ashby.   ISBN: 1-884564-30-5 $16.95

26.   *HEALING THE CRIMINAL HEART.* Introduction to Maat Philosophy, Yoga and Spiritual Redemption Through the Path of Virtue   Who is a criminal? Is there such a thing as a criminal heart? What is the source of evil and sinfulness and is there any way to rise above it? Is there redemption for those who have committed sins, even the worst crimes?   Ancient Egyptian mystical psychology holds important answers to these questions. Over ten thousand years ago mystical psychologists, the Sages of Ancient Egypt, studied and charted the human mind and spirit and laid out a path which will lead to spiritual redemption, prosperity and Enlightenment.   This introductory volume brings forth the teachings of the Asarian Resurrection, the most important myth of Ancient Egypt, with relation to the faults of human existence: anger, hatred, greed, lust, animosity, discontent, ignorance, egoism jealousy, bitterness, and a myriad of psycho-spiritual ailments which keep a human being in a state of negativity and adversity   ISBN: 1-884564-17-8 $15.95

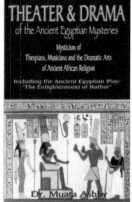

27.   *TEMPLE RITUAL OF THE ANCIENT EGYPTIAN MYSTERIES--THEATER & DRAMA OF THE ANCIENT EGYPTIAN MYSTERIES*: Details the practice of the mysteries and ritual program of the temple and the philosophy an practice of the ritual of the mysteries, its purpose and execution. Featuring the Ancient Egyptian stage play-"The Enlightenment of Hathor' Based on an Ancient Egyptian Drama, The original Theater -Mysticism of the Temple of Hetheru 1-884564-14-3 $19.95   By Dr. Muata Ashby

28.   *GUIDE TO PRINT ON DEMAND: SELF-PUBLISH FOR PROFIT,* SPIRITUAL FULFILLMENT AND SERVICE TO HUMANITY Everyone asks us how we produced so many books in such a short time. Here are the secrets to writing and producing books that uplift humanity and

how to get them printed for a fraction of the regular cost. Anyone can become an author even if they have limited funds. All that is necessary is the willingness to learn how the printing and book business work and the desire to follow the special instructions given here for preparing your manuscript format. Then you take your work directly to the non-traditional companies who can produce your books for less than the traditional book printer can. ISBN: 1-884564-40-2 $16.95 U. S.

9.   *Egyptian Mysteries: Vol. 1,* Shetaut Neter What are the Mysteries? For thousands of years the spiritual tradition of Ancient Egypt, *Shetaut Neter,* "The Egyptian Mysteries," "The Secret Teachings," have fascinated, tantalized and amazed the world. At one time exalted and recognized as the highest culture of the world, by Africans, Europeans, Asiatics, Hindus, Buddhists and other cultures of the ancient world, in time it was shunned by the emerging orthodox world religions. Its temples desecrated, its philosophy maligned, its tradition spurned, its philosophy dormant in the mystical *Medu Neter*, the mysterious hieroglyphic texts which hold the secret symbolic meaning that has scarcely been discerned up to now. What are the secrets of *Nehast* {spiritual awakening and emancipation, resurrection}. More than just a literal translation, this volume is for awakening to the secret code *Shetitu* of the teaching which was not deciphered by Egyptologists, nor could be understood by ordinary spiritualists. This book is a reinstatement of the original science made available for our times, to the reincarnated followers of Ancient Egyptian culture and the prospect of spiritual freedom to break the bonds of *Khemn,* "ignorance," and slavery to evil forces: *Såaa* . ISBN: 1-884564-41-0 $19.99

80.   *EGYPTIAN MYSTERIES VOL 2:* Dictionary of Gods and Goddesses This book is about the mystery of neteru, the gods and goddesses of Ancient Egypt (Kamit, Kemet). Neteru means "Gods and Goddesses." But the Neterian teaching of Neteru represents more than the usual limited modern day concept of "divinities" or "spirits." The Neteru of Kamit are also metaphors, cosmic principles and vehicles for the enlightening teachings of Shetaut Neter (Ancient Egyptian-African Religion). Actually they are the elements for one of the most advanced systems of spirituality ever conceived in human history. Understanding the concept of neteru provides a firm basis for spiritual evolution and the pathway for viable culture, peace on earth and a healthy human society.   Why is it important to have gods and goddesses in our lives? In order for spiritual evolution to be possible, once a human being has accepted that there is existence after death and there is a transcendental being who exists beyond time and space knowledge, human beings need a connection to that which transcends the ordinary experience of human life in time and space and a means to understand the transcendental reality beyond the mundane reality. ISBN: 1-884564-23-2 $21.95

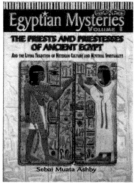

31.   *EGYPTIAN MYSTERIES VOL. 3* The Priests and Priestesses of Ancient Egypt This volume details the path of Neteria priesthood, the joys, challenges and rewards of advanced Neterian life, the teachings that allowed the priests and priestesse to manage the most long lived civilization in human history and how that path can be adopted today; for those who want t tread the path of the Clergy of Shetaut Neter. ISBN: 1-884564-53-4 $24.95

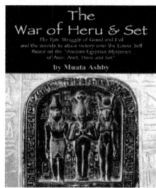

32.   *The War of Heru and Set:* The Struggle of Good and Evil for Control of the World and The Human Soul This volum contains a novelized version of the Asarian Resurrection myth that is based on the actual scriptures presented in the Boo Asarian Religion (old name –Resurrecting Osiris). This volume is prepared in the form of a screenplay and can be easil adapted to be used as a stage play. Spiritual seeking is a mythic journey that has many emotional highs and lows, ecstasie and depressions, victories and frustrations. This is the War of Life that is played out in the myth as the struggle of Heru an Set and those are mythic characters that represent the human Higher and Lower self. How to understand the war and emerg victorious in the journey o life? The ultimate victory and fulfillment can be experienced, which is not changeable or lost i time. The purpose of myth is to convey the wisdom of life through the story of divinities who show the way to overcome th challenges and foibles of life. In this volume the feelings and emotions of the characters of the myth have been highlighted t show the deeply rich texture of the Ancient Egyptian myth. This myth contains deep spiritual teachings and insights into th nature of self, of God and the mysteries of life and the means to discover the true meaning of life and thereby achieve the tru purpose of life. To become victorious in the battle of life means to become the King (or Queen) of Egypt.Have you seer movies like The Lion King, Hamlet, The Odyssey, or The Little Buddha? These have been some of the most popular movie in modern times. The Sema Institute of Yoga is dedicated to researching and presenting the wisdom and culture of ancien Africa. The Script is designed to be produced as a motion picture but may be addapted for the theater as well. $21.9 copyright 1998 By Dr. Muata Ashby ISBN 1-8840564-44-5

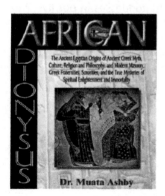

33.   *AFRICAN DIONYSUS: FROM EGYPT TO GREECE:* The Kamitan Origins of Greek Culture and Religion ISBN: 1-884564-47-X   FROM EGYPT TO GREECE   This insightful manual is a reference to Ancient Egyptian mythology and philosophy and its correlation to what later became known as Greek and Rome mythology and philosophy. It outlines the basic tenets of the mythologies and shoes the ancient origins of Greek culture in Ancient Egypt. This volume also documents the origins of the Greek alphabet in Egypt as well as Greek religion, myth and philosophy of the gods and goddesses from Egypt from the myth of Atlantis and archaic period with the Minoans to the Classical period. This volume also acts as a resource for Colleges students who would like to set up fraternities and sororities based on the original Ancient Egyptian principles of Sheti and Maat philosophy. ISBN: 1-884564-47-X $22.95 U.S.

34.   THE FORTY TWO PRECEPTS OF MAAT, THE PHILOSOPHY OF RIGHTEOUS ACTION AND THE ANCIENT EGYPTIAN WISDOM TEXTS <u>ADVANCED STUDIES</u> This manual is designed for use with the 1998 Maat Philosophy Class conducted by Dr. Muata Ashby. This is a detailed study of Maat Philosophy. It contains a compilation of the 42 laws or precepts of Maat and the corresponding principles which they represent along with the teachings of the ancient Egyptian Sages relating to each. Maat philosophy was the basis of Ancient Egyptian society and government as well as the heart of Ancient Egyptian myth and spirituality. Maat is at once a goddess, a cosmic force and a living social doctrine, which promotes social harmony and thereby paves the way for spiritual evolution in all levels of society. ISBN: 1-884564-48-8 $16.95 U.S.

35.   **THE SECRET LOTUS: *Poetry of Enlightenment***
Discover the mystical sentiment of the Kemetic teaching as expressed through the poetry of Sebai Muata Ashby. The teaching of spiritual awakening is uniquely experienced when the poetic sensibility is present. This first volume contains the poems written between 1996 and 2003. **1-884564--16 -X $16.99**

36. The Ancient Egyptian Buddha: The Ancient Egyptian Origins of Buddhism

This book is a compilation of several sections of a larger work, a book by the name of African Origins of Civilization, Religion, Yoga Mysticism and Ethics Philosophy. It also contains some additional evidences not contained in the larger work that demonstrate the correlation between Ancient Egyptian Religion and Buddhism. This book is one of several compiled short volumes that has been compiled so as to facilitate access to specific subjects contained in the larger work which is over 680 pages long. These short and small volumes have been specifically designed to cover one subject in a brief and low cost format. This present volume, The Ancient Egyptian Buddha: The Ancient Egyptian Origins of Buddhism, formed one subject in the larger work; actually it was one chapter of the larger work. However, this volume has some new additional evidences and comparisons of Buddhist and Neterian (Ancient Egyptian) philosophies not previously discussed. It was felt that this subject needed to be discussed because even in the early 21st century, the idea persists that Buddhism originated only in India independently. Yet there is ample evidence from ancient writings and perhaps more importantly, iconographical evidences from the Ancient Egyptians and early Buddhists themselves that prove otherwise. This handy volume has been designed to be accessible to young adults and all others who would like to have an easy reference with documentation on this important subject. This is an important subject because the frame of reference with which we look at a culture depends strongly on our conceptions about its origins. in this case, if we look at the Buddhism as an Asiatic religion we would treat it and it's culture in one way. If we id as African [Ancient Egyptian] we not only would see it in a different light but we also must ascribe Africa with a glorious legacy that matches any other culture in human history and gave rise to one of the present day most important religious philosophies. We would also look at the culture and philosophies of the Ancient Egyptians as having African insights that offer us greater depth into the Buddhist philosophies. Those insights inform our knowledge about other African traditions and we can also begin to understand in a deeper way the effect of Ancient Egyptian culture on African culture and also on the Asiatic as well. We would also be able to discover the glorious and wondrous teaching of mystical philosophy that Ancient Egyptian Shetaut Neter religion offers, that is as powerful as any other mystic system of spiritual philosophy in the world today. ISBN: 1-884564-61-5 $28.95

37. The Death of American Empire: Neo-conservatism, Theocracy, Economic Imperialism, Environmental Disaster and the Collapse of Civilization

This work is a collection of essays relating to social and economic, leadership, and ethics, ecological and religious issues that are facing the world today in order to understand the course of history that has led humanity to its present condition and then arrive at positive solutions that will lead to better outcomes for all humanity. It surveys the development and decline of major empires throughout history and focuses on the creation of American Empire along with the social, political and economic policies that led to he prominence of the United States of America as a Superpower including the rise of the political control of the neo-con political hilosophy including militarism and the military industrial complex in American politics and the rise of the religious right into and merican Theocracy movement. This volume details, through historical and current events, the psychology behind the dominance of estern culture in world politics through the "Superpower Syndrome Mandatory Conflict Complex" that drives the Superpower ulture to establish itself above all others and then act hubristically to dominate world culture through legitimate influences as well as oercion, media censorship and misinformation leading to international hegemony and world conflict. This volume also details the nancial policies that gave rise to American prominence in the global economy, especially after World War II, and promoted merican preeminence over the world economy through Globalization as well as the environmental policies, including the oil conomy, that are promoting degradation of the world ecology and contribute to the decline of America as an Empire culture. This olume finally explores the factors pointing to the decline of the American Empire economy and imperial power and what to expect in e aftermath of American prominence and how to survive the decline while at the same time promoting policies and social-economic-eligious-political changes that are needed in order to promote the emergence of a beneficial and sustainable culture. **$25.95soft** 1-84564-25-9, Hard Cover **$29.95** 1-884564-45-3

38. The African Origins of Hatha Yoga: And its Ancient Mystical Teaching

he subject of this present volume, The Ancient Egyptian Origins of Yoga Postures, formed one subject in the larger works, African Origins of Civilization Religion, Yoga Mysticism and Ethics Philosophy and the Book Egypt and India is the section of the book frican Origins of Civilization. Those works contain the collection of all correlations between Ancient Egypt and India. This volume lso contains some additional information not contained in the previous work. It was felt that this subject needed to be discussed more lirectly, being treated in one volume, as opposed to being contained in the larger work along with other subjects, because even in the arly 21st century, the idea persists that the Yoga and specifically, Yoga Postures, were invented and developed only in India. The ncient Egyptians were peoples originally from Africa who were, in ancient times, colonists in India. Therefore it is no surprise that nany Indian traditions including religious and Yogic, would be found earlier in Ancient Egypt. Yet there is ample evidence from ncient writings and perhaps more importantly, iconographical evidences from the Ancient Egyptians themselves and the Indians hemselves that prove the connection between Ancient Egypt and India as well as the existence of a discipline of Yoga Postures in ncient Egypt long before its practice in India. This handy volume has been designed to be accessible to young adults and all others vho would like to have an easy reference with documentation on this important subject. This is an important subject because the rame of reference with which we look at a culture depends strongly on our conceptions about its origins. In this case, if we look at the ncient Egyptians as Asiatic peoples we would treat them and their culture in one way. If we see them as Africans we not only see hem in a different light but we also must ascribe Africa with a glorious legacy that matches any other culture in human history. We vould also look at the culture and philosophies of the Ancient Egyptians as having African insights instead of Asiatic ones. Those nsights inform our knowledge bout other African traditions and we can also begin to understand in a deeper way the effect of Ancient gyptian culture on African culture and also on the Asiatic as well. When we discover the deeper and more ancient practice of the ostures system in Ancient Egypt that was called "Hatha Yoga" in India, we are able to find a new and expanded understanding of the ractice that constitutes a discipline of spiritual practice that informs and revitalizes the Indian practices as well as all spiritual lisciplines. $19.99 ISBN 1-884564-60-7

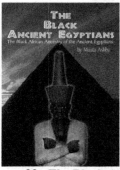

39. The Black Ancient Egyptians

This present volume, The Black Ancient Egyptians: The Black African Ancestry of the Ancient Egyptians, formed one subject in the larger work: The African Origins of Civilization, Religion, Yoga Mysticism and Ethics Philosophy. It was felt that this subject needed to be discussed because even in the early 21st century, the idea persists that the Ancient Egyptians were peoples originally from Asia Minor who came into North-East Africa. Yet there is ample evidence from ancient writings and perhaps more importantly iconographical evidences from the Ancient Egyptians themselves that proves otherwise. This handy volume has been designed to be accessible to young adults and all others who would like to have an easy reference with documentation on this important subject. This is an important subject because the frame of reference with which we look at a culture depends strongly on our conceptions about its origins. in this case, if we look at the Ancient Egyptians as Asiatic peoples we would treat them and their culture in one way. If we see them as Africans we not only see them in a different light but we also must ascribe Africa with a glorious legacy that matches any other culture in human history. We would also look at the culture and philosophies of the Ancient Egyptians as having African insights instead of Asiatic ones. Those insights inform our knowledge bout other African traditions and we can also begin to understand in a deeper way the effect of Ancient Egyptian culture on African culture and also on the Asiatic as well. ISBN 1-884564-21-6 $19.99

40. The Limits of Faith: The Failure of Faith-based Religions and the Solution to the Meaning of Life

Is faith belief in something without proof? And if so is there never to be any proof or discovery? If so what is the need of intellect? If faith is trust in something that is real is that reality historical, literal or metaphorical or philosophical? If knowledge is an essential element in faith why should there by so much emphasis on believing and not on understanding in the modern practice of religion? This volume is a compilation of essays related to the nature of religious faith in the context of its inception in human history as well as its meaning for religious practice and relations between religions in modern times. Faith has come to be regarded as a virtuous goal in life. However, many people have asked how can it be that an endeavor that is supposed to be dedicated to spiritual upliftment has led to more conflict in human history than any other social factor? ISBN 1884564631 SOFT COVER - $19.99, ISBN 1884564623 HARD COVER -$28.95

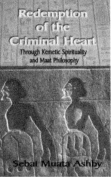

41. Redemption of The Criminal Heart Through Kemetic Spirituality and Maat Philosophy

Special book dedicated to inmates, their families and members of the Law Enforcement community. ISBN: 1-884564-70-4

$5.00

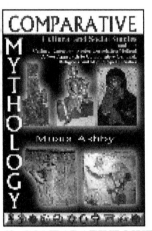

42. COMPARATIVE MYTHOLOGY

What are Myth and Culture and what is their importance for understanding the development of societies, human evolution and the search for meaning? What is the purpose of culture and how do cultures evolve? What are the elements of a culture and how can those elements be broken down and the constituent parts of a culture understood and compared? How do cultures interact? How does enculturation occur and how do people interact with other cultures? How do the processes of acculturation and cooptation occur and what does this mean for the development of a society? How can the study of myths and the elements of culture help in understanding the meaning of life and the means to promote understanding and peace in the world of human activity? This volume is the exposition of a method for studying and comparing cultures, myths and other social aspects of a society. It is an expansion on the Cultural Category Factor Correlation method for studying and comparing myths, cultures, religions and other aspects of human culture. It was originally introduced in the year 2002. This volume contains an expanded treatment as well as several refinements along with examples of the application of the method. the apparent. I hope you enjoy these art renditions as serene reflections of the mysteries of life. ISBN: 1-884564-72-0

Book price $21.95

43. CONVERSATION WITH GOD: Revelations of the Important Questions of Life
$24.99 U.S.

This volume contains a grouping of some of the questions that have been submitted to Sebai Dr. Muata Ashby. They are efforts by many aspirants to better understand and practice the teachings of mystical spirituality. It is said that when sages are asked spiritual questions they are relaying the wisdom of God, the Goddess, the Higher Self, etc. There is a very special quality about the Q & A process that does not occur during a regular lecture session. Certain points come out that would not come out otherwise due to the nature of the process which ideally occurs after a lecture. Having been to a certain degree enlightened by a lecture certain new questions arise and the answers to these have the effect of elevating the teaching of the lecture to even higher levels. Therefore, enjoy these exchanges and may they lead you to enlightenment, peace and prosperity. Available Late Summer 2007 ISBN: 1-884564-68-2

44. MYSTIC ART PAINTINGS

(with Full Color images) This book contains a collection of the small number of paintings that I have created over the years. Some were used as early book covers and others were done simply to express certain spiritual feelings; some were created for no purpose except to express the joy of color and the feeling of relaxed freedom. All are to elicit mystical awakening in the viewer. Writing a book on philosophy is like sculpture, the more the work is rewritten the reflections and ideas become honed and take form and become clearer and imbued with intellectual beauty. Mystic music is like meditation, a world of its own that exists about 1 inch above ground wherein the musician does not touch the ground. Mystic Graphic Art is meditation in form, color, image and reflected image which opens the door to the reality behind the apparent. I hope you enjoy these art renditions and my reflections on them as serene reflections of the mysteries of life, as visual renditions of the philosophy I have written about over the years. ISBN 1-884564-69-0 $19.95

45. ANCIENT EGYPTIAN HIEROGLYPHS FOR BEGINNERS

This brief guide was prepared for those inquiring about how to enter into Hieroglyphic studies on their own at home or in study groups. First of all you should know that there are a few institutions around the world which teach how to read the Hieroglyphic text but due to the nature of the study there are perhaps only a handful of people who can read fluently. It is possible for anyone with average intelligence to achieve a high level of proficiency in reading inscriptions on temples and artifacts; however, reading extensive texts is another issue entirely. However, this introduction will give you entry into those texts if assisted by dictionaries and other aids. Most Egyptologists have a basic knowledge and keep dictionaries and notes handy when it comes to dealing with more difficult texts. Medtu Neter or the Ancient Egyptian hieroglyphic language has been considered as a "Dead Language." However, dead languages have always been studied by individuals who for the most part have taught themselves through various means. This book will discuss those means and how to use them most efficiently. ISBN 1884564429 **$28.95**

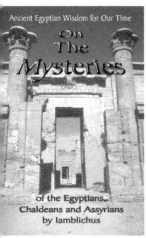

6. ON THE MYSTERIES: Wisdom of An Ancient Egyptian Sage -with Foreword by Muata Ashby

This volume, On the Mysteries, by Iamblichus (Abamun) is a unique form or scripture out of the Ancient Egyptian religious tradition. It is written in a form that is not usual or which is not usually found in the remnants of Ancient Egyptian scriptures. It is in the form of teacher and disciple, much like the Eastern scriptures such as Bhagavad Gita or the Upanishads. This form of writing may not have been necessary in Ancient times, because the format of teaching in Egypt was different prior to the conquest period by the Persians, Assyrians, Greeks and later the Romans. The question and answer format can be found but such extensive discourses and corrections of misunderstandings within the context of a teacher - disciple relationship is not usual. It therefore provides extensive insights into the times when it was written and the state of practice of Ancient Egyptian and other mystery religions. This has important implications for our times because we are today, as in the Greco-Roman period, also besieged with varied religions and new age philosophies as well as social strife and war. How can we understand our times and also make sense of the forest of spiritual traditions? How can we cut through the cacophony of religious fanaticism, and ignorance as well as misconceptions about the mysteries on the other in order to discover the true purpose of religion and the secret teachings that open up the mysteries of life and the way to enlightenment and immortality? This book, which comes to us from so long ago, offers us transcendental wisdom that applied to the world two thousand years ago as well as our world today. ISBN 1-884564-64-X $25.95

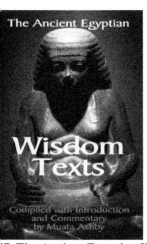

7. The Ancient Egyptian Wisdom Texts -Compiled by Muata Ashby

The Ancient Egyptian Wisdom Texts are a genre of writings from the ancient culture that have survived to the present and provide vibrant record of the practice of spiritual evolution otherwise known as religion or yoga philosophy in Ancient Egypt. The principl focus of the Wisdom Texts is the cultivation of understanding, peace, harmony, selfless service, self-control, Inner fulfillment an spiritual realization. When these factors are cultivated in human life, the virtuous qualities in a human being begin to manifest an sinfulness, ignorance and negativity diminish until a person is able to enter into higher consciousness, the coveted goal of a civilizations. It is this virtuous mode of life which opens the door to self-discovery and spiritual enlightenment. Therefore, th Wisdom Texts are important scriptures on the subject of human nature, spiritual psychology and mystical philosophy. The teaching presented in the Wisdom Texts form the foundation of religion as well as the guidelines for conducting the affairs of every area c social interaction including commerce, education, the army, marriage, and especially the legal system. These texts were sources fc the famous 42 Precepts of Maat of the Pert-m-Heru (Book of the Dead), essential regulations of good conduct to develop virtue an purity in order to attain higher consciousness and immortality after death. ISBN1-884564-65-8 $18.95

48. THE KEMETIC TREE OF LIFE

THE KEMETIC TREE OF LIFE: Newly Revealed Ancient Egyptian Cosmology and Metaphysics for Higher Consciousness The Tree o Life is a roadmap of a journey which explains how Creation came into being and how it will end. It also explains what Creation i composed of and also what human beings are and what they are composed of. It also explains the process of Creation, how Creatio develops, as well as who created Creation and where that entity may be found. It also explains how a human being may discove that entity and in so doing also discover the secrets of Creation, the meaning of life and the means to break free from the patheti condition of human limitation and mortality in order to discover the higher realms of being by discovering the principles, the level of existence that are beyond the simple physical and material aspects of life. This book contains color plates **ISBN: 1-884564-74-7** **$27.95 U.S.**

49-MATRIX OF AFRICAN PROVERBS: The Ethical and Spiritual Blueprint

This volume sets forth the fundamental principles of African ethics and their practical applications for use by individuals and organizations seeking to model their ethical policies using the Traditional African values and concepts of ethical human behavior for the proper sustenance and management of society. Furthermore, this book will provide guidance as to how the Traditional African Ethics may be viewed and applied, taking into consideration the technological and social advancements in the present. This volume also presents the principles of ethical culture, and references for each to specific injunctions from Traditional African Proverbial Wisdom Teachings. These teachings are compiled from varied Pre-colonial African societies including Yoruba, Ashanti, Kemet, Malawi, Nigeria, Ethiopia, Galla, Ghana and many more. ISBN 1-884564-77-1

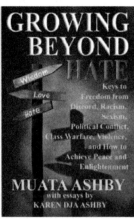

50- <u>**Growing Beyond Hate: Keys to Freedom from Discord, Racism, Sexism, Political Conflict, Class Warfare, Violence, and How to Achieve Peace and Enlightenment**</u>---INTRODUCTION: WHY DO WE HATE? Hatred is one of the fundamental motivating aspects of human life; the other is desire. Desire can be of a worldly nature or of a spiritual, elevating nature. Worldly desire and hatred are like two sides of the same coin in that human life is usually swaying from one to the other; but the question is why? And is there a way to satisfy the desiring or hating mind in such a way as to find peace in life? Why do human beings go to war? Why do human beings perpetrate violence against one another? And is there a way not just to understand the phenomena but to resolve the issues that plague humanity and could lead to a more harmonious society? Hatred is perhaps the greatest scourge of humanity in that it leads to misunderstanding, conflict and untold miseries of life and clashes between individuals, societies and nations. Therefore, the riddle of Hatred, that is, understanding the sources of it and how to confront, reduce and even eradicate it so as to bring forth the fulfillment in life and peace for society, should be a top priority for social scientists, spiritualists and philosophers. This book is written from the perspective of spiritual philosophy based on the mystical wisdom and sema or yoga philosophy of the Ancient Egyptians. This philosophy, originated and based in the wisdom of Shetaut Neter, the Egyptian Mysteries, and Maat, ethical way of life in society and in spirit, contains Sema-Yogic wisdom and understanding of life's predicaments that can allow a human being of any ethnic group to understand and overcome the causes of hatred, racism, sexism, violence and disharmony in life, that plague human society. ISBN: 1-884564-81-X

52. Guide to Creating a Kemetic Marriage Contract

This marital contract guide reflects actual Ancient Egyptian Principles for Kemetic Marriage as they are to be applied for our times. The marital contract allows people to have a framework with which to face the challenges of marital relations instead of relying on hopes or romantic dreams that everything will workout somehow; in other words, love is not all you need. The latter is not an evolved, mature way of handling one of the most important aspects of human life. Therefore, it behooves anyone who wishes to enter into a marriage to explore the issues, express their needs and seek to avoid costly mistakes, and resolve conflicts in the normal course of life or make sure that their rights and dignity will be protected if any eventuality should occur. Marital relations in Ancient Egypt were not like those in other countries of the time and not like those of present day countries. The extreme longevity of Ancient Egyptian society, founded in Maat philosophy, allowed the social development of marriage to evolve and progress to a high level of order and balance. Maat represents truth, righteous, justice and harmony in life. This meant that the marital partner's rights were to be protected with equal standing before the law. So there was no disparity between rights of men or rights of women. Therefore, anyone who wants to enter into a marriage based on Kemetic principles must first and foremost adhere to this standard…equality in the rights of men and women. This guide demonstrates procedures for following the Ancient Egyptian practice of formalizing marriage with a contract that spells out the important concerns of each partner in the marital relationship, based on Maatian principles [of righteous, truth, harmony and justice] so that the rights and needs of each partner may be protected within the marriage. It also allows the partners to think about issues that arise out of the marital relations so that they may have a foundation to fall back on in the event that those or other unforeseen issues arise and cause conflict in the relationship. By having a document of expressed concerns, needs and steps to be taken to address them, it is less likely that issues which affect the relationship in a negative way will arise, and when they do, they will be better handled, in a more balanced, just and amicable way.

EBOOK ISBN 978-1-937016-59-3, HARDCOPY BOOK ISBN: 1-884564-82-8

53-Ancient Egyptian Mysteries of The Kybalion: A Hermetic Mystic Psychology Primer Paperback – November 28, 2014

This Volume is a landmark study by a renounced mystic philosopher, Sebai Dr. Muata Ashby. It is study not just to philosophize but to be practiced for the purpose of attaining enlightenment. The book is divided into three sections. Part 1 INTRODUCTION presents a brief history of Hermeticism, its origins in the Ancient Egyptian Mysteries (Neterianism) the Kybalion and the origins of the personality known as Hermes Trismegistus. Part 2 presents the essential teachings of the Kybalion text, a set of MAXIMS, without interpretation. Part 3 presents glosses (commentary and explanation) on the essential teachings of the Kybalion based on the philosophy of the Ancient Egyptian Mysteries as determined by Sebai Dr. Muata Ashby based on studies and translations of original Ancient Egyptian Hieroglyphic texts; the source from which the Kybalion teaching is derived. The Glosses are an edited and expanded version of Lessons given by Sebai Dr. Muata Ashby in the form of lectures on the teachings of the Kybalion.

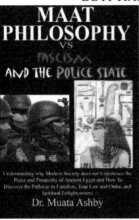

4-Maat Philosophy Versus Fascism and the Police State: Understanding why Modern Society does not Experience the Peace and Prosperity of Ancient Egypt ... Law and Order, and Spiritual Enlightenment Paperback – January 1, 2014

Understanding why Modern Society does not Experience the Peace and Prosperity of Ancient Egypt and How To Discover the Pathway to Freedom, True Law and Order, and Spiritual Enlightenment. Understanding the Corporate State and How Maatian Philosophy can Leads to Freedom, Prosperity and Enlightenment

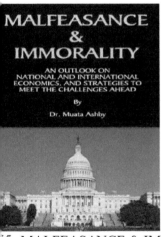

55- MALFEASANCE & IMMORALITY: An Analysis of the World Economic Crash of 2008, the Corrupt Political and Financial Institutions that Caused it and Strategies to Survive the Future Collapse of the Economy

The following is a first ever publication, by the Sema Institute, of a �White Paper�. The term is defined as: A white paper is an authoritative report or guide that often addresses issues and how to solve them. White papers are used to educate readers and help people make decisions. They are often used in politics and business. This paper serves as an update to the book Dollar Crisis: The Collapse of Society and Redemption Through Ancient Egyptian Fiscal & Monetary Policy (2008). That book was a continuation and expansion of issues presented in the book The Collapse of Civilization and the Death of American Empire (2006). Those books contained a detailed analysis of economic and political as well as social issues and how Maat Philosophy could offer insights into the nature of the problem, its sources and possible solutions as well as a means to develop an economic system (Fiscal and Monetary policies) that can work for all members of society. This paper contains an analysis of economic events and possible future outcomes based on those events as well as ideas individuals or groups may use in order to develop plans of action to deal with the possible detrimental events that may occur in the near and intermediate future. It serves as an update to the previous publications. This paper is divided into two parts. The first section is a summary which contains the conclusions of each section of Part 2.

This was done so that the reader may have a quick and easy understanding of what is happening with the economy and finally, the actions that should be considered to meet the challenges ahead

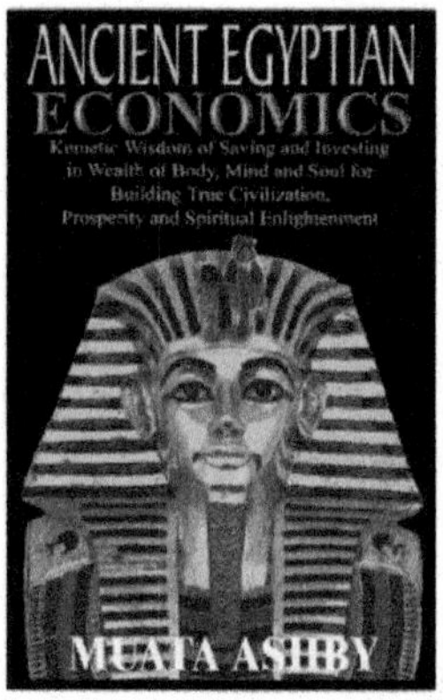

56- ANCIENT EGYPTIAN ECONOMICS
Ancient Egyptian Economics: Kemetic Wisdom of Saving and Investing in Wealth of Body, Mind and Soul for Building True Civilization, Prosperity and Spiritual Enlightenment------Question: Why has the subject of finances and economics become important, I thought the spiritual teachings and Ancient Egyptian Philosophy and money were separate? Answer: Finances and money are an integral part of Ancient Egyptian culture as an instrument for promoting Maat ethics in the form of the well-being of the 'hekat'. The hekat are the people and the "Heka" is the Pharaoh. The Pharaoh was like a shepherd leading a flock and moneys were controlled righteously to promote the welfare of the people. In that tradition we have applied the philosophy of maatian economics to promote the well-being of those who are following this path as well as those who may read the books so they may avoid financial trouble as much as possible and have better capacity to practice the teachings. In order to have a successful life, human beings need a certain amount of money and wealth, but money and wealth are not the goal. They are a foundation that enables the true goal of life, enlightenment, to be realized. Therefore, we are only fulfilling the duty of transmitting wisdom about wealth to promote Maat, righteousness, truth and well-being, for all. This volume explores the mysteries of wealth based on the teachings of the sages of Ancient Egypt and the means to promote prosperity that allows a person to create the conditions for discovering inner peace and spiritual enlightenment. HTP-Peace

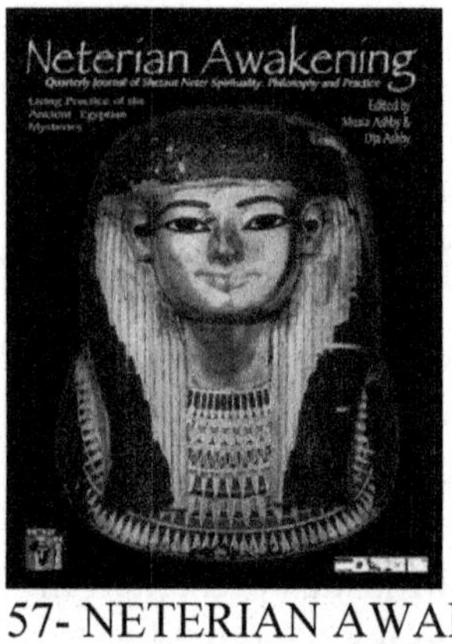

57- NETERIAN AWAKENING Journal of Neterian Culture Vol 1-12 In one Volume

This is a single file containing 12 volumes of The Neterian Awakening Journal. The Neterian Awakening Journal was a publication where the culture and community of Shetaut Neter spirituality was explored. In it Sebai Dr. Muata Ashby and Dr. Dja Ashby along with members of the Temple of Shetaut Neter presented articles, festival reviews, Questions and Answer columns and many other important aspects of Neterian culture and spirituality beyond those presented in other volumes of the book series that are useful in understanding the practice of Neterian Spirituality and the path to achieving a �Neterian Spiritual Awakening.� Part of its mission was: To promote the study of Shetaut Neter (Neterianism, Neterian Religion) as a spiritual path. Instruct the serious followers of Shetaut Neter spirituality who would like to receive literature in between the publication of major books that will fill the needs of their daily spiritual practice. Neterian Awakening Journal explores the varied aspects of Shetaut Neter spirituality not covered in the books. NAJ provides a forum for the development of a Neterian Community of those who wish to follow the Neterian Spiritual Path of African Religious Culture

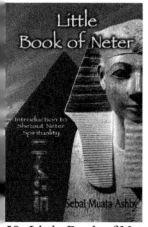

58- Little Book of Neter: Introduction to Shetaut Neter Spirituality and Religion Paperback – June 7, 2007

The Little Book of Neter is a summary of the most important teachings of Shetaut Neter for all aspirants to have for easy reference and distribution. It is designed to be portable and low cost so that all can have the main teachings of Shetaut Neter at easy access for personal use and also for sharing with others the basic tenets of Neterian spirituality.

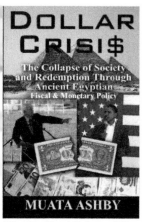

59- Dollar Crisis: The Collapse of Society and Redemption Through Ancient Egyptian Monetary Policy by Muata Ashby (2008-07-24)

This book is about the problems of the US economy and the imminent collapse of the U.S. Dollar and its dire consequences for the US economy and the world. It is also about the corruption in government, economics and social order that led to this point. Also it is about survival, how to make it through this perhaps most trying period in the history of the United States. Also it is about the ancient wisdom of life that allowed an ancient civilization to grow beyond the destructive corruptions of ignorance and power so that the people of today may gain insight into the nature of their condition, how they got there and what needs to be done in order to salvage what is left and rebuild a society that is sustainable, beneficial and an example for all humanity.

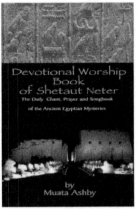

60- Devotional Worship Book of Shetaut Neter: Medu Neter song, chant and hymn book for daily practice [Paperback] [2007] (Author) Muata Ashby Paperback – 2007

Ushet Hekau Shedi Sema Taui Uashu or Ushet means "to worship the Divine," "to propitiate the Divine." Ushet is of two types, external and internal. When you go to pilgrimage centers, temples, spiritual gatherings, etc., you are practicing external worship or spiritual practice. When you go into your private meditation room on your own and your utter words of power, prayers and meditation you are practicing internal worship or spiritual practice. Ushet needs to be understood as a process of not only an outer show of spiritual practice, but it is also a process of developing love for the Divine. Therefore, Ushet really signifies a development in Devotion towards the Divine. This practice is also known as sma uash or Yoga of Devotion. Ushet is the process of discovering the Divine and allowing your heart to flow towards the Divine. This program of life allows a spiritual aspirant to develop inner peace, contentment and universal love, and these qualities lead to spiritual enlightenment or union with the Divine. It is recommended that you see the book "The Path of Divine Love" by Dr. Muata Ashby. This volume will give details into this form of Sema or Yoga.

61- Initiation Into Egyptian Yoga and Neterian Religion Workbook for Beginning and Advancing Aspirants

 What is Initiation? The great personalities of the past known to the world as Isis, Hathor, Jesus, Buddha and many other great Sages and Saints were initiated into their spiritual path but how did initiation help them and what were they specifically initiated into? This volume is a template for such lofty studies, a guidebook and blueprint for aspirants who want to understand what the path is all about, its requirements and goals, as they work with a qualified spiritual guide as they tread the path of Kemetic Spirituality and Yoga disciplines. This workbook helps by presenting the fundamental teachings of Egyptian Yoga and Neterian Spirituality with questions and exercises to help the aspirant gain a foundation for more advanced studies and practices

CPSIA information can be obtained
at www.ICGtesting.com
Printed in the USA
LVOW02s1910100717
540827LV00016B/670/P

9 781884 564918